"Some Greek professors excel in scholarship, while others excel in pedagogy. It is rare to encounter Greek professors who combine thorough knowledge of the language with evident classroom skills. Merkle and Plummer admirably join academic excellence with pedagogical expertise. Years of honing their skills in the classroom are evident in this valuable volume. First-year Greek students will be informed and challenged to put to work what they have learned through the exercises drawn from the text of 1 John. In my opinion this reader will eventually become a standard textbook in elementary Greek instruction."

—**Will Varner,** professor of biblical languages and
Bible exposition, The Master's University

"This book ranks among the very best as a carefully structured bridge from learning the basics of Greek to actual reading with comprehension. With attention to textual criticism and vocabulary, and incorporating valuable review of grammar and syntax, the authors have produced a guide that will enhance both teaching and learning of 1 John and beyond. Students will love the clarity, succinctness, and organization. This is destined to become a classroom staple."

—**Robert W. Yarbrough,** professor of New Testament, Covenant Theological Seminary

1 JOHN

1 JOHN

A New Testament
Greek Reader

Benjamin L. **Merkle** and Robert L. **Plummer**

ACADEMIC
BRENTWOOD, TENNESSEE

CONTENTS

//////////////

ABBREVIATIONS

//////////////

acc.	accusative
act.	active (voice)
aor.	aorist
Bateman and Peer, *John's Letters*	Bateman, Herbert W., and Aaron C. Peer. *John's Letters*. Big Greek Idea Series. Grand Rapids: Kregel Academic, 2018.
Baugh, *First John Reader*	Baugh, S. M. *A First John Reader: Intermediate Greek Reading Notes and Grammar*. Phillipsburg, NJ: P&R, 1999.
BDAG	Bauer, Walter, Frederick Danker, William F. Arndt, and F. Wilbur Gingrich. *A Greek-English Lexicon of the New Testament and Other Early Christian Literature*. 3rd ed. Chicago: University of Chicago Press, 2000.
BDF	Blass, F., A. Debrunner, and Robert W. Funk. *A Greek Grammar of the New Testament and Other Early Christian Literature*. Chicago: University of Chicago Press, 1961.
Culy, *I, II, III John*	Culy, Martin M. *I, II, III John*. Baylor Handbook on the Greek New Testament. Waco, TX: Baylor University Press, 2005.
Dana and Mantey, *Manual Grammar*	Dana, H. E., and Julius R. Mantey. *A Manual Grammar of the Greek New Testament*. Toronto: Macmillan, 1927.
dat.	dative
Derickson, *1, 2, & 3 John*	Derickson, Gary W. *1, 2, & 3 John*. Evangelical Exegetical Commentary. Bellingham, WA: Lexham, 2014.

EDNT	Balz, H., and G. Schneider. *Exegetical Dictionary of the New Testament*. 3 vols. Grand Rapids: Eerdmans, 1990–1993.
e.g.	*exempli gratia* (Lat.), for example
Fanning, *Verbal Aspect*	Fanning, Buist M. *Verbal Aspect in New Testament Greek*. Oxford: Clarendon, 1990.
fem.	feminine
fut.	future
i.e.	*id est* (Lat.), that is
impf.	imperfect (tense)
impv.	imperative (mood)
ind.	indicative (mood)
inf.	infinitive
KJV	King James Version
KMP, *Deeper Greek*	Köstenberger, Andreas J., Benjamin L. Merkle, and Robert L. Plummer. *Going Deeper with New Testament Greek: An Intermediate Study of the Grammar and Syntax of the New Testament*. Rev. ed. Nashville: B&H Academic, 2020.
LN	Louw, Johannes P., and Eugene A. Nida. *Greek-English Lexicon of the New Testament Based on Semantic Domains*. 2 vols. New York: United Bible Societies, 1988.
LXX	Septuagint (Greek Old Testament)
masc.	masculine
Metzger, *Textual Commentary*	Metzger, Bruce. *Textual Commentary on the Greek New Testament*. 2nd ed. Stuttgart: UBS, 1994.
mid.	middle (voice)
NA	*Novum Testamentum Graece*, Nestle-Aland
NASB	New American Standard Bible®, Copyright © 1960, 1971, 1977, 1995, 2020 by The Lockman Foundation. All rights reserved.
NASB1995	New American Standard Bible®, Copyright © 1960, 1971, 1977, 1995 by The Lockman Foundation. All rights reserved.

NIDNTTE	Silva, Moisés, ed. *New International Dictionary of New Testament Theology and Exegesis.* 5 vols. Grand Rapids: Zondervan, 2014.
NIV	Holy Bible, New International Version®, NIV® Copyright ©1973, 1978, 1984, 2011 by Biblica, Inc.® Used by permission. All rights reserved worldwide.
NLT	*Holy Bible*, New Living Translation, copyright © 1996, 2004, 2015 by Tyndale House Foundation. Used by permission of Tyndale House Publishers, Inc., Carol Stream, Illinois 60188. All rights reserved.
nom.	nominative
NRSV	New Revised Standard Version of the Bible, copyright © 1989 Division of Christian Education of the National Council of the Churches of Christ in the USA. Used by permission. All rights reserved.
neut.	neuter
opt.	optative
pass.	passive (voice)
per.	perfect
pl.	plural
plpf.	pluperfect
pres.	present
ptc.	participle
Porter, *Idioms*	Porter, Stanley E. *Idioms of the Greek New Testament.* 2nd ed. Sheffield: Sheffield Academic Press, 1994.
Robertson, *Grammar*	Robertson, A. T. *A Grammar of the Greek New Testament in the Light of Historical Research.* 4th ed. Nashville: Broadman, 1934.

RSV	
sg.	singular
subjunc.	subjunctive
UBS	*The Greek New Testament*, United Bible Society
v(v).	verse(s)
Wallace, *Greek Grammar*	Wallace, Daniel B. *Greek Grammar beyond the Basics: An Exegetical Syntax of the New Testament*. Grand Rapids: Zondervan, 1996.
Young, *Intermediate Greek*	Young, Richard A. *Intermediate New Testament Greek: A Linguistic and Exegetical Approach*. Nashville: B&H, 1994.
Zerwick, *Biblical Greek*	Zerwick, Maximilian. *Biblical Greek: Illustrated by Examples*. Rome: Scripta Pontificii Instituti Biblici, 1963.

INTRODUCTION

//////////////

G reek professors have long seen the advantage of studying the book of 1 John with their students due to its simple syntax and its manageable length and vocabulary. So, after completing the basics of Greek grammar, students usually continue their journey in Koine Greek by translating and studying 1 John. But why another textbook on 1 John? What does this book offer that others do not? Please allow us to share some unique features of this book.

First, this book divides the text of 1 John into fourteen sections, corresponding to fourteen chapters of the textbook. This means that, on average, the student will translate and work through seven verses per chapter. Because there are fourteen chapters, a professor could assign one chapter per week for a manageable semester-long load, or even two a week over the course of a half semester.

Second, each chapter of this book contains twelve vocabulary words (a total of 180 words). The words chosen for each chapter include two groups of terms: (1) words in the designated 1 John passage that occur fewer than fifty times throughout the NT (words that occur more than fifty times have presumably already been learned) and (2) words from a descending frequency list. By the time the student finishes the textbook, he or she will have encountered every word appearing thirty times or more in the NT. This means that a student could self-sufficiently use a NT Greek reader with the aid of the footnotes. The twelve words contained in these lists are grouped together into three categories: (1) nouns; (2) adjectives, adverbs, conjunctions, participles, etc.; and (3) verbs. Words that are grouped together are typically easier to memorize.

Third, this book includes not just verse-by-verse (phrase-by-phrase) reading notes of 1 John, but it also includes a brief summary of NT Greek syntax. Each summary follows the order and basic content of *Going Deeper with New Testament Greek*. Furthermore, all of the examples that illustrate each particular syntax category are taken from 1 John (when applicable). This aids in the reinforcement and retention of the material.

Fourth, this book provides appropriate-level reading notes of the text. Although the notes cover various syntactical features of each passage, attention is also given to the particular syntactical focus of that chapter. So, for example, because chapter 4 focuses on the dative case, the notes of 1 John 2:7–14 will highlight the use of the dative in the text.

In drawing some portions of this book from our previously published works, we have endeavored to carry over essential footnotes, but readers are referred to those other publications for more extensive footnotes and references. I (Ben) and Rob are close friends and have worked on many projects together. In writing this *1 John Reader*, I took lead on the draft, with Rob coming back through, making revisions and edits. It was a collaborative effort. At points, we did not always agree on an interpretation or syntactical function, but we recognize legitimate grounds for our differing interpretations. We want to thank our editor, Renée Chavez; B&H Academic staff; volunteer proofreader Christian Hedland; designer Trina Fulton; and the many freelancers involved in this volume for their skillful assistance. Finally, unless otherwise noted, the English translations are by us (Merkle or Plummer) and the Greek text is from the Nestle-Aland 28th edition.

///////////////

1 JOHN 1:1–4

KOINE GREEK AND TEXTUAL CRITICISM

1.1 Vocabulary

ἀνάστασις, -εως, ἡ	resurrection (42)
ἔρημος, ἡ	desert, wilderness (48)
ἡμέτερος, -α, -ον	our (7)
κοινωνία, ἡ	fellowship, communion (19)
μέρος, -ους, τό	part, share, district (42)
διέρχομαι	I go through, cross over (43)
εὐλογέω	I bless, praise (42)
θεάομαι	I see, look at, behold (22)
παραλαμβάνω	I take (to oneself), take with/along (49)
πάσχω	I suffer (42)
φωνέω	I call (43)
ψηλαφάω	I touch, handle (4)

1.2 Text: 1 John 1:1–4

¹ Ὃ ἦν ἀπ' ἀρχῆς, ὃ ἀκηκόαμεν, ὃ ἑωράκαμεν τοῖς ὀφθαλμοῖς ἡμῶν, ὃ ἐθεασάμεθα καὶ αἱ χεῖρες ἡμῶν ἐψηλάφησαν περὶ τοῦ λόγου τῆς ζωῆς—² καὶ ἡ ζωὴ ἐφανερώθη, καὶ ἑωράκαμεν καὶ μαρτυροῦμεν καὶ ἀπαγγέλλομεν ὑμῖν τὴν ζωὴν τὴν αἰώνιον ἥτις ἦν πρὸς τὸν πατέρα καὶ ἐφανερώθη ἡμῖν—³ ὃ ἑωράκαμεν καὶ ἀκηκόαμεν, ἀπαγγέλλομεν καὶ ὑμῖν, ἵνα καὶ ὑμεῖς κοινωνίαν ἔχητε μεθ' ἡμῶν. καὶ ἡ κοινωνία δὲ ἡ ἡμετέρα μετὰ τοῦ πατρὸς καὶ μετὰ τοῦ υἱοῦ αὐτοῦ Ἰησοῦ Χριστοῦ. ⁴ καὶ ταῦτα γράφομεν ἡμεῖς, ἵνα ἡ χαρὰ ἡμῶν ᾖ πεπληρωμένη.

1.3 Syntax: Koine Greek and Textual Criticism

1.3.1 Koine Greek

The Greek of the NT is also called Koine (or "common") Greek. It was the spoken language in Greece and throughout the ancient Mediterranean world from roughly 300 BC to AD 330. The Greek spoken *before* the Koine period is known as classical Greek, whose usage spanned from about 1000 BC to 300 BC. The dialect spoken *after* the Koine period is known as Byzantine Greek. This linguistic era lasted for more than a millenium (AD 330–1453). Today's modern Greek is much different from Koine Greek. Just as a modern English speaker has difficulty understanding the King James Version (1611) or the plays of William Shakespeare (1564–1616), the modern student of Koine Greek will have difficulty understanding modern Greek.

The Koine period began during the military conquests of Alexander the Great, son of Philip II of Macedon. Alexander, who had studied under Aristotle (384–322 BC), made it his goal to permeate the lands he conquered with the culture and language of Greece. By 326 BC Alexander had conquered much of the known world from Eastern Europe to India. Thus, the Koine period spans from the unifying effects of Alexander's conquests (c. 300 BC) to the moving of the capital of Rome to Constantinople (AD 330).

The NT reflects the common Greek of its time and is not a unique "Holy Spirit" Greek. Several changes to the language occurred during the Koine period, partly fueled by the spread of the language to non-native speakers. Some of the changes from classical to Koine are (1) the rapidly diminishing use of the optative mood (employed only sixty-eight times in the NT); (2) the increased use of prepositions (instead of merely case endings) to communicate syntactical relationships more explicitly; (3) the virtual disappearance of the letters *digamma* (ϝ) and *koppa* (ϙ), except in numbers and some inscriptions; (4) the increased use of the paratactic (coordinate) style over the hypotactic (subordinate) style of writing (e.g., the style of 1 John is composed in paratactic style); and (5) the increased use of the positive form of the adjective to express comparative and superlative meanings, comparative adjectives to express superlative meanings, and superlative forms to express elative meanings.

1.3.2 Textual Criticism

Textual criticism can be defined as the study of different ancient manuscripts of the same literary work with the goal of determining what the author originally wrote. Because there are slight differences (i.e., variants) among the more than 5,000 ancient NT Greek manuscripts (or portions of manuscripts) available today, we sometimes need to adjudicate which of the readings reflects the author's original wording. In order to determine the most likely reading, it is important to consider both external and internal evidence.[1]

External evidence relates to the age, location, and quantity of the manuscripts that support a particular variant. Here are three principles for adjudicating the external evidence:

1. *Favor the older manuscripts.* Typically, the older a manuscript is, the fewer the opportunities there are for errors to creep in. Conversely, the younger (newer) a manuscript is, the further separated in time it is from the original, and thus, though multiple copies might exist, there is a greater opportunity for errors to be introduced into the manuscript. Thus, manuscripts that are often favored include א (Sinaiticus, fourth century), A (Alexandrinus, fifth century), B (Vaticanus, fourth century), C (Ephraemi Rescriptus, fifth century), and D (Claromontanus, sixth century).

2. *Favor the reading supported by the majority of (significant) manuscripts.* Because most of the manuscripts that we possess today are from the Byzantine tradition, and because these are relatively young manuscripts (eighth through fifteenth centuries), we have to qualify this principle with the term *significant.* These later manuscripts are often not considered as significant since they have gone through centuries of transmission (copying the copies of copies) and the potential introduction of errors. Occasionally a later manuscript can be a direct copy of a very early one and thus be a more significant witness for the original text. Thus, manuscripts must be weighed and not merely counted.

3. *Favor the reading best attested across various families of manuscripts.* Over time, recognizable, distinct streams of text transmission developed. Within these streams (delineated by geographical provenance) flowed manuscripts with similar patterns of variants. There are three main families of manuscripts based upon geographic provenance: (1) Byzantine, (2) Alexandrian, and (3) Western. The manuscripts in these families often betray a "family" resemblance which indicates a common source. The Alexandrian family (which includes large portions of א, A, B, C) is often considered the most reliable. A disputed reading found in manuscripts from several families is considered more weighty.

Internal evidence relates to the literary and grammatical context of where the disputed variants are found. Below are a few general principles of how to judge the internal evidence:

---

[1] The presentation below follows a traditional approach to NT textual criticism, though the field is changing rapidly. With digitized transcriptions of ancient manuscripts and powerful computer algorithms, text critics have a growing confidence in determining more precisely the genealogical relationships among manuscripts without classifying them into broad families. Cutting-edge text critics generally adhere to this Coherence-Based Genealogical Method (CBGM).

1. *Favor the reading that best explains the origin of the other variants.* This is perhaps the most important internal criterion since it is helpful to deduce what might have caused the variant in the first place. It is sometimes possible to reconstruct a series of mistakes or attempted fixes that all flow from a scribal alteration of the original reading.
2. *Favor the reading that best fits the literary context.* This holds true as a general rule. Of course, sometimes NT authors wrote shocking or unexpected things, so this criterion must not be rigidly applied.
3. *Favor the reading that best corresponds with writings by the same NT author.* Authors have general stylistic patterns and theological motifs. As noted above, however, authors are not always predictable. The use of an amanuensis (ancient secretary) and differing purposes can explain stylistic variations within the same text.
4. *Favor the more difficult reading.* Later additions often attempt to "fix" a perceived problem. This criterion cannot be applied in isolation from the other principles mentioned above, but scribes, when not making mistakes of hearing or sight, were prone to smooth out difficulties rather than introduce them.
5. *Favor the shorter reading.* As texts were often lengthened or clarified, the shorter reading should usually be preferred. This is especially true when investigating parallel passages within the Synoptic Gospels.

Two somewhat significant textual variants are found in 1 John 1:4. The first involves the pronoun ἡμεῖς in the phrase καὶ ταῦτα γράφομεν ἡμεῖς, "*We* are writing these things." The first-person personal pronoun functions emphatically, stressing the subject of the verb (i.e., "we"). Some manuscripts, however, read: καὶ ταῦτα γράφομεν ὑμῖν, "We are writing these things *to you.*" In this case, the second-person personal pronoun functions as the indirect object of the verb. Which reading is correct?

The evidence is split. The external manuscript evidence for ἡμεῖς includes ℵ A* B P Ψ 33 it² cop^ms, whereas the evidence for ὑμῖν includes A^c C K L *Byz.* The former has earlier support, but the latter has both Alexandrian and Byzantine support. The internal evidence is also not easy to adjudicate. In favor of the first reading (ἡμεῖς) is the fact that it is the more difficult reading. This type of construction typically includes a dative indirect object (cf. v. 3, ἀπαγγέλλομεν καὶ ὑμῖν).[2] So, it could be that a scribe attempted to "fix" (consciously or unconsciously) the text and make it conform to expectations. In favor of ὑμῖν, if John wanted to use the pronoun ἡμεῖς emphatically, he perhaps would have placed it before the main verb. In the end, although it is important for us to seek to determine the text closest to the original, the variant readings in no way obscure the overall message of the text.

The second major variant involves the pronoun ἡμῶν in the phrase ἵνα ἡ χαρὰ ἡμῶν ᾖ πεπληρωμένη, "so that *our* joy may be complete." The variant reads "so

---

2 Metzger, *Textual Commentary*, 639.

that your [ὑμῶν] joy may be complete." The external evidence of ἡμῶν has stronger Alexandrian support (ℵ B L Ψ 049 88 181 326 426 1241 Lect^m it^{p,t,z} vg^{ww} cop^{sa}). On the other hand, ὑμῶν is found in some Alexandrian manuscripts and in the Byzantine tradition (A C^{vid} K P *Byz* et al.). The internal evidence favors ἡμῶν since it is the more difficult reading (perhaps some scribes thought it came across as a bit selfish to write for "our own joy" and not for the joy of others). For example, Derickson, favoring ὑμῶν, writes, "It seems more likely [the apostle's] focus would be on the heart and hope of his readers rather than his own satisfaction" (an argument solely from internal evidence).[3] Yet, Derickson also asserts, "In both instances either word makes sense in the sentence, and neither changes its basic meaning nor impacts any doctrines."[4]

1.4 Reading Notes

1 John 1:1

- Ὃ ἦν ἀπ' ἀρχῆς

  John begins his epistle in an unusual manner. He does not begin with his name, the name of the recipients (church), or with a formal greeting. Instead, he begins with the neuter relative pronoun ὅ. Because ὅ is the first word, it does not have an expressed literary antecedent (i.e., it is a "headless" relative pronoun), but most scholars agree that it refers to the person and work of Jesus. Although a masculine form might be expected (i.e., ὅς), the neuter form "is sometimes used with reference to persons if it is not the individuals but a general quality that is to be emphasized" (BDF §138).[5] The first occurrence of ὅ functions as the nominative subject, but the other four uses (three in v. 1 and one in v. 3) function as the accusative direct objects of the verb ἀπαγγέλλομεν (v. 3).

  The verb ἦν (impf. ind. 3rd sg. εἰμί) is common, occurring in this form 413 times in the NT and eleven times in 1 John.

  The prepositional phrase ἀπ' ἀρχῆς can be considered definite, even though the article is not included: "from *the* beginning." Anarthrous objects of prepositions are often definite (as determined from contextual analysis).

---

[3] Derickson, *1, 2, & 3 John*, 46.
[4] Derickson, 45–46.
[5] It is also possible that the neuter form is a matter of John's idiolect since he sometimes uses neuter forms where masculine forms are expected (e.g., John 3:6; 4:22; 6:37, 39; 17:2, 10; 1 John 5:4).

- ὃ ἀκηκόαμεν

The neuter relative pronoun is repeated for the second time (of five) in this verse.

The verb ἀκηκόαμεν (per. act. ind. 1st pl. ἀκούω) has somewhat of an irregular form. As a perfect verb that begins with a vowel, the first two letters are reduplicated instead of the first letter (as with verbs beginning with consonants). This reduplication of the first syllable is called "Attic reduplication" and is rare in the NT. Also, the expected *kappa* (χ) added to the end of the stem is lacking, probably due to an overabundance of *kappas* that would affect pronunciation (ἀκουόμεν → ακακοκαμεν → ἀκηκόαμεν). In Koine Greek, the perfect tense (stative aspect) often signifies ongoing relevance of a prior action, as here, where it undergirds John's role of announcing and bearing witness (1:2).

- ὃ ἑωράκαμεν τοῖς ὀφθαλμοῖς ἡμῶν

The verb ἑωράκαμεν (per. act. ind. 1st pl. ὁράω) is parsed identically as the previous verb (ἀκηκόαμεν) and occurs twice more in this passage (vv. 2, 3). The *epsilon* (ε) at the beginning of the word is not an augment (which communicates past time) but is part of the reduplication process. But because the word begins with a vowel and not a consonant, the only part of the reduplication remaining is the added vowel (i.e., vocalic reduplication), and the original *omicron* (o) vowel is lengthened to an *omega* (ω). The perfect tense (stative aspect) likely draws attention to these verbs.[6] "The first person plural verbs in verses 1–4 probably (1) highlight the writer's status as one of a limited group of eyewitnesses, and (2) bolster the authority of the letter by linking it to that group."[7]

The phrase τοῖς ὀφθαλμοῖς is a dative of means or instrument (see §4.3). It specifies the *means* by which the verb is accomplished: "*with* our eyes."

- ὃ ἐθεασάμεθα καὶ αἱ χεῖρες ἡμῶν ἐψηλάφησαν περὶ τοῦ λόγου τῆς ζωῆς—

The verb ἐθεασάμεθα (aor. mid. ind. 1st pl θεάομαι) denotes a shift in tense from the perfect (ἀκηκόαμεν, ἑωράκαμεν) to the aorist. Louw and Nida suggest that θεάομαι differs from ὁράω in that the former includes the nuance of "continuity and attention, often with the implication that what is observed is something unusual" (LN §24.14).

---

6 Wallace, *Greek Grammar*, 578.
7 Culy, *I, II, III John*, 2–3.

The verb ἐψηλάφησαν (aor. act. ind. 3rd pl. ψηλαφάω) is used only three other times in the NT (Luke 24:39; Acts 17:27; Heb 12:18). Most notably, in Luke 24:39 Jesus states, "Look at my hands and my feet, that it is I myself! Touch [ψηλαφήσατε] me and see, because a ghost does not have flesh and bones as you can see I have" (CSB). John is emphasizing that he and the other apostles physically touched the body of Jesus. He was no mere ghost or phantom. That is, at the beginning of his epistle, John is stressing that Jesus Christ has come in the flesh.

The prepositional phrase περὶ τοῦ λόγου τῆς ζωῆς contains an example of Apollonius's Canon. This canon (rule) states that two nouns joined in a genitive phrase are either both articular (including the article) or are both anarthrous (omitting the article).

1 John 1:2

- καὶ ἡ ζωὴ ἐφανερώθη

The dash added before and after verse 2 indicates that the editors of the Greek text view this verse as a parenthetical comment that expands on the meaning of ζωή at the end of verse 1. Thus, the conjunction καί at the beginning of this verse has a parenthetical or explanatory function (BDAG 495).

The use of the article in ἡ ζωή is likely communicating "previous reference" (also called the anaphoric use of the article; see §5.3.1). That is, the article points back to the previous appearance of ζωή in verse 1 (περὶ τοῦ λόγου τῆς ζωῆς). To communicate this function of the article in translation, several English versions rightly translate the phrase "that life," referring back to the previous mention of ζωή. The "life" is a personification of Jesus (see John 11:25; 14:6; Rev 1:18). Many times when a noun appears with an anaphoric article, the previous (and initial) appearance of that noun is anarthrous. That is not the case in 1 John 1:2.

The verb ἐφανερώθη (aor. pass. ind. 3rd sg. φανερόω) is used twice in this verse—at the beginning and at the end, forming an *inclusio*.

- καὶ ἑωράκαμεν καὶ μαρτυροῦμεν καὶ ἀπαγγέλλομεν ὑμῖν τὴν ζωὴν τὴν αἰώνιον

The author shifts from the perfect tense (ἑωράκαμεν) to the present tense with the verbs μαρτυροῦμεν (pres. act. ind. 1st pl. μαρτυρέω) and ἀπαγγέλλομεν (pres. act. ind. 1st pl. ἀπαγγέλλω). These uses of the present tense suggest that John sees the letter he is writing as an example of testi-fying and proclaiming.[8]

The phrase τὴν ζωὴν τὴν αἰώνιον follows a common Greek pattern for an attributive adjective (article + noun + article + adjective).

- ἥτις ἦν πρὸς τὸν πατέρα καὶ ἐφανερώθη ἡμῖν—

The feminine relative pronoun ἥτις refers back to the antecedent feminine noun τὴν ζωήν. The relative pronoun must agree with its antecedent in gender and number but case is determined from syntactical function. The alternate form ἥτις, an indefinite relative pronoun in earlier time periods (ἥ + τις = ἥτις), is a virtual synonym to ἥ in most appearances in the Koine period. That is, the indefinite relative pronoun (usually in nominative case) is used synonymously with the simple relative pronoun in many places in the NT (BDAG 730).

1 John 1:3

- ὃ ἑωράκαμεν καὶ ἀκηκόαμεν

After John provides the fifth (and final) neuter relative pronoun (ὃ), he then repeats the ἑωράκαμεν for a third time and ἀκηκόαμεν for a second time. The repetition of the verbs demonstrate a chiastic pattern:[9]

> A ἀκηκόαμεν (v. 1)
>   B ἑωράκαμεν (v. 1)
>   C ἐφανερώθη (v. 2)
>   B ἑωράκαμεν (v. 2)
>   C ἐφανερώθη (v. 2)
>   B ἑωράκαμεν (v. 3)
> A ἀκηκόαμεν (v. 3)

This pattern demonstrates two key elements. First, it signifies that ἐφανερώθη, "he/it was revealed," is the focus of the passage. Second, it brings closure to the introductory section and sets up the main verb that follows.

- ἀπαγγέλλομεν καὶ ὑμῖν

The verb ἀπαγγέλλομεν is the main verb in verses 1–3: "that which . . .

---

[8] See Baugh, *First John Reader*, 4.
[9] See Baugh, 2.

we declare to you." The function of καί here cannot be as a mere connector (i.e., "*and* we are declaring to you") due to the word order. Another option is to take καί as "also" (i.e., "we are declaring *also* to you"). But this interpretation is probably not best since it places emphasis on the act of the author previously declaring this message to others and now also to his readers. Thus, taking καί as "even" is the best option: "we are declaring *even* to you" (BDAG 495–96). Some find this interpretation attractive if John is writing from the perspective of a Jewish apostle to a primarily Gentile audience. He is then boldly proclaiming a message about Jesus (a Jewish Messiah) even to those who are Gentiles. In the early church, the distinction between Jews and Gentiles was often *the* central issue that could divide the church.

- ἵνα καὶ ὑμεῖς κοινωνίαν ἔχητε μεθ᾽ ἡμῶν

The conjunction ἵνα introduces a purpose clause and triggers the subjunctive mood (ἔχητε: pres. act. subjunc. 2nd pl. ἔχω). Here, John provides the first stated purpose of writing this epistle—that his readers would have fellowship with him and others. Because the pronoun is implied and embedded in the verb ἔχητε, "*you* have," the addition of the pronoun ὑμεῖς makes it emphatic.

The καί once again cannot be translated as "and" but can be translated as "also" or "even." If the latter is correct, then once again John is emphasizing the significance of him writing to Gentiles: "in order that *even you* might have fellowship with *us*."

- καὶ ἡ κοινωνία δὲ ἡ ἡμετέρα μετὰ τοῦ πατρὸς καὶ μετὰ τοῦ υἱοῦ αὐτοῦ Ἰησοῦ Χριστοῦ.

John further elaborates on the fellowship that he and other eyewitnesses have. This sentence has no verb, and thus the verb (ἐστίν) is implied: "our fellowship *is* with the Father." Forms of the verb εἰμί are often implied in Greek.

The "and" found in English versions translates δέ: "*and* our fellowship." Again, that leaves us with the question of the function of καί. In this context, "and," "also," and "even" do not fit. Instead, καί explains a previous statement (see BDAG 495). Consequently, several English versions translate καί as "indeed" (CSB, ESV, NASB, NET) or "truly" (NKJV, NRSV).

The pronominal adjective ἡμετέρα, "our," is uncommon, occurring only seven times in the NT. The more common way to express first-person plural possession is with the genitive ἡμῶν. Perhaps John is once again highlighting the contrast between "our" and "your" by using the less common term. Indeed, it may be the rare (and arguably emphatic) form ἡμετέρα that influenced English translations to add "indeed" or "truly."

The genitive phrase Ἰησοῦ Χριστοῦ is in apposition to τοῦ υἱοῦ αὐτοῦ (see §3.3). When a word is in apposition to another word, it appears in the same case and points to the same referent, providing additional explanation to the reader. In English, we can add the words *that is* or *namely* to convey the appositional function: "his son, *that is*, Jesus Christ."

1 John 1:4

- καὶ ταῦτα γράφομεν ἡμεῖς

  The text critical issues in this verse were discussed earlier (see §1.3.2). If the correct reading is ἡμεῖς, then John is stating emphatically that he (on behalf of other eyewitnesses) is writing (γράφομεν: pres. act. ind. 1st pl. γράφω) to his readers.

- ἵνα ἡ χαρὰ ἡμῶν ᾖ πεπληρωμένη.

  The conjunction ἵνα introduces a second purpose statement and triggers the subjunctive mood (ᾖ: pres. subjunc. 3rd sg. εἰμί). The verb ᾖ is in a periphrastic construction with πεπληρωμένη (per. pass. ptc. fem. nom. sg. πληρόω). Because the aorist and present tense are essentially John's only choices for a subjunctive-mood verb, a periphrastic construction (see §10.3.5) is needed to convey stative aspect (pres. subjunc. + per. ptc. = stative aspect).

CHAPTER 2

///////////////////

1 JOHN 1:5–10

NOMINATIVE, VOCATIVE, AND ACCUSATIVE CASES

2.1 Vocabulary

ἀγγελία, ἡ	message (2)
σκοτία, ἡ	darkness (16)
ἀδικία, ἡ	unrighteousness, injustice (25)
σκότος, -ους, τό	darkness (31)
ψεύστης, ὁ	liar (10)
ἄξιος, -ία, -ον	worthy, fit, deserving (41)
πάντοτε	always (41)
ἀναγγέλλω	I report, announce, proclaim (cf. ἀπαγγέλλω) (14)
καθαρίζω	I cleanse, purify (31)
ὁμολογέω	I confess, profess (26)
πλανάω	I go astray, am misled, wander (39)
ψεύδομαι	I lie (12)

2.2 Text: 1 John 1:5–10

⁵ Καὶ ἔστιν αὕτη ἡ ἀγγελία ἣν ἀκηκόαμεν ἀπ' αὐτοῦ καὶ ἀναγγέλλομεν ὑμῖν, ὅτι ὁ θεὸς φῶς ἐστιν καὶ σκοτία ἐν αὐτῷ οὐκ ἔστιν οὐδεμία. ⁶ Ἐὰν εἴπωμεν ὅτι κοινωνίαν ἔχομεν μετ' αὐτοῦ καὶ ἐν τῷ σκότει περιπατῶμεν, ψευδόμεθα καὶ οὐ ποιοῦμεν τὴν ἀλήθειαν· ⁷ ἐὰν ἐν τῷ φωτὶ περιπατῶμεν, ὡς αὐτός ἐστιν ἐν τῷ φωτί, κοινωνίαν ἔχομεν μετ' ἀλλήλων, καὶ τὸ αἷμα Ἰησοῦ τοῦ υἱοῦ αὐτοῦ καθαρίζει ἡμᾶς ἀπὸ πάσης ἁμαρτίας. ⁸ ἐὰν εἴπωμεν ὅτι ἁμαρτίαν οὐκ ἔχομεν, ἑαυτοὺς πλανῶμεν καὶ ἡ ἀλήθεια οὐκ ἔστιν ἐν

ἡμῖν. ⁹ἐὰν ὁμολογῶμεν τὰς ἁμαρτίας ἡμῶν, πιστός ἐστιν καὶ δίκαιος, ἵνα ἀφῇ ἡμῖν τὰς ἁμαρτίας καὶ καθαρίσῃ ἡμᾶς ἀπὸ πάσης ἀδικίας. ¹⁰ἐὰν εἴπωμεν ὅτι οὐχ ἡμαρτήκαμεν, ψεύστην ποιοῦμεν αὐτὸν καὶ ὁ λόγος αὐτοῦ οὐκ ἔστιν ἐν ἡμῖν.

2.3 Syntax: Nominative, Vocative, and Accusative Cases

2.3.1 Nominative Case

Beginning Greek students learn that the nominative case functions as the subject of a sentence. Although this is true in many instances, the nominative case is not limited to one function. The following represent several key uses:

- **Subject.** The subject of the finite verb.

  - ἔστιν **αὕτη** ἡ ἀγγελία, "**this** is the message" (1 John 1:5).[1]
  - **ὁ θεὸς** φῶς ἐστιν, "**God** is light" (1 John 1:5).
  - **αὐτός** ἐστιν ἐν τῷ φωτί, "**he** is in the light" (1 John 1:7).

- **Predicate Nominative.** Expresses a characteristic or state of the subject with a copulative verb.

  - ἔστιν αὕτη **ἡ ἀγγελία**, "this is **the message**" (1 John 1:5).
  - ὁ θεὸς **φῶς** ἐστιν, "God is **light**" (1 John 1:5).
  - **πιστός** ἐστιν καὶ **δίκαιος**, "he is **faithful** and **just**" (1 John 1:9).[2]

- **Apposition.** Provides an additional substantive with the same referent as another nominative noun.

  - καὶ αὕτη ἐστὶν ἡ νίκη ἡ νικήσασα τὸν κόσμον, **ἡ πίστις** ἡμῶν, "and this is the conquering which conquers the world, **that is**, our **faith**" (1 John 5:4). "Faith" (ἡ πίστις) is in apposition to αὕτη.
  - οὗτός ἐστιν ὁ ἐλθὼν δι᾽ ὕδατος καὶ αἵματος, **Ἰησοῦς Χριστός**, "This is the one who came by water and blood, **Jesus Christ**" (1 John 5:6).

- **Other Categories** (not found in 1 John):

  - **Absolute.** Grammatically independent and often used in greetings: Παῦλος δοῦλος Χριστοῦ Ἰησοῦ, "**Paul**, a servant of Christ Jesus" (Rom 1:1).

---

[1] The English translation here takes αὕτη as the subject, though αὕτη could also be attributive, modifying ἡ ἀγγελία: "this message is."

[2] Technically, these are predicate adjectives.

○ **Address.** A nominative (usually articular) used in the place of a vocative: οἱ ἄνδρες, ἀγαπᾶτε τὰς γυναῖκας, "**Husbands**, love your wives" (Eph 5:25).

Most verbs take a direct object in the accusative case (with some verbs, the direct object can be in the genitive or the dative case). With equative or copulative verbs (such as εἰμί, γίνομαι, or ὑπάρχω), the reader can expect two substantives in the nominative case: the subject *and* the predicate nominative. Because word order in Greek is flexible, in situations where there are two substantives in the nominative case, how do we determine which is the subject and which is the predicate nominative? Wallace provides the following guidelines to determine the subject:[3]

1. If one is a pronoun (whether stated or embedded in the verb), it is the subject.
2. If one is articular, it is the subject.
3. If one is a proper name, it is the subject.

Additionally, Wallace lists a "pecking order" for when both nouns have one of these qualities: the pronoun has the highest priority and articular nouns and proper names have an equal status in determining the subject.

2.3.2 Vocative Case

The vocative case indicates the person (or group) that is being directly addressed. In 1 John 1, the vocative case occurs fourteen times with a total of five different terms. It always appears as a plural noun: τεκνία (2:1, 12, 28; 3:18; 4:4; 5:21), πατέρες (2:13, 14), νεανίσκοι (2:13, 14), παιδία (2:14, 18; 3:7), and ἀδελφοί (3:13). In nearly every instance, the vocative occurs at the beginning of a new paragraph (and always at the beginning of a sentence). Although not used in 1 John, the most common distinct ending in the vocative case is the masculine singular ending –ε (e.g., κύριε).

2.3.3 Accusative Case

The accusative case is the case of *limitation* or *extension*, delimiting the action of a verb. More specifically, it can convey the end, direction, or extent of an action, often answering the question, How far?[4] As Wallace states, "The *accusative* limits as to *quantity* . . . the accusative is concerned about the extent and the scope of the verb's action."[5] Students initially learn that the accusative case functions as the direct object of the verb. But, as with the nominative (and the genitive and dative) case, there are several important uses:

---

[3] Wallace, *Greek Grammar*, 42–46.
[4] Dana and Mantey, *Manual Grammar*, 91–92.
[5] Wallace, *Greek Grammar*, 178.

- **Direct Object.** Indicates the recipient/object of the verbal action.

  ○ κοινωνίαν ἔχομεν, "we have **fellowship**" (1 John 1:6).

  ○ οὐ ποιοῦμεν **τὴν ἀλήθειαν**, "we do not practice **the truth**" (1 John 1:6).

- **Double Accusative.** Sometimes a verb has more than one accusative object to complete the thought. The words *to be* or *as* are often added to an English translation.

  ○ ψεύστην ποιοῦμεν **αὐτὸν**, "we make **him** [to be] **a liar**" (1 John 1:10).

  ○ ἀπέστειλεν τὸν υἱὸν αὐτοῦ **ἱλασμὸν** περὶ τῶν ἁμαρτιῶν ἡμῶν, "he sent his **Son** as a **propitiation** for our sins" (1 John 4:10).

  ○ ὁ πατὴρ ἀπέσταλκεν **τὸν υἱὸν σωτῆρα** τοῦ κόσμου, "the Father has sent **the Son** [to be] **the Savior** of the world" (1 John 4:14).

- **Apposition.** Provides an additional substantive with the same referent as another noun in the accusative case.

  ○ παράκλητον ἔχομεν πρὸς τὸν πατέρα **Ἰησοῦν Χριστὸν δίκαιον**, "we have an advocate with the Father, **Jesus Christ, the righteous one**" (1 John 2:1). Here, Ἰησοῦν Χριστόν is in apposition to παράκλητον, and δίκαιον is in apposition to Ἰησοῦν Χριστόν.

- **Respect.** Limits or qualifies the extent of the verbal action.

  ○ καὶ ἐὰν οἴδαμεν ὅτι ἀκούει ἡμῶν **ὃ ἐὰν αἰτώμεθα**, οἴδαμεν, "and if we know that he hears us **with respect to whatever** we ask, we know" (1 John 5:15).

- **Other Categories** (not found in 1 John):

  ○ **Measure.** Indicates the extent (time or space) of a verbal action: καὶ προσελθὼν **μικρόν**, ἔπεσεν ἐπὶ πρόσωπον αὐτοῦ, "And going **a little farther**, he fell on his face" (Matt 26:39).

  ○ **Manner.** Specifies the way in which a verbal action is performed: **δωρεὰν** δότε, "give **freely**" (Matt 10:8).

  ○ **Subject of Infinitive.** Functions as the subject of an infinitive, indicating the agent performing the action conveyed by the infinitive: διὰ τὸ ἔχειν **με** ἐν τῇ καρδίᾳ ὑμᾶς, "because **I** have you in my heart" (Phil 1:7).

2.4 Reading Notes

1 John 1:5

- Καὶ ἔστιν αὕτη ἡ ἀγγελία

  The verb ἔστιν (pres. ind. 3rd sg. εἰμί) is common in 1 John, occurring seventy-four times in this specific form.

  The feminine near demonstrative pronoun αὕτη is the subject of the verb (ἔστιν), with ἡ ἀγγελία functioning as the predicate nominative. Typically, the noun that possesses the article will serve as the subject, but when one of the substantives is a pronoun, it will function as the subject.[6]

- ἣν ἀκηκόαμεν ἀπ’ αὐτοῦ καὶ ἀναγγέλλομεν ὑμῖν

  The antecedent of the feminine relative pronoun ἣν (not to be confused with the imperfect third person singular form of εἰμί = ἦν) is ἡ ἀγγελία. This pronoun functions as the direct object of the verb ἀκηκόαμεν (per. act. ind. 1st pl. ἀκούω; this verb has already appeared in 1:1, 3). The verb ἀναγγέλλομεν (pres. act. ind. 1st pl. ἀναγγέλλω) is most likely employed for stylistic variation (cf. ἀπαγγέλλω, 1:2, 3).[7] John’s idiolect is marked by the interchangeable use of near synonyms.

- ὅτι ὁ θεὸς φῶς ἐστιν

  After a verb of speaking (such as ἀναγγέλλομεν), ὅτι will typically introduce a content clause (translated “that”; see BDAG 732; BDF §397[3]).

  In the phrase ὁ θεὸς φῶς ἐστιν, ὁ θεός functions as the subject, whereas φῶς functions as the predicate nominative. This phrase is also possibly an example of Colwell’s Canon (see §5.3.1). This rule observes that when the predicate nominative is definite *from context* and *precedes* the copulative verb (usually εἰμί), then nearly 90 percent of the time the predicate nominative is anarthrous. In the phrase above, it seems more likely that φῶς is anarthrous to convey a qualitative sense. That is, God is, in essence, light (holy).

---

[6] Wallace, *Greek Grammar*, 44. It is possible that αὕτη functions attributively, with αὕτη ἡ ἀγγελία (“this message”) as the subject of ἔστιν.

[7] Culy writes, “It is unlikely . . . that a different meaning, however slight, is intended. . . . The shift to the synonym here may have been motivated by a stylistic desire to avoid repeating the morpheme ἀπ– on the heels of the proposition ἀπ’ three words earlier” (*I, II, III John,* 12).

- καὶ σκοτία ἐν αὐτῷ οὐκ ἔστιν οὐδεμία.

Again, John uses the anarthrous noun σκοτία (the subject of ἔστιν) to focus on the quality of God's character. In this case, he emphatically states that God has no darkness by using a double negation (οὐκ and οὐδεμία). Modern English versions rightly attempt to capture this emphasis: "there is *absolutely no* darkness in him" (CSB); "in him [there] is *no* darkness *at all*" (ESV, NASB, NIV; see BDF §431).

1 John 1:6

- Ἐὰν εἴπωμεν ὅτι κοινωνίαν ἔχομεν μετ' αὐτοῦ καὶ ἐν τῷ σκότει περιπατῶμεν

The conjunction ἐάν introduces the protasis (the "if" statement) of a third class conditional clause (a hypothetical projection) and triggers the subjunctive mood (εἴπωμεν: aor. act. subjunc. 1st pl. λέγω). Ἐάν is common in 1 John, occurring twenty-two times and found in every chapter. This passage (1:6–10) contains five uses of ἐάν, one at the beginning of each verse. John uses an alternating pattern in which the negative examples (vv. 6, 8, 10) alternate with a positive example (vv. 7, 9).[8] Additionally, the passage is bracketed by an *inclusio*, with ἐὰν εἴπωμεν ὅτι . . . ψευδόμεθα (v. 6) and ἐὰν εἴπωμεν ὅτι . . . ψεύστην ποιοῦμεν αὐτὸν (v. 10).[9]

Again, ὅτι introduces a content clause following a verb of speech (εἴπωμεν). The term κοινωνίαν is the accusative direct object of the verb ἔχομεν.

The verb περιπατῶμεν (pres. act. subjunc. 1st pl. περιπατέω) is parallel to εἴπωμεν (connected by καί) and is likewise controlled by ἐάν, making it subjunctive. After a word introducing the subjunctive (e.g., ἐάν), expect the subjunctive mood to govern the discourse until there is a grammatical pause or break with a punctuation mark.

- ψευδόμεθα καὶ οὐ ποιοῦμεν τὴν ἀλήθειαν·

The verbs ψευδόμεθα (pres. mid. ind. 1st pl. ψεύδομαι) and ποιοῦμεν (pres. act. ind. 1st pl. ποιέω) form the apodosis (the "then" statement) of the condition.[10] The accusative τὴν ἀλήθειαν is the direct object of the verb ποιοῦμεν. The expression οὐ ποιοῦμεν τὴν ἀλήθειαν, "we do not practice the

---

[8] See Baugh, *First John Reader*, 10.
[9] See Culy, *I, II, III John*, 13–14.
[10] Verbs of reciprocity that involve two essential parties (such as ψεύδομαι) are often found in the middle voice. See Neva F. Miller, "Appendix 2: A Theory of Deponent Verbs," in *Analytical Lexicon of the Greek New Testament*, ed. Timothy Friberg, Barbara Friberg, and Neva F. Miller (Grand Rapids: Baker, 2000), 427.

truth," is a Semitic idiom meaning to practice covenantal fidelity (see Gen 32:10 [32:11 LXX]; 47:29; Isa 26:10).

1 John 1:7

- ἐὰν ἐν τῷ φωτὶ περιπατῶμεν ὡς αὐτός ἐστιν ἐν τῷ φωτί

The text of the NA²⁷/UBS⁴ includes δέ (a postpositive conjunction) following ἐάν. The editors of the NA²⁸/UBS⁵, following the *ECM* (*Editio Critica Maior*), have concluded that the δέ, which is found in some manuscripts, is not original.

In this verse, John provides the first positive conditional statement (and the second of the five in this chapter). The verb περιπατῶμεν is a metaphor for one's conduct in life. To walk in the light means to live according to God's standards.

The personal pronoun αὐτός functions as the subject of the verb ἔστιν. Although personal pronouns as subjects of verbs usually convey emphasis (since the pronoun information is already embedded in the verb), such is not usually the case with εἰμί.[11] Explicit pronoun subjects should be expected with forms of εἰμί without any emphasis. The particular context of any passage, however, is determinative in the final analysis of a pronoun's inclusion.

- κοινωνίαν ἔχομεν μετ᾽ ἀλλήλων

The noun κοινωνίαν functions as the accusative direct object of the verb ἔχομεν, "we have *fellowship*."

The term ἀλλήλων, "one another," is a reciprocal pronoun expressing mutual action.

- καὶ τὸ αἷμα Ἰησοῦ τοῦ υἱοῦ αὐτοῦ καθαρίζει ἡμᾶς ἀπὸ πάσης ἁμαρτίας.

The noun τὸ αἷμα functions as the subject of the verb καθαρίζει, whereas the personal pronoun ἡμᾶς functions as the accusative direct object. Τὸ αἷμα functions as metonymy (a figure of speech in which one thing stands for something closely associated with it). In this case, the blood that Jesus shed on the cross stands for his atoning sacrificial death. The genitive phrase τοῦ υἱοῦ αὐτοῦ is in apposition to Ἰησοῦ: "the blood of Jesus, *his*

---

[11] See Baugh, *First John Reader*, 12.

son" (see §3.3). The personal pronoun αὐτοῦ is classified as a genitive of relationship.

Although not reflected in most English versions, πάσης ἁμαρτίας is best translated "every sin" since the forms are singular.

The verb καθαρίζει (pres. act. ind. 3rd sg. καθαρίζω) is a gnomic present, meaning that it is a generic statement that is always true (see §8.3.1).

1 John 1:8

- ἐὰν εἴπωμεν ὅτι ἁμαρτίαν οὐκ ἔχομεν

  The noun ἁμαρτίαν is the accusative direct object of the verb ἔχομεν, "we have *sin.*" Although most English versions translate this phrase, "If we say that we have no sin," the verb (ἔχομεν) is negated and not the noun (ἁμαρτίαν). Thus, more literally the phrase reads, "If we say that we do not have sin" (cf. οὐχ ἡμαρτήκαμεν in 1:10). The Greek phrase to "have sin" means simply to be in a state of having committed sin.

- ἑαυτοὺς πλανῶμεν καὶ ἡ ἀλήθεια οὐκ ἔστιν ἐν ἡμῖν.

  The reflexive pronoun ἑαυτούς functions as the accusative direct object of the verb πλανῶμεν: "we deceive *ourselves.*"

  Although the verb πλανῶμεν (pres. act. ind. 1st pl. πλανάω) looks like it might be subjunctive, it is not. The ending is –ωμεν and not –ομεν because the verb is an *alpha*-contract verb. When the *alpha* (α) of the verb's stem comes into contact with the *omicron* (ο) of the ending, they contract to an *omega* (πλανα + ομεν → πλανῶμεν). To be clear, the first-person plural present active subjunctive forms of *alpha*-contract verbs will be spelled the same as their present active indicative forms. Context must distinguish them. See 3:18, where the contract verb ἀγαπῶμεν is used as a (hortatory) subjunctive.

  The noun ἡ ἀλήθεια functions as the nominative subject of the verb ἔστιν.

1 John 1:9

- ἐὰν ὁμολογῶμεν τὰς ἁμαρτίας ἡμῶν

  In context, the verb ὁμολογῶμεν (pres. act. subjunc. 1st pl. ὁμολογέω) conveys a confession with a "focus on admission of wrongdoing" (BDAG 708).

The noun ἁμαρτίας is the accusative direct object of the verb ὁμολογῶμεν: "if we confess our *sins*." The plural ἁμαρτίας "probably points to confession of specific sins rather than confession of sinfulness in general."[12]

- πιστός ἐστιν καὶ δίκαιος

Both πιστός and δίκαιος function as predicate adjectives with the verb ἔστιν. The word order may place additional emphasis on δίκαιος, a word that is somewhat unexpected in the context. One might expect something like "God is faithful and *merciful* or *gracious*," but instead the text reads, "God is faithful and *just* or *righteous*." But how can God be just (righteous) in forgiving sinners? The answer is found in what follows where John speaks of Christ being a propitiatory sacrifice. It is the atoning death of his Son that allows God to be both "just and the justifier of the one who has faith in Jesus" (Rom 3:26 ESV). Consequently, "For God *not* to forgive in such circumstances would be *un*just, presumably because justice has already been fully satisfied through the cleansing effects of τὸ αἷμα Ἰησοῦ τοῦ υἱοῦ αὐτου (v. 7) and the concomitant act of confession."[13] In the Psalms, "righteousness" language often includes the nuance of God intervening to deliver his people from peril. That nuance also seems present here.

- ἵνα ἀφῇ ἡμῖν τὰς ἁμαρτίας καὶ καθαρίσῃ ἡμᾶς ἀπὸ πάσης ἀδικίας.

The conjunction ἵνα introduces two result clauses and triggers the subjunctive mood (ἀφῇ: aor. act. subjunc. 3rd sg. ἀφίημι; καθαρίσῃ: aor. act. subjunc. 3rd sg. καθαρίζω). "As a result of God's fidelity and justice, he forgives our sins. Forgiveness results from God's character."[14]

The pronoun ἡμῖν can be classified as a dative of advantage ("for us"; see §4.3).

The noun τὰς ἁμαρτίας is the accusative direct object of the verb ἀφῇ: "to forgive us our *sins*." Also note that the article τάς functions as a possessive pronoun ("our sins"; see §5.3.1). Another way to think about this construction is that a possessive pronoun is clearly implied from context. In constructions like this, the noun with an implied possessive pronoun usually is articular.

The pronoun ἡμᾶς is the accusative direct object of the verb καθαρίσῃ, "to cleanse *us*."

---

[12] Culy, *I, II, III John*, 18.
[13] Culy, 19.
[14] Baugh, *First John Reader*, 13.

1 John 1:10

- ἐὰν εἴπωμεν ὅτι οὐχ ἡμαρτήκαμεν

  The perfect tense verb ἡμαρτήκαμεν (per. act. ind. 1st pl. ἁμαρτάνω) conveys "not only the fact that the act was completed but that there is some implied consequence as well."[15] Baugh adds that the speakers are essentially claiming, "We have not committed sin (and thereby have not incurred any guilt)."[16]

- ψεύστην ποιοῦμεν αὐτὸν

  This is an example of a double accusative: "we make him [to be] a liar" or "we make him [appear to be] a liar" (since someone cannot actually make God a liar).

- καὶ ὁ λόγος αὐτοῦ οὐκ ἔστιν ἐν ἡμῖν.

  The noun ὁ λόγος is the nominative subject of the verb ἔστιν.

---

[15] Baugh, 14.
[16] Baugh, 14.

///////////////////

CHAPTER 3

1 JOHN 2:1–6
GENITIVE CASE

3.1 Vocabulary

ἱλασμός, ὁ	propitiation, atoning sacrifice (2)
παράκλητος, ὁ	advocate, mediator, helper (5)
τεκνίον, τό	(little) child (8)
τιμή, ἡ	honor, value, price (41)
ἀληθῶς	truly, really (18)
καινός, -ή, -όν	new, unused (42)
σήμερον	today (41)
χωρίς	without, apart from (41)
κλαίω	I weep, cry (40)
ὀφείλω	I owe, ought (35)
παρίστημι	I place beside, present (41)
τελειόω	I complete, make perfect (23)

3.2 Text: 1 John 2:1–6

¹ Τεκνία μου, ταῦτα γράφω ὑμῖν ἵνα μὴ ἁμάρτητε. καὶ ἐάν τις ἁμάρτῃ, παράκλητον ἔχομεν πρὸς τὸν πατέρα Ἰησοῦν Χριστὸν δίκαιον· ² καὶ αὐτὸς ἱλασμός ἐστιν περὶ τῶν ἁμαρτιῶν ἡμῶν, οὐ περὶ τῶν ἡμετέρων δὲ μόνον ἀλλὰ καὶ περὶ ὅλου τοῦ κόσμου. ³ Καὶ ἐν τούτῳ γινώσκομεν ὅτι ἐγνώκαμεν αὐτόν, ἐὰν τὰς ἐντολὰς αὐτοῦ τηρῶμεν. ⁴ ὁ λέγων ὅτι Ἔγνωκα αὐτόν καὶ τὰς ἐντολὰς αὐτοῦ μὴ τηρῶν, ψεύστης ἐστίν, καὶ ἐν τούτῳ ἡ ἀλήθεια οὐκ ἔστιν ⁵ ὃς δ' ἂν τηρῇ αὐτοῦ τὸν λόγον, ἀληθῶς ἐν τούτῳ ἡ ἀγάπη τοῦ

23

θεοῦ τετελείωται, ἐν τούτῳ γινώσκομεν ὅτι ἐν αὐτῷ ἐσμεν. ⁶ ὁ λέγων ἐν αὐτῷ μένειν ὀφείλει, καθὼς ἐκεῖνος περιεπάτησεν, καὶ αὐτὸς [οὕτως] περιπατεῖν.

3.3 Syntax: Genitive Case

The genitive case is the most versatile or flexible of the cases. Beginning students learn that when the genitive case is used, *of* should be added to the translation. Although this advice is helpful most of the time, the word *of* is also a notably versatile word. A "house of people" means a house *containing* people. A "house of wood" means a house *made of* wood. And a "house of Mary" means a house *belonging to* Mary. Just as the word *of* has many different uses, so also the genitive case has a plethora of uses.

The genitive is the case of restriction, description, or separation. Whereas the accusative case restricts verbs, the genitive limits or restricts *nouns*, often denoting a quality of a person or thing (thus similar to an adjective). For example, "the birth of Jesus Christ" (τοῦ Ἰησοῦ Χριστοῦ ἡ γένεσις; Matt 1:18) specifies whose birth was referenced, and "the Father of glory" (ὁ πατὴρ τῆς δόξης; Eph 1:17) is best understood as adjectivally meaning "glorious Father." Although the word *of* is often appropriate in translation, it is important to grasp the specific relationship between the head noun and the genitive term. As seen in the examples below, other terms, such as *from*, *in*, *by*, and *than* convey more precisely that relationship. The genitive noun will typically follow the noun that it qualifies, though this order is sometimes reversed for emphasis or contrast.

In his grammar, Wallace includes thirty-three distinct categories of the genitive case (though some of the categories are quite debated). This proliferation of categories for the genitive case can be bewildering. Here, we will limit the categories to those that are the most common and the most significant.

- **Possession.** Identifies ownership of the head noun.
  - τὸ αἷμα Ἰησοῦ . . . καθαρίζει ἡμᾶς, "the blood **of Jesus** . . . cleanses us" = Jesus's blood cleanses us (1 John 1:7).
  - τὸ ὄνομα τοῦ υἱοῦ τοῦ θεοῦ, "the name **of the Son of God**" = the Son of God's name (1 John 5:13).

- **Relationship.** Signifies a family relationship (e.g., a parent, spouse, or sibling).
  - Τεκνία μου, "**my** little children" (1 John 2:1).
  - ὁ υἱὸς τοῦ θεοῦ, "the son **of God**" (1 John 3:8).

- **Attributive.** Coveys an attribute or quality of the head noun.

  ○ τὸν βίον τοῦ κόσμου, "the possessions **of the world**" = worldly posses-sions (1 John 3:17).

  ○ τὸ πνεῦμα τῆς ἀληθείας καὶ τὸ πνεῦμα τῆς πλάνης, "the spirit **of truth** and the spirit **of deception**" = a truthful spirit and a deceptive spirit (1 John 4:6).

  ○ ἐν τῇ ἡμέρᾳ τῆς κρίσεως, "in the day **of judgment**" = on judgment day (1 John 4:17).

- **Source.** Designates the origin or source of the head noun.

  ○ ἡ ἐπιθυμία τῆς σαρκός, "The lust **of the flesh**" (1 John 2:16). This could mean lust that comes from the flesh (source) or that the flesh itself lusts (subjective genitive, see below).

  ○ τὸ πνεῦμα τοῦ θεοῦ, "the Spirit **of God**" = the Spirit from God (1 John 4:2).

- **Partitive.** Denotes the whole of which the head noun is a part.[1]

  ○ οὐκ ἦσαν ἐξ ἡμῶν, "they were not **of us**" = they were not part of us (1 John 2:19).[2]

- **Subjective.** Functions as the subject of the verbal idea implied in the head noun.

  ○ περὶ τῶν ἁμαρτιῶν ἡμῶν, "concerning **our** sins" (1 John 2:2). Thus, "our sins" refers to sins that we commit.

  ○ ἐὰν τὰς ἐντολὰς αὐτοῦ τηρῶμεν, "if we keep **his** commands" (1 John 2:3; see also 2:4; 3:22, 24; 5:2, 3). Although this example (as well as the previous one) might appear to indicate possession, the idea is not merely that the commands belong to God. Rather, the genitive com-municates that God commands (verbal idea) others to keep his law.

  ○ ἐν τούτῳ ἐφανερώθη ἡ ἀγάπη τοῦ θεοῦ ἐν ἡμῖν, "In this the love **of God** was revealed among us" (1 John 4:9). This refers to God's love for us (not our love for God) based on the following content that specifies

---

[1] This category is arguably misnamed. Wallace notes that the term *partitive* "is confusing, for it suggests that the gen. itself will designate the part of which the head noun is the whole" (*Greek Grammar*, 84). Thus, some suggest it should be called a "wholeative genitive" since we are describ-ing the function of the genitive (the whole) and not the function of the head noun (the part).

[2] In this scriptural example, the prepositional phrase ἐξ ἡμῶν communicates a partitive idea, though the genitive pronoun ἡμῶν alone could have conveyed the same nuance.

God's love for us and not our love for God: "God sent his one and only Son into the world so that we might live through him" (CSB).[3]

- **Objective.** Functions as the direct object of the verbal idea implied in the head noun.

    ○ ἀληθῶς ἐν τούτῳ ἡ ἀγάπη τοῦ θεοῦ τετελείωται, "truly in this one, the love **of God** has been perfected" (1 John 2:5). Here, it seems that the meaning is not God's love for us, but our love for God. The verse begins by stating, "But whoever keeps his words," demonstrating that the focus is on a person's love for God.

    ○ ἐάν τις ἀγαπᾷ τὸν κόσμον, οὐκ ἔστιν ἡ ἀγάπη τοῦ πατρὸς ἐν αὐτῷ, "If anyone loves the world, the love **of the Father** is not in him" (1 John 2:15). From context, we see that "the love of the Father" refers to someone's love of the Father and not the Father's love of someone.[4]

- **Separation.** Indicates movement away from, whether literally or figuratively.

    ○ καθαρίζει ἡμᾶς ἀπὸ **πάσης ἁμαρτίας**, "he cleanses us **from every sin**" (1 John 1:7). The idea of separation in this example (and the following two verses) is aided by the preposition ἀπό (see also 1:9).

    ○ κλείσῃ τὰ σπλάγχνα αὐτοῦ ἀπ' **αὐτοῦ**, "he closes his heart **from him**" (1 John 3:17).

    ○ φυλάξατε ἑαυτὰ ἀπὸ **τῶν εἰδώλων**, "keep yourselves **from idols**" (1 John 5:21).

- **Comparison.** Denotes a comparison with a comparative adjective (e.g., μείζων).

    ○ μείζων ἐστὶν ὁ θεὸς **τῆς καρδίας** ἡμῶν, "God is greater **than** our **heart**" (1 John 3:20).

- **Apposition.** Provides an additional genitive noun with the same referent as an earlier genitive noun.

---

[3] See also 1 John 2:16 (ἡ ἐπιθυμία τῶν ὀφθαλμῶν, "the lust of the eyes" = the eyes lust); 2:17 (τὸ θέλημα τοῦ θεοῦ, "the will of God" = God wills); 5:9 (τὴν μαρτυρίαν τῶν ἀνθρώπων, "the testimony of men" = men testify; ἡ μαρτυρία τοῦ θεοῦ, "the testimony of God" = God testifies).

[4] See also 1 John 2:16 (ἡ ἀλαζονεία τοῦ βίου, "the pride in possessions"); 3:17 (ἡ ἀγάπη τοῦ θεοῦ, "the love of God"); 4:14 (σωτῆρα τοῦ κόσμου, "Savior of the world" = he saves the world); 5:3 (ἡ ἀγάπη τοῦ θεοῦ).

○ μετὰ τοῦ υἱοῦ αὐτοῦ Ἰησοῦ Χριστοῦ, "with his son, **Jesus Christ**" (1 John 1:3; see also 3:23). "Jesus Christ" is in apposition to "his son" (τοῦ υἱοῦ αὐτοῦ).

○ τὸ αἷμα Ἰησοῦ **τοῦ υἱοῦ αὐτοῦ** καθαρίζει ἡμᾶς, "the blood of Jesus **his son** cleanses us**"** (1 John 1:7).

● **Direct Object.** Verbs of sensation, emotion or volition, sharing, ruling, or separation sometimes take their direct object in the genitive case. Some grammarians call this the "genitive complement" rather than a genitive direct object.

○ ὁ κόσμος **αὐτῶν** ἀκούει, "the world hears **them**" (1 John 4:5). The pronoun αὐτῶν is the direct object and is not translated "of them" (see also 4:6; 5:14, 15).

○ ὁ πονηρὸς οὐχ ἅπτεται **αὐτοῦ**, "the evil one does not touch **him**" (1 John 5:18).

● **Other Categories** (not found in 1 John):

○ **Material.** Indicates the material of which an object is made: γόμον χρυσοῦ, "cargo **of gold**" = cargo made of gold (Rev 18:12).

○ **Content.** Indicates the content of an object: τὸ δίκτυον τῶν ἰχθύων, "the net **of fish**" = a net containing fish (John 21:8).

3.4 Reading Notes

1 John 2:1

● Τεκνία μου, ταῦτα γράφω ὑμῖν ἵνα μὴ ἁμάρτητε

The familial term τεκνία is in the vocative case, which is used for direct address. It occurs seven times in 1 John (2:1, 12, 28; 3:7, 18; 4:4; 5:21) and is a diminutive form of τέκνον, conveying endearment or affection (thus often translated "little/dear children"). It may also convey a position of authority within the relationship. The genitive pronoun μου conveys a personal relationship (in this case, spiritual—not biological—kinship, is intended).

Notice that the author has shifted from using plural verbs in chapter 1 (e.g., ἀπαγγέλλομεν, "we are proclaiming," 1:3) to a singular verb here (γράφω: pres. act. ind. 1st sg. γράφω). Thus, after establishing that he is a member of the apostolic band of eyewitnesses, he now shifts to the first person, demonstrating that he alone is the author of the letter.

The conjunction ἵνα conveys purpose and triggers the subjunctive mood (ἁμάρτητε: aor. act. subjunc. 2nd pl. ἁμαρτάνω). Note that ἁμάρτητε is a second aorist form that has a stem spelling change. Also note that this verb (like almost all nonindicative verbs) is negated by μή and not οὐ.

- καὶ ἐάν τις ἁμάρτῃ

The conjunction ἐάν communicates a conditional statement and triggers the subjunctive mood (ἁμάρτῃ: aor. act. subjunc. 3rd sg. ἁμαρτάνω). The indefinite pronoun τις is often found in subjunctive constructions and is apropos since the subjunctive mood often conveys something indefinite. It is helpful to recall that about 75 percent of all subjunctive verbs are aorist. The aorist does not convey that the time of the action is in the past (only indicative forms inherently communicate time). Indeed, all conditional statements are future from the perspective of the author.

- παράκλητον ἔχομεν πρὸς τὸν πατέρα Ἰησοῦν Χριστὸν δίκαιον·

The noun παράκλητον functions as the direct object of the verb ἔχομεν: "we have *an advocate.*" This term occurs only four other times in the NT, all in the Gospel of John (14:16, 26; 15:26; 16:7) and all referring to the Holy Spirit.

The phrase Ἰησοῦν Χριστόν is in apposition to παράκλητον, "an advocate, *that is,* Jesus Christ," and the term δίκαιον is in apposition to Ἰησοῦν Χριστόν "Jesus Christ, *that is,* the righteous one." The reader might have expected an article in front of the substantive adjective δίκαιον, but perhaps the word is anarthrous in parallel construction with the nouns in which it is in apposition (παράκλητον and Ἰησοῦν Χριστόν). It has also been suggested that δίκαιον could be an attributive adjective modifying Ἰησοῦν Χριστόν, "the righteous Jesus Christ."

1 John 2:2

- καὶ αὐτὸς ἱλασμός ἐστιν περὶ τῶν ἁμαρτιῶν ἡμῶν

The predicate nominative ἱλασμός lacks the article due to Colwell's Canon (see §5.3.1). The term, therefore, can rightly be translated as "the propitiation" since there is no other means of a wrath-absorbing sacrifice available, as the author of 1 John makes clear.

The genitive noun τῶν ἁμαρτιῶν is in the genitive case due to the preposition περί, conveying reference/respect (i.e., "with reference to our sins").

The personal pronoun ἡμῶν is a subjective genitive ("our sins" = we sin, or the sins we commit).

• οὐ περὶ τῶν ἡμετέρων δὲ μόνον ἀλλὰ καὶ περὶ ὅλου τοῦ κόσμου.

The use of the pronoun ἡμετέρων is perhaps emphatic (cf. 1:3). The two genitive phrases (τῶν ἡμετέρων and ὅλου τοῦ κόσμου) are genitive because of the preposition περί. That is, in order for περί to mean "with reference to" or "concerning," the preposition must be followed by an object in the genitive case. If περί were followed by an accusative, we would expect it to convey the nuance of "around" (spatially).

The phrase δὲ μόνον . . . ἀλλὰ καί conveys the inclusion of an unexpected item. Here, John states that Jesus is the propitiation *not only* for our sins (perhaps the sins of Jewish believers whom John represents) *but also* those of the whole world. The author could be making a claim related to the inclusion of Gentiles into the people of God. The sacrifice and atonement of Jesus is not restricted to a small group of Jews but is available for people all over the world, including Gentiles.

1 John 2:3

• Καὶ ἐν τούτῳ γινώσκομεν ὅτι ἐγνώκαμεν αὐτόν

The phrase ἐν τούτῳ occurs fourteen times in 1 John (including four times in 2:1–6) and can be either anaphoric (pointing back to something previously stated) or cataphoric (pointing forward to something that will be stated). Only the literary context can guide us as to which way ἐν τούτῳ is pointing. Here it points forward to the next phrase (ἐὰν τὰς ἐντολὰς αὐτοῦ τηρῶμεν).

The shift in the tenses of the two verbs γινώσκομεν (pres. act. ind. 1st pl. γινώσκω) and ἐγνώκαμεν (per. act. ind. 1st pl. γινώσκω) is evidence that John is using them differently. The first use, "we know," relates to a cognitive affirmation of something (i.e., "we know this in our minds to be true"). John is writing about knowing a particular proposition: "we know *that we know him.*" The second relates to relational or interpersonal knowledge of God (i.e., "we have come to know him").[5] Happily for English readers, the verb "know" is also used for both cognitive and relational knowledge.

---

[5] See Baugh, *First John Reader*, 20.

- ἐὰν τὰς ἐντολὰς αὐτοῦ τηρῶμεν.

The conjunction ἐάν introduces a conditional clause and triggers the subjunctive mood (τηρῶμεν: pres. act. subjunc. 1st pl. τηρέω).

The genitive personal pronoun αὐτοῦ is a subjective genitive ("his commands/commandments" = he commands).

1 John 2:4

- ὁ λέγων ὅτι Ἔγνωκα αὐτόν

The author shifts from using ἐάν plus a subjunctive, "if we say," to using a substantival participle, "the one who says." The participle ὁ λέγων (pres. act. ptc. masc. nom. sg. λέγω) is one of around fifty substantival participles used in 1 John. This particular participle occurs two other times in 1 John (2:6, 9).

The verb ἔγνωκα (per. act. ind. 1st sg. γινώσκω) introduces a direct quotation (first person) and thus is capitalized in the Greek, "the one who says, 'I know him.'" Thus, ὅτι functions (and can correctly be rendered) as opening quotation marks.

- καὶ τὰς ἐντολὰς αὐτοῦ μὴ τηρῶν

The verb τηρῶν (pres. act. ptc. masc. nom. sg. τηρέω) functions as part of a compound subject of two substantival participles governed by the initial ὁ prior to λέγων (ὁ λέγων . . . καὶ . . . μὴ τηρῶν). John is talking about one person—the person who says X and does not keep Y. The participle τηρῶν is negated with μή as is the case with almost all nonindicative verbs.[6]

- ψεύστης ἐστίν καὶ ἐν τούτῳ ἡ ἀλήθεια οὐκ ἔστιν·

The term ψεύστης is a predicate nominative and belongs to a classification called occupation nouns. These have a unique declension in that they look feminine (first declension) but are actually masculine. Other common nouns in this category include μαθητής, "disciple," and προφήτης, "prophet."

The near demonstrative pronoun τούτῳ functions substantivally and could be translated "this one/person."

---

[6] Another interpretation sees τηρῶν as a temporal adverbial participle: "the one who says . . . while not keeping his commands." In this case, the action of the participle occurs contemporaneously with the action of the main verb.

1 John 2:5

- ὃς δ' ἂν τηρῇ αὐτοῦ τὸν λόγον

The particle ἄν turns the relative pronoun (ὅς) into an indefinite relative pronoun, triggering the subjunctive mood (τηρῇ: pres. act. subjunc. 3rd sg. τηρέω). Indefinite relative pronouns have no antecedent (i.e., are headless). The construction (relative pronoun + ἄν + subjunctive) is virtually equivalent to the earlier use of a substantival participle (ὁ λέγων, "the one who says," 2:4).

Notice that the word order of αὐτοῦ τὸν λόγον does not follow the normal pattern (which would be τὸν λόγον αὐτοῦ; see e.g., τὰς ἐντολὰς αὐτοῦ in 2:4). This change in word order could be for emphasis or variation of style. Similar to the construction "his commands" above, in the phrase "his word," the pronoun αὐτοῦ should be taken as a subjective genitive. Although John frequently employs near synonyms interchangeably, it is worth reflecting on whether λόγον is used here with an intentionally broader referent for God's communication to humans (i.e., not only God's moral demands but his promises).

- ἀληθῶς ἐν τούτῳ ἡ ἀγάπη τοῦ θεοῦ τετελείωται

The term ἀληθῶς is an adverb, a word that (usually) modifies a verb, does not decline, and often ends in –ῶς (e.g., οὕτως). As with the previous verse, the near demonstrative pronoun τούτῳ functions substantivally and could be translated "this one/person."

The genitive construction in the phrase ἡ ἀγάπη τοῦ θεοῦ could be either an objective genitive (i.e., "the love of God" = someone's love for God)[7] or a subjective genitive (i.e., "God's love for us").[8] We think the context favors the objective genitive label.

The verb τετελείωται (per. pass. ind. 3rd sg. τελειόω) conveys not moral perfection but that a person's actions and beliefs are consistent with their profession.

- ἐν τούτῳ γινώσκομεν ὅτι ἐν αὐτῷ ἐσμεν.

The prepositional phrase ἐν τούτῳ could either be anaphoric, referring to the first part of the verse (i.e., keeping his word), or cataphoric, pointing to the next verse (2:6).

[7] Wallace, *Greek Grammar*, 121 n. 136.
[8] Baugh, *First John Reader*, 72.

1 John 2:6

- ὁ λέγων ἐν αὐτῷ μένειν

  The substantival participle ὁ λέγων is the subject of the verb ὀφείλει: "the one who says . . . ought."

  The phrase ἐν αὐτῷ μένειν functions as the object of the participle. The verb μένειν (pres. act. inf. μένω) is an infinitive of indirect discourse, and as such, it is translated with a third-person pronoun "the one who says that he abides in him" (see 2:9; §11.3.2). If λέγω is translated as "claim," the beginning student can find reassurance in translating the infinitive with "to + verb": "The one who claims *to remain* in him."

- ὀφείλει καθὼς ἐκεῖνος περιεπάτησεν καὶ αὐτὸς [οὕτως] περιπατεῖν.

  The verb ὀφείλει (pres. act. ind. 3rd sg. ὀφείλω) usually takes a complementary infinitive, which in this verse is found at the end of the sentence (περιπατεῖν: pres. act. inf. περιπατέω). Thus, the heart of the sentence reads, "The one who says . . . ought to walk." In the middle of the phrase is a comparison: καθὼς ἐκεῖνος περιεπάτησεν (aor. act. ind. 3rd sg. περιπατέω) καὶ αὐτὸς [οὕτως], "just as that one walked so also he in this manner [ought to walk]." The far demonstrative pronoun ἐκεῖνος occurs six times (in masc. nom. sg. form), and each time it refers to Jesus (2:6; 3:3, 5, 7, 16; 4:17).

////////////////

CHAPTER 4

1 JOHN 2:7–14

DATIVE CASE

4.1 Vocabulary

νεανίσκος, ὁ	youth, young man (11)
σκάνδαλον, τό	stumbling block, trap, temptation (15)
ἀληθής, -ές	true, honest, genuine (26)
ἀληθινός, -ή, -όν	true, real, genuine (28)
ἄρτι	now (36)
ἰσχυρός, -ά, -όν	strong, mighty, powerful (29)
παλαιός, -ά, -όν	old (19)
μισέω	I hate, detest (40)
νικάω	I conquer, overcome (28)
παράγω	I pass away/by, disappear (10)
τυφλόω	I make blind (3)
φαίνω	I shine, appear (31)

4.2 Text: 1 John 2:7–14

⁷ Ἀγαπητοί, οὐκ ἐντολὴν καινὴν γράφω ὑμῖν ἀλλ᾽ ἐντολὴν παλαιὰν ἣν εἴχετε ἀπ᾽ ἀρχῆς· ἡ ἐντολὴ ἡ παλαιά ἐστιν ὁ λόγος ὃν ἠκούσατε. ⁸ πάλιν ἐντολὴν καινὴν γράφω ὑμῖν ὅ ἐστιν ἀληθὲς ἐν αὐτῷ καὶ ἐν ὑμῖν, ὅτι ἡ σκοτία παράγεται καὶ τὸ φῶς τὸ ἀληθινὸν ἤδη φαίνει. ⁹ ὁ λέγων ἐν τῷ φωτὶ εἶναι καὶ τὸν ἀδελφὸν αὐτοῦ μισῶν ἐν τῇ σκοτίᾳ ἐστὶν ἕως ἄρτι. ¹⁰ ὁ ἀγαπῶν τὸν ἀδελφὸν αὐτοῦ ἐν τῷ φωτὶ μένει καὶ σκάνδαλον ἐν αὐτῷ οὐκ ἔστιν· ¹¹ ὁ δὲ μισῶν τὸν ἀδελφὸν αὐτοῦ ἐν τῇ σκοτίᾳ ἐστὶν καὶ ἐν τῇ σκοτίᾳ

περιπατεῖ καὶ οὐκ οἶδεν ποῦ ὑπάγει, ὅτι ἡ σκοτία ἐτύφλωσεν τοὺς ὀφθαλμοὺς αὐτοῦ. [12] Γράφω ὑμῖν, τεκνία, ὅτι ἀφέωνται ὑμῖν αἱ ἁμαρτίαι διὰ τὸ ὄνομα αὐτοῦ. [13] γράφω ὑμῖν, πατέρες, ὅτι ἐγνώκατε τὸν ἀπ' ἀρχῆς. γράφω ὑμῖν, νεανίσκοι, ὅτι νενικήκατε τὸν πονηρόν. [14] ἔγραψα ὑμῖν, παιδία, ὅτι ἐγνώκατε τὸν πατέρα. ἔγραψα ὑμῖν, πατέρες, ὅτι ἐγνώκατε τὸν ἀπ' ἀρχῆς. ἔγραψα ὑμῖν, νεανίσκοι, ὅτι ἰσχυροί ἐστε καὶ ὁ λόγος τοῦ θεοῦ ἐν ὑμῖν μένει καὶ νενικήκατε τὸν πονηρόν.

4.3 Syntax: Dative Case

The dative case limits the action of the verb by one of three main ways: (1) by specifying the *person* involved (to/for whom?); (2) by designating the *location* of the action (where?); or (3) by indicating the *means* by which an action is accomplished (how?). Generally, the dative case is less ambiguous than the genitive case, making it easier to classify. One of the reasons for this distinction is that dative nouns are typically related to verbs, whereas genitive nouns are typically related to other nouns.

- **Indirect Object.** Indicates to whom or for whom an act is performed.

  ○ ταῦτα γράφω **ὑμῖν**, "I write these things **to you**" (1 John 2:1). The direct object of the verb "I write" is "these things" (ταῦτα) with ὑμῖν functioning as the indirect object.

  ○ ἔδωκεν ἐντολὴν **ἡμῖν**, "he gave a command **to us**" (1 John 3:23).

- **Advantage or Disadvantage.** Denotes the person for whose benefit (advantage) or detriment (disadvantage) a verbal action occurs.

  ○ ἵνα ἀφῇ **ἡμῖν** τὰς ἁμαρτίας, "that he might forgive **us** our sins" (1 John 1:9).

  ○ ἀφέωνται **ὑμῖν** αἱ ἁμαρτίαι διὰ τὸ ὄνομα αὐτοῦ, "your sins have been forgiven **you** on account of his name" (1 John 2:12).

- **Reference (Respect).** Limits or qualifies the extent of the verbal action.

  ○ ὅμοιοι **αὐτῷ** ἐσόμεθα, "we shall be similar **[with respect] to him**" (1 John 3:2).

- **Sphere (or Place).** Identifies the literal or figurative (metaphorical) location.

  ○ αὐτός ἐστιν **ἐν τῷ φωτι**, "he is **in the light**" (1 John 1:7).*

  ○ Μὴ ἀγαπᾶτε . . . τὰ **ἐν τῷ κόσμῳ**, "Do not love . . . the things **in the world**" (1 John 2:15).

* In both this example and some additional examples below, a prepositional phrase governed by ἐν functions in the same way a noun in the dative case would.

- **Time.** Indicates the time when the action of a verb is accomplished.[1]

  ○ ἵνα . . . μὴ αἰσχυνθῶμεν ἀπ᾽ αὐτοῦ **ἐν τῇ παρουσίᾳ** αὐτοῦ, "so that we might not be ashamed before him **at** his **coming**" (1 John 2:28).

  ○ ἵνα παρρησίαν ἔχωμεν **ἐν τῇ ἡμέρᾳ** τῆς κρίσεως, "so that we may have confidence **in the day** of judgment" (1 John 4:17).

- **Means.** Denotes the impersonal means by which the action of a given verb is accomplished.

  ○ ὃ ἑωράκαμεν **τοῖς ὀφθαλμοῖς** ἡμῶν, "which we have seen **with** our **eyes**" (1 John 1:1).

  ○ μὴ ἀγαπῶμεν **λόγῳ** μηδὲ **τῇ γλώσσῃ** ἀλλὰ **ἐν ἔργῳ** καὶ ἀληθείᾳ, "let us not love **with word** or **tongue** but **in deed** and truth" (1 John 3:18).

  ○ οὐκ **ἐν τῷ ὕδατι** μόνον ἀλλ᾽ **ἐν τῷ ὕδατι** καὶ **ἐν τῷ αἵματι**, "not **by water** only but **by water** and **by blood**" (1 John 5:6). The three bold prepositional phrases communicate means/instrument, but the dative case by itself would communicate the same idea.

- **Manner.** Signifies the way (manner) in which the action of a given verb is accomplished.

  ○ πᾶν πνεῦμα ὃ ὁμολογεῖ Ἰησοῦν Χριστὸν **ἐν σαρκὶ** ἐληλυθότα ἐκ τοῦ θεοῦ ἐστιν, "every spirit that confesses Jesus Christ having come **in the flesh** is from God" (1 John 4:2). The bold prepositional phrase communicates manner, but the dative case by itself would communicate the same idea.

- **Apposition.** An additional dative substantive with the same referent as an earlier dative substantive.

  ○ αἰτήσει καὶ δώσει αὐτῷ ζωήν, **τοῖς ἁμαρτάνουσιν** μὴ πρὸς θάνατον, "he will ask and he will give to him life, **to those who sin** not leading to death" (1 John 5:16). The phrase τοῖς ἁμαρτάνουσιν is in apposition to αὐτῷ, which is a somewhat irregular since the τοῖς ἁμαρτάνουσιν is plural and the pronoun αὐτῷ is singular.

  ○ ἐν τῷ υἱῷ αὐτοῦ Ἰησοῦ Χριστῷ, "in his Son, **Jesus Christ**" (1 John 5:20).

---

[1] According to Wallace, the genitive expresses the *kind* of time, the accusative expresses the *extent* of time, and the dative expresses a *point* in time. *Greek Grammar*, 156.

- **Direct Object.** Some verbs of trusting (e.g., πιστεύω), obeying, serving, worshiping, thanksgiving, or following can take their direct object in the dative case. Some grammarians call this a "dative complement" rather than a dative direct object.

  - ἵνα πιστεύσωμεν **τῷ ὀνόματι** τοῦ υἱοῦ αὐτοῦ, "that we might believe in **the name** of his son" (1 John 3:23). Although it might seem that the dative is not a direct object in the example because of the word "in" appears before the noun (i.e., "*in* the name"), here the verb means "to believe *in*." Consequently, the "in" is part of the verb and "the name" functions as the direct object (see also 5:13).

  - μὴ **παντὶ πνεύματι** πιστεύετε, "do not believe **every spirit**" (1 John 4:1; see also 1 John 5:10).

- **Other Categories** (not found in 1 John):

  - **Possession.** The dative possesses the subject of an equative verb (εἰμί or γίνομαι): ἐὰν γένηταί **τινι ἀνθρώπῳ** ἑκατὸν πρόβατα, "If **a certain man** has a hundred sheep" (Matt 18:12).

  - **Agency.** Indicates the personal agency by which the action of a given verb is accomplished: ὤφθη **ἀγγέλοις**, "he was seen **by angels**" (1 Tim 3:16). Personal agency is more commonly expressed by ὑπό + genitive.

  - **Association.** Denotes the person or thing with whom (or which) someone is associated: συνεζωοποίησεν **τῷ Χριστῷ**, "he made us alive together **with Christ**" (Eph 2:5).

4.4 Reading Notes

1 John 2:7

- Ἀγαπητοί, οὐκ ἐντολὴν καινὴν γράφω ὑμῖν

  Most English versions rightly begin a new paragraph here, a decision that is partly made based on the vocative ἀγαπητοί (a term that occurs six times in this form: 2:7; 3:2, 21; 4:1, 7, 11). The adjective ἀγαπητοί, "Beloved ones," functions substantivally (see §5.3.2).

  Interestingly, the particle οὐκ negates the noun ἐντολήν (based on word order) and not the verb (as is customary).

  The personal pronoun ὑμῖν functions as the indirect object of the verb γράφω, with ἐντολὴν καινὴν serving as the direct object.

- ἀλλ᾽ ἐντολὴν παλαιὰν ἣν εἴχετε ἀπ᾽ ἀρχῆς·

The conjunction ἀλλά indicates a contrast with what was previously stated (not this *but instead* that: "not a new command *but instead* an old command").

The phrase γράφω ὑμῖν is elided (omitted), a common practice in Greek. We allow this type of omission in English (e.g., "your *car* is red, mine is black"). Because it is clear from context, the words γράφω ὑμῖν do not need to be repeated.

The relative pronoun ἥν agrees with its antecedent (ἐντολήν) in gender and number (fem. sg.) and ἥν is in the accusative case because it functions as a direct object in its clause: "that you have had" = "you have had an old command."

The verb εἴχετε (impf. act. ind. 2nd pl. ἔχω) is irregular. The verb ἔχω does not augment to ἤχετε but to εἴχετε. This apparent exception is due to the original stem of the verb (which is not found in the present tense form). The root form of ἔχω is σεχ–. When the *epsilon* (ε) augment is added to the form (εσεχον), it causes the intervocalic *sigma* (i.e., a *sigma* [σ] between two vowels) to drop out (εεχον). The two *epsilons* then contract to form a diphthong (εἶχον).

- ἡ ἐντολὴ ἡ παλαιά ἐστιν ὁ λόγος ὃν ἠκούσατε.

The previous use of ἐντολὴν παλαιάν was anarthrous (i.e., it had no article). This time an article is used that points back to the previous reference (ἐντολὴν παλαιάν . . . ἡ ἐντολὴ ἡ παλαιά).

The antecedent for the masculine relative pronoun ὅν is ὁ λόγος. Here, notice that the relative pronoun is in the accusative case (since it functions as the direct object of ἠκούσατε: aor. act. ind. 2nd pl. ἀκούω), whereas ὁ λόγος functions as the predicate nominative with the verb ἐστιν. A definite predicate nominative that *follows* the copulative verb is expected to be articular (Colwell's Canon; see §5.3.1).

1 John 2:8

- πάλιν ἐντολὴν καινὴν γράφω ὑμῖν

The term πάλιν is probably not best translated "again" since it would seem to contradict what the author stated in the previous verse when he indicated that he was not writing a new command. Words have a range of meanings, and here πάλιν is best understood as meaning "conversely" or "on the other hand" (BDAG 753). Baugh paraphrases: "*But from another perspective*, the commandment I am writing to you *is* new."[2]

- ὅ ἐστιν ἀληθὲς ἐν αὐτῷ καὶ ἐν ὑμῖν

The antecedent for the neuter relative pronoun ὅ is difficult to determine. We know that it is not ἐντολήν because that is a feminine noun and the relative pronoun is neuter. Consequently, it is probably best to interpret the pronoun not as pointing back (antecedent) but pointing forward (postcedent). The neuter is used to refer to the next phrase that begins with ὅτι (such clauses were often considered neuter; see Gal 3:10).[3]

The relative pronoun ὅ functions as the subject with ἀληθές functioning as the predicate adjective.

- ὅτι ἡ σκοτία παράγεται καὶ τὸ φῶς τὸ ἀληθινὸν ἤδη φαίνει.

The reason that there is a sense in which the command is new is found in this phrase and is eschatological in nature. That is, the darkness is "passing away" and the true light is "already shining." The verbs παράγεται (pres. mid. ind. 3rd sg. παράγω) and φαίνει (pres. act. ind. 3rd sg. φαίνω) can be interpreted as progressive present verbs (see §8.3.1). This interpretation is confirmed by the use of the adverb ἤδη, "already." In the love of Jesus— and derivative love of his followers as well—the light of the new age breaks into this dark world.

1 John 2:9

- ὁ λέγων ἐν τῷ φωτὶ εἶναι

The prepositional phrase ἐν τῷ φωτί communicates the sphere or metaphorical location.

The verb εἶναι (pres. inf. εἰμί) is an infinitive of indirect discourse, and as such it is translated with a third-person pronoun: "the one who says that he is in the light" (see 2:6; also §11.3.2). As we noted earlier, λέγω may be translated as "claim" in order to still translate the Greek infinitive into English as "to + verb": "The one who claims to be in the light."

---

[2] Baugh, *First John Reader*, 25.
[3] See also Baugh, *First John Reader*, 26. Others, such as Culy, maintain that the most likely antecedent is the entire preceding statement (ἐντολὴν καινὴν γράφω ὑμῖν) (*I, II, III John*, 33).

- καὶ τὸν ἀδελφὸν αὐτοῦ μισῶν

It is best to take the participle μισῶν (pres. act. ptc. masc. nom. sg. μισέω) as substantival and thus parallel with ὁ λέγων, being connected by καί: "the one who says . . . and *who hates* his brother."[4]

- ἐν τῇ σκοτίᾳ ἐστὶν ἕως ἄρτι.

The prepositional phrase ἐν τῇ σκοτίᾳ communicates the sphere or metaphorical location and is "another Johannine label for those outside the community of believers."[5]

The temporal marker ἕως ἄρτι indicates that one cannot claim to be in the light (i.e., a Christian) and at the same time hate his brother.

1 John 2:10

- ὁ ἀγαπῶν τὸν ἀδελφὸν αὐτοῦ ἐν τῷ φωτὶ μένει

The substantival participle ὁ ἀγαπῶν (pres. act. ptc. masc. nom. sg. ἀγαπάω) functions as the subject of the verb μένει (pres. act. ind. 3rd sg. μένω) and is used seven other times in 1 John (3:10, 14; 4:7, 8, 20, 21; 5:1).

The personal pronoun αὐτοῦ is a genitive of relation (i.e., "his brother").

- καὶ σκάνδαλον ἐν αὐτῷ οὐκ ἔστιν·

It is uncertain whether the personal pronoun αὐτῷ is masculine (referring to the one who loves his brother) or neuter (referring to the light)— remember that there is no difference in forms between a masculine dative singular and a neuter dative singular. Although nearly all English versions opt for the masculine "in him," the RSV opts for the neuter "and *in it* there is no cause for stumbling."

Regarding the phrase σκάνδαλον ἐν αὐτῷ οὐκ ἔστιν, Culy notes, "The idiom means something like, 'there is no fault in him,' or better, 'there is not something within him that will lead him to fall away, i.e., fail to remain in the light.' The writer appears to be concerned with 'hatred' of one's brother being a potential σκάνδαλον, rather than claiming that those

---

[4] Another interpretation sees μισῶν as a temporal adverbial participle ("the one who says . . . *while hating* his brother").

[5] Culy, *I, II, III John*, 36.

who love their brother are free from *anything* that could cause them to stumble."[6]

1 John 2:11

- ὁ δὲ μισῶν τὸν ἀδελφὸν αὐτοῦ ἐν τῇ σκοτίᾳ ἐστὶν

The conjunction δέ is adversative "but," contrasting with the previous verse. The substantival participle ὁ μισῶν (pres. act. ptc. masc. nom. sg. μισέω) functions as the subject of the verb ἐστίν and is also used in this way in 3:15 (cf. 2:9).

- καὶ ἐν τῇ σκοτίᾳ περιπατεῖ καὶ οὐκ οἶδεν ποῦ ὑπάγει

The verbs περιπατεῖ (pres. act. ind. 3rd sg. περιπατέω) and ὑπάγει (pres. act. ind. 3rd sg. ὑπάγω) can be interpreted as gnomic present verbs (see §8.3.1). A gnomic verb conveys a general statement that is always true. The verb οἶδεν (per. act. ind. 3rd sg. οἶδα) is a present state perfect (see §9.3.2).

- ὅτι ἡ σκοτία ἐτύφλωσεν τοὺς ὀφθαλμοὺς αὐτοῦ.

The conjunction ὅτι functions as a causal marker, "because," and not a content marker, "that."

The verb ἐτύφλωσεν (aor. act. ind. 3rd sg. τυφλόω) conveys a past action as a whole (constative aorist; see §9.3.1), and, based on the semantic meaning of the verb, the result is enduring (i.e., blindness). Thus, many English versions render this verb "has blinded."

1 John 2:12

- Γράφω ὑμῖν, τεκνία

The verse division of 2:12–14 is unfortunate. Based on the Greek text, it is best to see two triads:

A[1] Γράφω ὑμῖν, τεκνία   B[1] ἔγραψα ὑμῖν, παιδία
   A[2] γράφω ὑμῖν, πατέρες . . .   B[2] ἔγραψα ὑμῖν, πατέρες
     A[3] γράφω ὑμῖν, νεανίσκοι   B[3] ἔγραψα ὑμῖν, νεανίσκοι

---

[6] Culy, 36.

Nevertheless, the text is divided into three verses: 2:12 (A¹), 2:13 (A², A³), and 2:14 (B¹, B², B³). There should either be two verses or six verses, but not three verses, especially with one verse given one stanza, the next verse given two stanzas, and the last verse given three stanzas.

The familial categories of τεκνία/παιδία, πατέρες, and νεανίσκοι are best understood as spiritual and not as physical categories for the following reasons. First, the author is fond of using familial terms to address his readers. He calls them τεκνία (2:1, 28; 3:7, 18; 4:4; 5:21), παιδία (2:18), and ἀδελφοί (3:13). Second, in 2 John the author writes "to the elect lady and to her children" (v. 1) and later adds that "the children of your elect sister send you greetings" (v. 13). Although this could be an elderly John writing to a woman and her children while referencing their cousins, it is best to see this as John writing to a local congregation ("elect lady" since the church is the bride of Christ; "children" since members are part of God's family) and as a reference to members from another congregation. It is also possible that a strict distinction of various groups in the church is not intended but that the three divisions are merely "a rhetorical device that is used to highlight key characteristics of the readers' experience."[7] In support of this view is the fact that all believers have their sins forgiven, know the One who is from the beginning, and have overcome the evil one.

- ὅτι ἀφέωνται ὑμῖν αἱ ἁμαρτίαι διὰ τὸ ὄνομα αὐτοῦ.

Although the conjunction ὅτι could be understood as introducing a content clause, "that," it is best to take it as introducing a causal clause, "because." This is true for the following five uses as well. John varies between rebuke and reassurance in his letter, and this passage circles back to reassure his addressees as to *why* he is writing to them.

The verb ἀφέωνται (per. pass. ind. 3rd sg. ἀφίημι) is classified as an intensive perfect (see §9.3.2). As such, the focus is on the present results from a past action and is typically translated as an English present, "your sins *are forgiven*."

The personal pronoun ὑμῖν is a dative of advantage ("your sins are forgiven **you**," i.e., "for your benefit"; see also 1:9) and the article αἱ functions like a personal pronoun, "*your* sins." We could also note that possessive pronouns are often implied and that in such cases the qualified nouns are almost always articular.

---

7 Culy, *I, II, III John*, 39.

1 John 2:13

- γράφω ὑμῖν, πατέρες

  The next two groups ("fathers" and "young men") are mentioned in this verse. The dative pronoun ὑμῖν functions as the indirect object.

- ὅτι ἐγνώκατε τὸν ἀπ᾽ ἀρχῆς.

  The verb ἐγνώκατε (per. act. ind. 2nd pl. γινώσκω) is a consummative perfect, which emphasizes the completed action that brought about the resulting state: "you have known" (see §9.3.2). Because the root of γινώσκω is a double consonant (γνο–), the initial consonant does not reduplicate leaving only the *epsilon* (ε) (i.e., vocalic reduplication).

  The article τόν functions as a substantizer, turning the prepositional phrase ἀπ᾽ ἀρχῆς into a noun: "the One from the beginning" (see §5.3.1).

- γράφω ὑμῖν, νεανίσκοι

  The noun νεανίσκοι only occurs twice in the NT and only here in this passage (2:13, 14). The term refers to "a young man beyond the age of puberty, but normally before marriage" (LN §9.32).

- ὅτι νενικήκατε τὸν πονηρόν.

  The verb νενικήκατε (per. act. ind. 2nd pl. νικάω) is a consummative perfect, which emphasizes the completed action that brought about the resulting state: "you conquered" (see §9.3.2).

  The adjective τὸν πονηρόν functions substantivally, referencing the devil, "the evil one" (see §5.3.2).

1 John 2:14

- ἔγραψα ὑμῖν, παιδία, ὅτι ἐγνώκατε τὸν πατέρα. ἔγραψα ὑμῖν, πατέρες, ὅτι ἐγνώκατε τὸν ἀπ᾽ ἀρχῆς.

  The shift in tense from the present (γράφω) to the aorist (ἔγραψα: aor. act. ind. 1st sg. γράφω) is best understood as a literary feature (i.e., a means of segmenting the text). The author is not referring to an earlier writing (e.g., the epistolary aorist) but is signaling a pattern of two triads.

- ἔγραψα ὑμῖν, νεανίσκοι, ὅτι ἰσχυροί ἐστε καὶ ὁ λόγος τοῦ θεοῦ ἐν ὑμῖν μένει καὶ νενικήκατε τὸν πονηρόν.

John adds a phrase (ἰσχυροί ἐστε καὶ ὁ λόγος τοῦ θεοῦ ἐν ὑμῖν μένει) to the last group. The term ἰσχυροί is a predicate adjective, "you are *strong*."

///////////////////

CHAPTER 5

1 JOHN 2:15–25
ARTICLES AND ADJECTIVES

5.1 Vocabulary

ἀλαζονεία, ἡ	arrogance (2)
ἀντίχριστος, ὁ	Antichrist (5)
βίος, ὁ	life, means of subsistence (10)
ἐπιθυμία, ἡ	lust, craving, desire (39)
μνημεῖον, τό	grave, tomb (40)
χρῖσμα, τό	anointing (3)
ψεῦδος, τό	a lie (10)
ὀλίγος, -η, -ον	little, few (40)
πόθεν	from where? (29)
ἀρνέομαι	I deny, reject (33)
ἐπαγγέλλομαι	I announce, proclaim, promise (15)
οἰκοδομέω	I build (up), erect, edify (40)

5.2 Text: 1 John 2:15–25

[15] Μὴ ἀγαπᾶτε τὸν κόσμον μηδὲ τὰ ἐν τῷ κόσμῳ. ἐάν τις ἀγαπᾷ τὸν κόσμον, οὐκ ἔστιν ἡ ἀγάπη τοῦ πατρὸς ἐν αὐτῷ· [16] ὅτι πᾶν τὸ ἐν τῷ κόσμῳ, ἡ ἐπιθυμία τῆς σαρκὸς καὶ ἡ ἐπιθυμία τῶν ὀφθαλμῶν καὶ ἡ ἀλαζονεία τοῦ βίου, οὐκ ἔστιν ἐκ τοῦ πατρὸς ἀλλ' ἐκ τοῦ κόσμου ἐστίν. [17] καὶ ὁ κόσμος παράγεται καὶ ἡ ἐπιθυμία αὐτοῦ, ὁ δὲ ποιῶν τὸ θέλημα τοῦ θεοῦ μένει εἰς τὸν αἰῶνα. [18] Παιδία, ἐσχάτη ὥρα ἐστίν, καὶ καθὼς ἠκούσατε ὅτι ἀντίχριστος ἔρχεται, καὶ νῦν ἀντίχριστοι πολλοὶ γεγόνασιν, ὅθεν

γινώσκομεν ὅτι ἐσχάτη ὥρα ἐστίν. [19] ἐξ ἡμῶν ἐξῆλθαν ἀλλ᾽ οὐκ ἦσαν ἐξ ἡμῶν, εἰ γὰρ ἐξ ἡμῶν ἦσαν, μεμενήκεισαν ἂν μεθ᾽ ἡμῶν, ἀλλ᾽ ἵνα φανερωθῶσιν ὅτι οὐκ εἰσὶν πάντες ἐξ ἡμῶν. [20] καὶ ὑμεῖς χρῖσμα ἔχετε ἀπὸ τοῦ ἁγίου καὶ οἴδατε πάντες. [21] οὐκ ἔγραψα ὑμῖν ὅτι οὐκ οἴδατε τὴν ἀλήθειαν ἀλλ᾽ ὅτι οἴδατε αὐτὴν καὶ ὅτι πᾶν ψεῦδος ἐκ τῆς ἀληθείας οὐκ ἔστιν. [22] Τίς ἐστιν ὁ ψεύστης εἰ μὴ ὁ ἀρνούμενος ὅτι Ἰησοῦς οὐκ ἔστιν ὁ Χριστός; οὗτός ἐστιν ὁ ἀντίχριστος, ὁ ἀρνούμενος τὸν πατέρα καὶ τὸν υἱόν. [23] πᾶς ὁ ἀρνούμενος τὸν υἱὸν οὐδὲ τὸν πατέρα ἔχει, ὁ ὁμολογῶν τὸν υἱὸν καὶ τὸν πατέρα ἔχει. [24] ὑμεῖς ὃ ἠκούσατε ἀπ᾽ ἀρχῆς, ἐν ὑμῖν μενέτω. ἐὰν ἐν ὑμῖν μείνῃ ὃ ἀπ᾽ ἀρχῆς ἠκούσατε, καὶ ὑμεῖς ἐν τῷ υἱῷ καὶ ἐν τῷ πατρὶ μενεῖτε. [25] καὶ αὕτη ἐστὶν ἡ ἐπαγγελία ἣν αὐτὸς ἐπηγγείλατο ἡμῖν, τὴν ζωὴν τὴν αἰώνιον.

5.3 Syntax: Articles and Adjectives

5.3.1 Articles

The article is the most frequent word in the NT, with nearly 20,000 occurrences (including more than 350 uses in 1 John alone). This means that about one in every seven words is an article. The article has at least three basic functions: (1) *Substantizer*: the article can transform various parts of speech into virtual nouns. (2) *Distinguisher*: the article can differentiate one substantive from another (or others). (3) *Definitizer*: the article can make a substantive definite. Below are some of the more specific uses of the article.[1]

- **Identification.** The article identifies a particular individual, group, or object from another (or others).

  ○ αὕτη ἐστὶν ἡ ἐπαγγελία, "this is **the** promise" (1 John 2:25).

  ○ αὕτη ἐστὶν ἡ ἀγγελία, "this is **the** message" (1 John 3:11).

- **Par Excellence.** The article identifies someone who is in a class by himself (or herself). Although there are others in this category, the one referenced is recognizably distinct.

  ○ παράκλητον ἔχομεν πρὸς τὸν πατέρα, "we have an advocate with **the** Father" (1 John 2:1).

  ○ οὗτός ἐστιν ὁ ἀντίχριστος, ὁ ἀρνούμενος τὸν πατέρα καὶ τὸν υἱόν, "This one is the antichrist, the one who denies **the** Father and **the** Son" (1 John 2:22).

- **Monadic.** The article identifies someone (or something) as unique or one of a kind.

---

[1] See Wallace, *Greek Grammar*, 209–10.

○ ἀπ᾽ ἀρχῆς ὁ διάβολος ἁμαρτάνει, "from the beginning **the** devil has been sinning" (1 John 3:8).

○ παρρησίαν ἔχομεν πρὸς **τὸν** θεόν, "we have confidence before God" (1 John 3:21).

○ πολλοὶ ψευδοπροφῆται ἐξεληλύθασιν εἰς **τὸν** κόσμον, "many false prophets have gone out into **the** world" (1 John 4:1).

- **With Abstract Nouns.** The article is often used with abstract nouns. When translating such nouns into English, it is appropriate to drop the article (since English does not typically use an article with abstract nouns).

○ γινώσκετε ὅτι καὶ πᾶς ὁ ποιῶν **τὴν** δικαιοσύνην ἐξ αὐτοῦ γεγέννηται, "we know that everyone who practices righteousness has been born of him " (1 John 2:29).

○ ἡ ἁμαρτία ἐστὶν ἡ ἀνομία, "sin is lawlessness" (1 John 3:4). Both "sin" (ἡ ἁμαρτία) and "lawlessness" (ἡ ἀνομία) are abstract nouns.

○ ἐν τούτῳ ἐγνώκαμεν **τὴν** ἀγάπην, "by this we know love" (1 John 3:16).

- **Previous Reference (Anaphoric).** The article points back to a substantive that was previously mentioned. It is often appropriate to add "this" or "that" to the translation (cf. the use of the article "As a Pronoun" below).

○ περὶ τοῦ λόγου τῆς ζωῆς—καὶ ἡ ζωὴ ἐφανερώθη, "concerning the word of life—and **this** life was revealed" (1 John 1:2).

○ ἠκούσατε ὅτι ἀντίχριστος ἔρχεται . . . οὗτός ἐστιν ὁ ἀντίχριστος, "you heard that an Antichrist is coming . . . This is **the** Antichrist" (1 John 2:18, 22).

○ φόβος οὐκ ἔστιν ἐν τῇ ἀγάπῃ . . . ὅτι ὁ φόβος κόλασιν ἔχει, "there is no fear in love . . . because **[this type of]** fear involves punishment" (1 John 4:18).

- **Generic.** The article identifies one group or a class from another (e.g., "the man on the street"). In English we communicate the generic idea with a noun modified by an indef. article ("a husband should love his wife") or with a plural form ("husbands should love their wives").

○ Τίς ἐστιν ὁ ψεύστης, "who is **the** liar" (1 John 2:22).

○ ὁ ὁμολογῶν τὸν υἱὸν καὶ τὸν πατέρα ἔχει, "**the** one who confesses the Son has also the Father" (1 John 2:23).

- **Substantizer.** The article is able to transform various parts of speech into a substantive (noun).

  ○ Μὴ ἀγαπᾶτε τὸν κόσμον μηδὲ **τὰ** ἐν τῷ κόσμῳ, "Do not love the world nor **the things** in the world" (1 John 2:15). The article τά turns the prepositional phrase ἐν τῷ κόσμῳ into a noun (literally, "the in-the-world things").

  ○ μείζων ἐστὶν **ὁ** ἐν ὑμῖν ἢ **ὁ** ἐν τῷ κόσμῳ, "Greater is **the one** in you than **the one** in the world" (1 John 4:4; see also 2:13, 14). Again, the article (ὁ) turns the two prepositional phrases into nouns (literally: "the in-you one" and "the in-the-world one").

- **As a Pronoun.** The article can function similar to (1) personal, (2) possessive, (3) demonstrative, and (4) alternate pronouns.

  ○ τὰ ἔργα αὐτοῦ πονηρὰ ἦν **τὰ** δὲ τοῦ ἀδελφοῦ αὐτοῦ δίκαια, "his works were evil but **those** of his brother [were] righteous" (1 John 3:12). Here, the article is functioning like a far demonstrative pronoun (ἐκεῖνα).

  ○ καὶ ἡμεῖς ὀφείλομεν ὑπὲρ **τῶν** ἀδελφῶν **τὰς** ψυχὰς θεῖναι, "we ought to lay down **our** lives for **our** brothers" (1 John 3:16). Here, we have two uses of the article functioning like a personal pronoun (ἡμῶν; see also 1:9; 3:5, 14).

- **Granville Sharp Rule.** This rule states that when a single article governs two nouns (substantives) of the same case that are connected by καί, they refer to the same person. This rule only applies to nouns that are (1) singular, (2) personal, and (3) non-proper.

  ○ ὁ λέγων ὅτι ἔγνωκα αὐτόν καὶ τὰς ἐντολὰς αὐτοῦ μὴ τηρῶν, "**the one** who says, 'I have known him' and who does not keep his commands" (1 John 2:4). The article ὁ governs both λέγων and τηρῶν (substantival participles). That is, "the one who says . . . and the one who does not keep . . ." both refer to the same individual.[2]

  ○ ὁ ἀρνούμενος **τὸν** πατέρα καὶ **τὸν** υἱόν, "the one who denies **the** Father and **the** Son" (1 John 2:22). This verse provides an example of something that is *not* the Granville Sharp Rule. Because two articles are provided, the Father and the Son are separate persons.

- **Colwell's Canon.** This rule states that when a predicate nominative *precedes* the copulative verb (usually εἰμί or γίνομαι), and that predicate

---

[2] Less likely, the second participle τηρῶν functions adverbially (see notes on 2:4).

nominative is definite (as determined by contextual analysis), the article should not be expected nearly 90 percent of the time: φῶς εἰμι τοῦ κόσμου, "I am **the light** of the world" (John 9:5). But, as a matter of stylistic pattern, if a definite predicate nominative *follows* the copulative verb, then the article is expected: Ἐγώ εἰμι τὸ φῶς τοῦ κόσμου "I am **the light** of the world" (John 8:12). Whether an anarthrous noun should be considered definite or not is based solely on context.

○ ἔστιν αὕτη ἡ ἀγγελία . . . ὅτι ὁ θεὸς φῶς ἐστιν, "this is **the message** . . . that God is **light**" (1 John 1:5; see also 2:25; 3:4). Here, we have two possible instances of Colwell's Canon. In the first use, the article (ἡ) is included since the predicate nominative (ἀγγελία) follows the verb (ἔστιν). In the second example, the article is *not* included since the predicate nominative (φῶς) precedes the verb (ἔστιν). In the second example, φῶς may also be anarthrous to communicate a qualitative sense (i.e., God is, in essence, light).

○ αὐτὸς ἱλασμός ἐστιν περὶ τῶν ἁμαρτιῶν ἡμῶν, "he is **the propitiation** for our sins" (1 John 2:2). The context unequivocally presents Jesus as the only propitiation for our sins. Though ἱλασμός is definite or specific in this way, it is anarthrous, as Colwell's Canon teaches us.

5.3.2 Adjectives

An adjective qualifies or describes a noun (or another substantive), distinguishing it from other nouns. In Greek, adjectives agree with the nouns that they modify in gender, case, and number. There are four main uses of the adjective: (1) predicate, (2) attributive, (3) substantival, or (4) adverbial.

- **Predicate.** Predicates a quality to the subject. The adjective is used in conjunction with a copulative verb (such as εἰμί or γίνομαι, stated or implied), and the article will never directly precede the adjective. If the adjective is immediately preceded by the article, it cannot be the predicate use.

  ○ πιστός ἐστιν καὶ δίκαιος, "he is **faithful** and **just**" (1 John 1:9).

  ○ ἰσχυροί ἐστε, "you are **strong**" (1 John 2:14).

- **Attributive.** Ascribes a certain quality to a noun or substantive. The adjective modifies an expressed noun.

  ○ ἀπαγγέλλομεν ὑμῖν τὴν ζωὴν τὴν αἰώνιον, "we proclaim to you **eternal** life" (1 John 1:2). Pattern: Article-noun-article-adjective.

  ○ καὶ νῦν ἀντίχριστοι πολλοὶ γεγόνασιν, ὅθεν γινώσκομεν ὅτι ἐσχάτη ὥρα ἐστίν, "Even now **many** antichrists have come, from this we know that it is the **last** hour" (1 John 2:18). Patterns: noun-adjective and adjective-noun.

○ οὗτός ἐστιν ὁ **ἀληθινὸς** θεὸς, "This one is the **true** God" (1 John 5:20). Pattern: article-adjective-noun.

- **Substantival.** Functions as a noun (substantive). That is, the adjective becomes a virtual noun.

  ○ ὑμεῖς χρῖσμα ἔχετε ἀπὸ τοῦ **ἁγίου**, "you have an anointing from the **Holy One**" (1 John 2:20).

  ○ νενικήκατε τὸν **πονηρόν**, "you have conquered the **evil one**" (1 John 2:13).

- **Adverbial.** Modifies a verb rather than a noun (thus functioning like an adverb).

  ○ ἡμεῖς ἀγαπῶμεν, ὅτι αὐτὸς **πρῶτος** ἠγάπησεν ἡμᾶς, "we love because he **first** loved us" (1 John 4:19).

  ○ οὗτός ἐστιν ὁ ἐλθὼν . . . οὐκ ἐν τῷ ὕδατι **μόνον**, "This is the one who came . . . not by water **only**" (1 John 5:6).

Finally, adjectives can be used to convey degree: (1) positive (strong); (2) comparative (stronger); (3) superlative (strongest); and (4) elative (very strong).

- **Positive.** Describes the properties of a noun in terms of kind rather than degree (e.g., "the strong man").

  ○ ἐντολὴν **καινήν**, "a **new** commandment" (1 John 2:7).

  ○ ἡ **τελεία** ἀγάπη, "**perfect** love" (1 John 4:18).

- **Comparative.** Compares two people or objects by specifying which is higher in degree in relation to the other (e.g., "the stronger man"). Two ways of forming a comparative adjective include (1) a third declension ending on a comparative noun (e.g., μείζων, "greater") or (2) adding -ερος to a positive degree adjective (e.g., πρέσβυς, "old" → πρεσβύτερος, "older"). These adjectives are often followed by a genitive of comparison or the particle ἤ, "than."

  ○ **μείζων** ἐστὶν ὁ θεὸς τῆς καρδίας ἡμῶν, "God is **greater** than our heart" (1 John 3:20).

  ○ **μείζων** ἐστὶν ὁ ἐν ὑμῖν ἢ ὁ ἐν τῷ κόσμῳ, "**greater** is the one in us than the one in the world" (1 John 4:4).

- **Superlative.** Compares three or more entities and indicates which is the highest in degree (e.g., "the strongest man"). Two common ways of forming a superlative include (1) adding -ιστος to a positive degree adjective (e.g., μέγας, "great" → μέγιστος, "greatest"); or (2) adding -τατος to a positive degree adjective (e.g., ἅγιος, "holy" → ἁγιώτατος, "holiest").

○ ἐσχάτη ὥρα ἐστίν, "it is the **last** hour" (1 John 2:18).

- **Elative.** Uses a comparative or superlative adjective to intensify the positive notion (e.g., "the very strong man").

○ συνάγεται πρὸς αὐτὸν ὄχλος **πλεῖστος**, "a **very large** crowd gathered to him" (Mark 4:1). This is an example of a superlative form functioning as an elative. Mark is not claiming that this was the largest crowd ever but that it was very large.

5.4 Reading Notes

1 John 2:15

- **Μὴ ἀγαπᾶτε τὸν κόσμον μηδὲ τὰ ἐν τῷ κόσμῳ.**

Although the verb ἀγαπᾶτε (pres. act. impv. 2nd pl. ἀγαπάω) is an imperative, the form itself could be indicative (as an *alpha*-contract verb, the contract vowel contracts with the connecting vowel, causing the *epsilon* [ε] to drop: ἀγαπα + ετε → ἀγαπᾶτε). The context, and especially the particle μή, clarify that it is a prohibition (i.e., a negated imperative). An indicative form would be negated with οὐ (e.g., οὐ ἀγαπᾶτε τὸν κόσμον, "you are not loving the world").

The article τόν (in τὸν κόσμον) is the monadic use (i.e., it refers to something that is unique or one of a kind). The article τά functions as a substantizer, turning the prepositional phrase ἐν τῷ κόσμῳ into a noun (literally "the in-the-world things").

- **ἐάν τις ἀγαπᾷ τὸν κόσμον**

The conjunction ἐάν introduces a (third class) conditional clause and triggers the subjunctive mood (ἀγαπᾷ: pres. act. subjunc. 3rd sg. ἀγαπάω).

- **οὐκ ἔστιν ἡ ἀγάπη τοῦ πατρὸς ἐν αὐτῷ·**

The genitive construction in the phrase ἡ ἀγάπη τοῦ πατρός is an objective genitive ("the love of the Father" = someone's love for the Father).

1 John 2:16

- ὅτι πᾶν τὸ ἐν τῷ κόσμῳ

The conjunction ὅτι functions as causal marker, "because." The adjective πᾶν modifies the phrase τὸ ἐν τῷ κόσμῳ (attributive use). The article τό functions as a substantizer, turning the prepositional phrase ἐν τῷ κόσμῳ into a noun (literally "the in-the-world thing").

- ἡ ἐπιθυμία τῆς σαρκὸς καὶ ἡ ἐπιθυμία τῶν ὀφθαλμῶν καὶ ἡ ἀλαζονεία τοῦ βίου

John now supplies three vices that are in apposition to πᾶν τὸ ἐν τῷ κόσμῳ, "everything in the world, that is." To better comprehend what John is saying, we need to understand the genitive forms. The first, τῆς σαρκός, is best taken as a subjective genitive ("the lust of flesh" = the flesh lusts) but could also be a genitive of source (i.e., "the lust from the flesh"). The second, τῶν ὀφθαλμῶν, is also a subjective genitive ("the lust of the eyes" = the eyes lust). The third, τοῦ βίου, is best interpreted as an objective genitive (i.e., "the pride in possessions"). The term βίος in this context refers not to "life" generally, but to "the resources which one has as a means of living" (LN §57.18) or the "resources needed to maintain life" (BDAG 177).

- οὐκ ἔστιν ἐκ τοῦ πατρὸς ἀλλ᾽ ἐκ τοῦ κόσμου ἐστίν.

The preposition ἐκ conveys source in both uses: "*from* the Father" or "*from* the world."

1 John 2:17

- καὶ ὁ κόσμος παράγεται καὶ ἡ ἐπιθυμία αὐτοῦ

The term κόσμος in this passage refers not to the physical world created by God but the world-system opposed to God. Words have a range of meaning, and it is too simplistic to suppose that a word has the same meaning or referent in every use. BDAG defines the κόσμος here as "that which is hostile to God, i.e., lost in sin, wholly at odds with anything divine, ruined and depraved" (BDAG 562).

The verb παράγεται (pres. mid. ind. 3rd sg. παράγω) is a progressive present (see §8.3.1), indicating that the world is destined for destruction and is even now beginning to pass away. This form is singular even though it has two subjects ("the world" and "its lusts"). Because of word order, the verb agrees with only the first subject (i.e., is singular), with the second subject following as an afterthought (cf. John 2:2, ἐκλήθη δὲ καὶ ὁ Ἰησοῦς καὶ οἱ μαθηταὶ αὐτοῦ εἰς τὸν γάμον, "And Jesus and his disciples were invited to a wedding"). A. T. Robertson called this construction (compound subject + singular verb) a "Pindaric construction," after the Greek poet Pindar who employed it frequently.

The genitive pronoun αὐτοῦ is an objective genitive ("its lust" = the lust/desire for things of the world).

- ὁ δὲ ποιῶν τὸ θέλημα τοῦ θεοῦ μένει εἰς τὸν αἰῶνα.

The conjunction δέ is adversative, "but," contrasting those who do the will of God with those who love the world.

The substantival participle ὁ ποιῶν (pres. act. ptc. masc. nom. sg. ποιέω) functions as the subject of the verb μένει (pres. act. ind. 3rd sg. μένω) and is used five other times in 1 John (2:29; 3:4, 7, 8, 10).

The noun τοῦ θεοῦ is a subjective genitive ("the will of God" = that which God wills). The phrase εἰς τὸν αἰῶνα is a temporal idiom meaning "to eternity" or "eternally" (BDAG 32).

1 John 2:18

- Παιδία, ἐσχάτη ὥρα ἐστίν

The vocative παιδία signals a new paragraph. The adjective ἐσχάτη (superlative in meaning) functions attributively modifying ὥρα, "*last* hour." Although they have different endings, the adjective agrees with its antecedent in gender, case, and number. The orthographic difference is due to the noun stem ending in the consonant *rho* (ρ), which takes an *alpha* (α) instead of the normal *eta* (η) ending. The phrase ἐσχάτη ὥρα is definite, even though the article is missing (note Colwell's Canon). This is made clear by the use of the adjective ἐσχάτη (there can only be one *last* hour).

- καὶ καθὼς ἠκούσατε ὅτι ἀντίχριστος ἔρχεται

The verb ἠκούσατε (aor. act. ind. 2nd pl. ἀκούω) is a constative aorist, viewing that action as a whole (see §9.3.1). John alone uses the term ἀντίχριστος in the NT (2:18, 22; 4:3; 2 John 7).

The conjunction ὅτι is a content marker, "that," introducing indirect discourse. The verb ἔρχεται (pres. mid. ind. 3rd sg. ἔρχομαι) is futuristic present, indicating not that the Antichrist is presently coming (from the perspective of the author) but that his coming is imminent (see §8.3.1)

- καὶ νῦν ἀντίχριστοι πολλοὶ γεγόνασιν

The adjective πολλοί functions attributively modifying ἀντίχριστοι, "*many antichrists.*"

The verb γεγόνασιν, "have appeared" (per. act. ind. 3rd pl. γίνομαι), is a consummative perfect, which emphasizes the completed action that brought about the resulting state (see §9.3.2).

- ὅθεν γινώσκομεν ὅτι ἐσχάτη ὥρα ἐστίν.

The term ὅθεν, "from which" or "whereby," is an inferential conjunction. The expression ἐσχάτη ὥρα reminds readers of the "imminent culmination of the ages. Such eschatological imminency is a frequent theme in the NT that serves rhetorically as a motivation both to perseverance and right living."[3]

1 John 2:19

- ἐξ ἡμῶν ἐξῆλθαν ἀλλ᾽ οὐκ ἦσαν ἐξ ἡμῶν,

The first use of the prepositional phrase ἐξ ἡμῶν communicates source (i.e., "*from* us") whereas the second use is a partitive genitive (i.e., "*part of* us"). This is another example of a word (or phrase) having two different meanings in the same immediate context. For John to mean "They went out *from* us, but they were not *from* us" is a contradiction. But for him to mean "They went out *from* us, but they were not *part of* us" is a profound statement regarding the background and character of this group of individuals who had been part of the community to which John writes but chose to leave and distance themselves from it and, sadly, from the apostolic gospel.

The verb ἐξῆλθαν (aor. act. ind. 3rd pl. ἐξέρχομαι) contains the first aorist ending instead of the second aorist ending (ἐξῆλθον). First aorist endings are increasingly found on second aorist stems in the Koine period.

The verb ἦσαν (impf. ind. 3rd pl. εἰμί) is common in the NT, occurring ninety times in this particular form.

---

[3] Culy, *I, II, III John*, 47.

- εἰ γὰρ ἐξ ἡμῶν ἦσαν, μεμενήκεισαν ἂν μεθ᾽ ἡμῶν—

  This clause introduces a second class conditional sentence (contrary to fact): "if they were part of us [but they are not], they would have remained with us" (see §13.3.1).

  The verb μεμενήκεισαν (plpf. act. ind. 3rd pl. μένω) is a pluperfect form, a tense form that is used only eighty-six times in the NT (see §9.3.3). The particle ἄν, often untranslated, conveys the indefinite and hypothetical nature of the phrase and the apodosis of the second class conditional statement.

- ἀλλ᾽ ἵνα φανερωθῶσιν ὅτι οὐκ εἰσὶν πάντες ἐξ ἡμῶν.

  There is an ellipsis here. The phrase ἐξ ἡμῶν ἐξῆλθαν, "they went out from us," is elided and should be supplied in translation for clarity: "but *they went out from us* that they might be revealed that they are not all part of us."

  The conjunction ἵνα introduces a purpose clause and triggers the subjunctive mood (φανερωθῶσιν: aor. pass. subjunc. 3rd pl. φανερόω).

1 John 2:20

- καὶ ὑμεῖς χρῖσμα ἔχετε ἀπὸ τοῦ ἁγίου

  The nominative pronoun ὑμεῖς is emphatic since that subject information is already embedded in the verb ἔχετε (pres. act. ind. 2nd pl. ἔχω: *"you have"*) and serves to contrast the readers from those who went out from them.

  The term χρῖσμα occurs only here and in 2:27 (twice) in the NT, and most likely refers to the Holy Spirit.

  The adjective ἁγίου functions substantivally, "the Holy One." Although "the Holy One" could refer to God the Father, it most likely refers to Jesus (see Mark 1:24; Luke 4:34; John 6:69; Acts 3:4; Rev 3:7).

- καὶ οἴδατε πάντες.

  The pronoun πάντες is emphatic and is the subject of the verb οἴδατε (per. act. ind. 2nd pl. οἶδα). Some manuscripts have πάντα (neut. acc. pl.), which would function as the direct object: "you know *all things*." The external evidence is split (though perhaps slightly favors πάντες), but the internal evidence favors the nominative reading (πάντες) because (1) the author is contrasting his readers with those who have abandoned the community, and (2) the nominative reading is more difficult since the text has no direct object.

1 John 2:21

- οὐκ ἔγραψα ὑμῖν ὅτι οὐκ οἴδατε τὴν ἀλήθειαν

The verb ἔγραψα (aor. act. ind. 1st sg. γράφω) is an epistolary aorist and refers not to an earlier letter but the letter the author was currently writing (see §9.3.1).

The conjunction ὅτι, "because," functions as a causal marker in all three occurrences in this verse (though it is possible that the third ὅτι introduces a content clause; so NKJV, NRSV).

- ἀλλ' ὅτι οἴδατε αὐτὴν καὶ ὅτι πᾶν ψεῦδος ἐκ τῆς ἀληθείας οὐκ ἔστιν.

The attributive adjective πᾶν modifies ψεῦδος (i.e., "*every* lie"), which is the subject of the verb ἔστιν. The feminine accusative singular personal pronoun αὐτήν must match its antecedent (ἀλήθειαν) in gender and number. The case of αὐτήν is determined by its syntactical function in the clause. As the direct object of οἴδατε, it is accusative.

1 John 2:22

- Τίς ἐστιν ὁ ψεύστης εἰ μὴ ὁ ἀρνούμενος ὅτι Ἰησοῦς οὐκ ἔστιν ὁ Χριστός;

Τίς is an interrogative pronoun introducing a rhetorical question (not to be confused with τις, the indefinite pronoun that has no accent in this form).

The article in the phrase ὁ ψεύστης is an example of the generic use. John is not pinpointing a particular person but is stating that anyone who denies the truth about Jesus is a liar. In contrast, the article in the phrase ὁ Χριστός is the monadic use (i.e., one of kind) since there is only one Messiah.

The substantival participle ὁ ἀρνούμενος (pres. mid. ptc. masc. nom. sg. ἀρνέομαι) is complemented by the phrase ὅτι Ἰησοῦς οὐκ ἔστιν ὁ Χριστός. John's statement seems to be lacking a verb of speech (e.g., λέγων, "saying"), but ἀρνέομαι here contains the idea of "denial by verbal expression." Otherwise, we might understand John's statement as conveying the opposite of what he intended. He writes, "Who is the liar except the one denying that Jesus is not the Christ." But the liar is not the one denying that Jesus is not the Christ (if you deny that Jesus is not the Christ, you are affirming that he is the Christ). Rather, John's statement should be read as follows: "Who is the liar except the one making the denial [i.e., saying] that Jesus is not the Christ."

- οὗτός ἐστιν ὁ ἀντίχριστος, ὁ ἀρνούμενος τὸν πατέρα καὶ τὸν υἱόν.

The use of the article in ὁ ἀντίχριστος is referenced previously. John is referring back to the coming Antichrist of v. 18.

The phrase ὁ ἀρνούμενος τὸν πατέρα καὶ τὸν υἱόν is not an example of the Granville Sharp rule because two articles are provided (τὸν πατέρα καὶ τὸν υἱόν). Consequently, the Father and the Son are separate persons. The use of the article with these two nouns is known as par excellence since the article identifies one who is in a class by oneself (see §5.3.1, "Par Excellence"). That is, there are other fathers and other sons, but the Father and the Son of the Godhead are like no other.

1 John 2:23

- πᾶς ὁ ἀρνούμενος τὸν υἱὸν οὐδὲ τὸν πατέρα ἔχει

The attributive adjective πᾶς modifies the substantival participle ὁ ἀρνούμενος, "*everyone* who denies," which is the subject of the verb ἔχει (pres. act. ind. 3rd sg. ἔχω).

- ὁ ὁμολογῶν τὸν υἱὸν καὶ τὸν πατέρα ἔχει.

The substantival participle ὁ ὁμολογῶν, "the one who confesses," contrasts with "everyone who denies." Both uses of the article ὁ are the generic use. In English, we often convey a generic or proverbial idea by placing an indefinite article in front of a noun or making it plural (e.g., "A person confessing the Son also has the Father" or "People who confess the Son also have the Father.")

1 John 2:24

- ὑμεῖς ὃ ἠκούσατε ἀπ' ἀρχῆς, ἐν ὑμῖν μενέτω.

The pronoun ὑμεῖς is emphatic since the second-person plural information is embedded in the verbal ending. John sharply contrasts his readers with the false brothers who deserted them.

The relative pronoun ὅ is "headless," having no antecedent (see also 1:1), and functions as the accusative direct object of ἠκούσατε. The verb ἀκούω can take a direct object in the genitive or accusative case.

There are only ten imperatives in 1 John, and μενέτω (pres. act. impv. 3rd sg.) is the first command (see 2:15 for the first prohibition). The third-person singular imperative, often translated "let him X," should be given the full imperatival force: "he must X."

- ἐὰν ἐν ὑμῖν μείνῃ ὃ ἀπ' ἀρχῆς ἠκούσατε, καὶ ὑμεῖς ἐν τῷ υἱῷ καὶ ἐν τῷ πατρὶ μενεῖτε.

The conjunction ἐάν introduces a third class conditional clause and triggers the subjunctive mood (μείνῃ: aor. act. subjunc. 3rd sg. μένω).

The verb μενεῖτε (fut. act. ind. 2nd pl. μένω) is in the future tense, lacking the *sigma* (σ) because it is a liquid verb.[4]

1 John 2:25

- καὶ αὕτη ἐστὶν ἡ ἐπαγγελία

The near demonstrative pronoun αὕτη is cataphoric, pointing forward to τὴν ζωὴν τὴν αἰώνιον. The article ἡ has the basic function of identifying a particular promise.

- ἣν αὐτὸς ἐπηγγείλατο ἡμῖν, τὴν ζωὴν τὴν αἰώνιον.

The antecedent of the relative pronoun ἣν is ἡ ἐπαγγελία. The personal pronoun αὐτός is emphatic and is the subject of the verb ἐπηγγείλατο (aor. mid. ind. 3rd sg. ἐπαγγέλλομαι). This is another liquid verb that rejected the *sigma*, which caused compensatory lengthening of the stem vowel (ε → ει).

The adjective τὴν αἰώνιον functions attributively, modifying τὴν ζωήν "*eternal* life." The noun τὴν ζωήν is in apposition to ἡ ἐπαγγελία.

---

[4] The tense formative is changed from a *sigma* (σ) to an *epsilon* + *sigma* (εσ). When the connecting vowel of the personal ending is placed beside the *sigma*, however, the *sigma* is then found between two vowels (intervocalic *sigma*). The *sigma* then drops out of the word. The two vowels that were separated by a *sigma* are then found together and contract: μεν + εσ + ετε → μενεσετε → μενεετε → μενεῖτε. A circumflex accent is placed over the contracted vowels.

////////////////

CHAPTER 6

1 JOHN 2:26–3:3
SUBJUNCTIVES AND IMPERATIVES

6.1 Vocabulary

θύρα, ἡ	door, gate, entrance (39)
παρουσία, ἡ	coming, arrival (24)
παρρησία, ἡ	confidence, boldness (31)
τέλος, -ους, τό	end, goal (40)
ἁγνός, -ή, -όν	pure, holy (8)
ἱκανός, -ή, -όν	qualified, able (39)
οὔπω	not yet (26)
ποταπός, -ή, -όν	how glorious (7)
ἁγνίζω	I purify (7)
αἰσχύνω	I am put to shame, disgraced (5)
ἐπιτίθημι	I lay upon, put upon (39)
περισσεύω	I exceed, overflow, abound (39)

6.2 Text: 1 John 2:26–3:3

²⁶ Ταῦτα ἔγραψα ὑμῖν περὶ τῶν πλανώντων ὑμᾶς. ²⁷ καὶ ὑμεῖς τὸ χρῖσμα ὃ ἐλάβετε ἀπ᾽ αὐτοῦ μένει ἐν ὑμῖν, καὶ οὐ χρείαν ἔχετε ἵνα τις διδάσκῃ ὑμᾶς, ἀλλ᾽ ὡς τὸ αὐτοῦ χρῖσμα διδάσκει ὑμᾶς περὶ πάντων, καὶ ἀληθές ἐστιν καὶ οὐκ ἔστιν ψεῦδος, καὶ καθὼς ἐδίδαξεν ὑμᾶς, μένετε ἐν αὐτῷ. ²⁸ Καὶ νῦν, τεκνία, μένετε ἐν αὐτῷ, ἵνα ἐὰν φανερωθῇ, σχῶμεν παρρησίαν καὶ μὴ αἰσχυνθῶμεν ἀπ᾽ αὐτοῦ ἐν τῇ παρουσίᾳ αὐτοῦ. ²⁹ ἐὰν εἰδῆτε ὅτι δίκαιός ἐστιν, γινώσκετε ὅτι καὶ πᾶς ὁ ποιῶν τὴν δικαιοσύνην ἐξ αὐτοῦ γεγέννηται.

³:¹ ἴδετε ποταπὴν ἀγάπην δέδωκεν ἡμῖν ὁ πατήρ, ἵνα τέκνα θεοῦ κληθῶμεν, καὶ ἐσμέν. διὰ τοῦτο ὁ κόσμος οὐ γινώσκει ἡμᾶς, ὅτι οὐκ ἔγνω αὐτόν. ² Ἀγαπητοί νῦν τέκνα θεοῦ ἐσμεν, καὶ οὔπω ἐφανερώθη τί ἐσόμεθα. οἴδαμεν ὅτι ἐὰν φανερωθῇ, ὅμοιοι αὐτῷ ἐσόμεθα, ὅτι ὀψόμεθα αὐτὸν, καθώς ἐστιν. ³ καὶ πᾶς ὁ ἔχων τὴν ἐλπίδα ταύτην ἐπ' αὐτῷ ἁγνίζει ἑαυτόν, καθὼς ἐκεῖνος ἁγνός ἐστιν.

6.3 Syntax: Subjunctives and Imperatives

6.3.1 Subjunctives

Although it is sometimes called the mood of uncertainty, the subjunctive mood is best described as the mood of indefiniteness (or the mood of probability). For example, John employs the subjunctive mood to describe the return of Christ: "so that *when he appears* [ἐὰν φανερωθῇ] we may have confidence and not be ashamed before him at his coming" (1 John 2:28 CSB) and "*when he appears* [ἐὰν φανερωθῇ], we will be like him because we will see him as he is" (1 John 3:2 CSB). In both verses, John uses the subjunctive mood not because the return of Christ is uncertain but because the time of his return is unknown to us.

When it comes to tense forms, with the subjunctive mood there is a binary choice: present (25 percent) or aorist (75 percent).[1] When in doubt, it is typically best to assume that a subjunctive form is aorist, since aorist subjunctives occur three times more frequently than present subjunctives (though 1 John has more present forms [28] than aorist [23]). Regardless of tense form, subjunctives do not communicate time. In fact, the action of most subjunctive mood verbs is future oriented. For example, conditional subjunctives (sometimes called future conditions), indicate something that will/could happen if certain conditions are met: Ἐάν τις ἴδῃ τὸν ἀδελφὸν αὐτοῦ ἁμαρτάνοντα, "if anyone sees his brother sinning [in the future]" (1 John 5:16).

Subjunctives are often used in combination with certain conjunctions (listed below in parentheses). Here are some of the main uses of the subjunctive:

- **Purpose or Result** (ἵνα or ὅπως + subjunctive).[2]

  ○ ἀπαγγέλλομεν καὶ ὑμῖν, **ἵνα** καὶ ὑμεῖς κοινωνίαν **ἔχητε** μεθ' ἡμῶν, "we proclaim to you, **that** you also **might have** fellowship with us" (1 John 1:3).

  ○ μένετε ἐν αὐτῷ, **ἵνα** . . . **σχῶμεν** παρρησίαν, "abide in him, **that** . . . **you might have** confidence" (1 John 2:28).

---

[1] Technically, there are ten perfect subjunctives (including two in 1 John), but these are all from the term οἶδα, and functionally they should be treated as present forms.

[2] Ἵνα occurs nineteen times in 1 John, though not always introducing a purpose clause (ὅπως does not occur in 1 John). Ἵνα frequently is used to introduce "content" in John's writings, similar to "i.e.," in English prose. This use is sometimes called the epexegetical use of ἵνα.

- **Conditional** (ἐάν or ἐὰν μή + subjunctive).[3]

  ○ ἐὰν εἴπωμεν ὅτι ἁμαρτίαν οὐκ ἔχομεν, ἑαυτοὺς πλανῶμεν, "**if we say** that we do not have sin, we deceive ourselves" (1 John 1:8).

  ○ ἐὰν εἰδῆτε ὅτι δίκαιός ἐστιν, γινώσκετε ὅτι, "**if you know** that he is righteous, you know that" (1 John 2:29).

- **Indefinite Relative** (ὅσ[τις] ἄν/ἐάν or ὃς [δ'] ἄν + subjunctive).

  ○ ὃς δ' ἂν τηρῇ αὐτοῦ τὸν λόγον, ἀληθῶς ἐν τούτῳ ἡ ἀγάπη τοῦ θεοῦ τετελείωται, "but **whoever keeps** his word, truly in this one the love of God is perfected" (1 John 2:5).

  ○ ὃς δ' ἂν ἔχῃ τὸν βίον τοῦ κόσμου καὶ θεωρῇ τὸν ἀδελφὸν αὐτοῦ χρείαν ἔχοντα καὶ κλείσῃ τὰ σπλάγχνα αὐτοῦ ἀπ' αὐτοῦ, πῶς ἡ ἀγάπη τοῦ θεοῦ μένει ἐν αὐτῷ; "but **whoever has** the possessions of the world and **sees** his brother having need and **closes** his heart to him, how does the love of God abide in him?" (1 John 3:17).

- **Temporal** (ὅταν [or ἕως, ἄχρι, μέχρι] + subjunctive).

  ○ ἐν τούτῳ γινώσκομεν ὅτι ἀγαπῶμεν τὰ τέκνα τοῦ θεοῦ, ὅταν τὸν θεὸν ἀγαπῶμεν καὶ τὰς ἐντολὰς αὐτοῦ ποιῶμεν, "by this we know that we love the children of God, **whenever we love** God and **practice** his commands" (1 John 5:2).

  ○ οἴδαμεν ὅτι ἐὰν φανερωθῇ, ὅμοιοι αὐτῷ ἐσόμεθα, "we know that **when he appears**, we will be like him" (1 John 3:2). Here, ἐάν introduces a temporal clause.[4]

- **Hortatory.** A first-person plural subjunctive functioning as an imperative.

  ○ Τεκνία, μὴ ἀγαπῶμεν λόγῳ μηδὲ τῇ γλώσσῃ, ἀλλὰ ἐν ἔργῳ καὶ ἀληθείᾳ, "Little children, **let us** not **love** with word or tongue but in deed and truth" (1 John 3:18).

---

[3] Ἐάν occurs twenty-two times in 1 John, though not always introducing a future conditional clause (ἐὰν μή does not occur in 1 John). Ἐάν sometimes functions as an indefinite particle alongside a relative pronoun.

[4] According to BDAG, ἐάν can function as a "marker of the prospect of an action in a point of time coordinated with another point of time." Consequently, sometimes the meaning of ἐάν "approaches closely that of ὅταν" (268). Likewise, according to Louw and Nida, this conjunction may refer to "a point of time which is somewhat conditional and simultaneous with another point of time" (§67.32). Culy posits that perhaps the normal conditional sense "if" is intended for rhetorical effect. He states, "The writer is arguing that if the readers need his warning to 'remain in him,' they will most certainly have confidence 'if' he appears" (*I, II, III John*, 63).

- ᾿Αγαπητοί, **ἀγαπῶμεν** ἀλλήλους, "Beloved, **let us love** one another" (1 John 4:7).

- **Other Uses** (not found in 1 John):

  - **Deliberative.** Asks a real or rhetorical question: τί εἴπω ὑμῖν; "What **shall I say** to you?" (1 Cor 11:22).

  - **Emphatic Negation.** Consists of a double negative (οὐ μή): ὁ πιστεύων εἰς ἐμὲ οὐ **μὴ διψήσει**, "the one who believes in me will **never thirst**" (John 6:35).

  - **Prohibitory.** A negated aorist subjunctive that functions as an imperative: **μὴ νομίσητε** ὅτι ἦλθον καταλῦσαι τὸν νόμον ἢ τοὺς προφήτας, "**Do not think** that I came to abolish the law or the prophets" (Matt 5:17).

6.3.2 Imperatives

The imperative mood is most commonly used to express a command. It can best be described, however, as the mood of intention, since it is used in contexts other than a command. The following categories represent the main uses of the imperative mood.

- **Command.** An exhortation or charge.

  - Καὶ νῦν, τεκνία, **μένετε** ἐν αὐτῷ, "And now, little children, **abide** in him" (1 John 2:28).

  - Τεκνία, **φυλάξατε** ἑαυτὰ ἀπὸ τῶν εἰδώλων, "Little children, **guard** yourselves from idols" (1 John 5:21).

- **Prohibition.** A negative command (using μή) that forbids an action.

  - **Μὴ ἀγαπᾶτε** τὸν κόσμον, "**Do not love** the world" (1 John 2:15).

  - **μὴ θαυμάζετε**, ἀδελφοί, εἰ μισεῖ ὑμᾶς ὁ κόσμος, "**Do not be surprised**, brothers, if the world hates you" (1 John 3:13).

- **Other Uses** (not found in 1 John).

  - **Request.** A plea given to someone with a higher social rank: Κύριε, **βοήθει** μοι, "Lord, **[please] help** me" (Matt 15:25).

  - **Permission.** Expresses permission, allowance, or toleration: εἰ δὲ ὁ ἄπιστος χωρίζεται, **χωριζέσθω**, "But if the unbeliever leaves, **let him leave**" (1 Cor 7:15).

  - **Conditional.** Conveys an implied conditional statement: **λύσατε** τὸν ναὸν τοῦτον καὶ ἐν τρισὶν ἡμέραις ἐγερῶ αὐτόν, "**Destroy** this temple, and in three days I will raise it" (John 2:19). The idea is "if you destroy this temple in three days, I will raise it."

6.4 Reading Notes

1 John 2:26

- Ταῦτα ἔγραψα ὑμῖν περὶ τῶν πλανώντων ὑμᾶς.

The verb ἔγραψα (aor. act. ind. 1st sg. γράφω) is an example of an epistolary aorist (see §9.3.1).

The substantival particle τῶν πλανώντων (pres. act. ptc. masc. gen. pl. πλανάω) functions as a tendential present tense form (see §8.3.1). That is, John is *not* claiming that the opponents are deceiving his readers, but that they are *trying* or *attempting* to do so. Consequently, it is appropriate (and even necessary) to translate the participle as "those *trying* to deceive." The present tense form of the participle does not *by itself* communicate this nuance (though this nuance is not possible if the aorist is used) but *allows* for this nuance, since it is the imperfective aspect. This aspect portrays the action as in process or ongoing. Thus, from the epistolary context, we discern that some are attempting to deceive John's readers, but so far these attempts have been unsuccessful.

1 John 2:27

- καὶ ὑμεῖς τὸ χρῖσμα ὃ ἐλάβετε ἀπ' αὐτοῦ

The personal pronoun ὑμεῖς is a hanging (or pendent) nominative because it is grammatically unconnected to the main verb (which is μένει, a third-person verb).

The article in τὸ χρῖσμα points back to the previous use of the noun in 2:20. The antecedent of the neuter relative pronoun ὅ is τὸ χρῖσμα.

The verb ἐλάβετε (aor. act. ind. 2nd pl. λαμβάνω) is a second aorist form.

- μένει ἐν ὑμῖν, καὶ οὐ χρείαν ἔχετε ἵνα τις διδάσκῃ ὑμᾶς

The subject of the verb μένει is τὸ χρῖσμα: "the anointing abides."

The prepositional phrases ἐν ὑμῖν and ἐν αὐτῷ (see below) are both examples of the metaphorical use of the dative of location.

The conjunction ἵνα introduces a content clause and triggers the subjunctive mood (διδάσκῃ: pres. act. subjunc. 3rd sg. διδάσκω). Typically, ἵνα introduces a purpose clause, but occasionally in the NT (and in a few places in 1 John) it functions similarly to a ὅτι content clause.

- **ἀλλ' ὡς τὸ αὐτοῦ χρῖσμα διδάσκει ὑμᾶς περὶ πάντων, καὶ ἀληθές ἐστιν καὶ οὐκ ἔστιν ψεῦδος**

The subject of the verb διδάσκει (pres. act. ind. 3rd sg. διδάσκω) is τὸ αὐτοῦ χρῖσμα: "his anointing."

There are a few textual issues in this verse. (1) τὸ αὐτοῦ χρῖσμα ("his anointing"; subjective genitive = he [i.e., the Holy Spirit] anoints) appears in some manuscripts as τὸ αὐτὸ χρῖσμα (i.e., "the same anointing"); (2) μένετε ("abide" or "you are abiding") appears in some manuscripts as μενεῖτε (i.e., "you will abide"). In both cases the reading given in the bold Greek text above is most likely John's original wording, but it is a good practice to consider these variants for yourself.

- **καὶ καθὼς ἐδίδαξεν ὑμᾶς, μένετε ἐν αὐτῷ.**

The implied subject of the verb ἐδίδαξεν (aor. act. ind. 3rd sg. διδάσκω) is τὸ χρῖσμα, referenced twice above, once with the same verb.

Although the verb μένετε (pres. act. ind./impv. 2nd pl. μένω) could be taken as an indicative, it is better to view it as an imperative in this context: "abide in him" (cf. 2:28).

1 John 2:28

- **Καὶ νῦν, τεκνία, μένετε ἐν αὐτῷ**

The verb μένετε (pres. act. impv. 2nd pl. μένω) is an imperative used as a command.

- **ἵνα ἐὰν φανερωθῇ, σχῶμεν παρρησίαν**

This clause contains two subjunctive phrases. The first (ἵνα . . . σχῶμεν), involves ἵνα, which introduces a purpose clause: "that you might have confidence." The verb σχῶμεν (aor. act. subjunc. 1st pl. ἔχω) comes from the root σεχ–. As typical with most subjunctives, the connecting vowel lengthens (ομεν → ωμεν).

The other subjunctive (ἐὰν φανερωθῇ: aor. pass. subjunc. 3rd sg. φανερόω), is sandwiched in the midst of the subjunctive purpose clause. Although ἐάν normally introduces a conditional statement, here it functions similar to the temporal marker ὅταν (i.e., "*when* he appears").[5] Indeed, it is reflecting on the time of Jesus's appearing and the confidence we hope to have before him that provides an impetus for faithful Christian living and stewardship in this life.

- καὶ μὴ αἰσχυνθῶμεν ἀπ' αὐτοῦ ἐν τῇ παρουσίᾳ αὐτοῦ.

The verb αἰσχυνθῶμεν (aor. pass. subjunc. 1st pl. αἰσχύνω) is connected by καί and is therefore controlled by ἵνα, introducing a second purpose clause: "and that you might not be ashamed," or perhaps, "and that you might not shrink back in shame from him."

The prepositional phrase ἀπ' αὐτοῦ expresses separation. The entire expression "appears to point to a negative judgment that involves removal from the Son's presence."[6]

The phrase ἐν τῇ παρουσίᾳ αὐτοῦ is a dative of time, "*at* his coming," and the personal pronoun αὐτοῦ functions as subjective genitive ("at his coming" = when he comes).

1 John 2:29

- ἐὰν εἰδῆτε ὅτι δίκαιός ἐστιν

The conjunction ἐάν introduces a third class conditional statement and triggers the subjunctive mood. The verb εἰδῆτε (per. act. subjunc. 2nd pl. οἶδα), although it is parsed as a perfect verb, should be treated as a present form for the following reasons: (1) Οἶδα is the only verb in the NT that occurs with a perfect tense subjunctive. (2) The verb οἶδα does not occur in the present tense. (3) The perfect εἰδῆτε is parallel to the present γινώσκετε in the next clause.

Students often mistake εἰδῆτε as a second aorist subjunctive form of ὁράω, but that form would be ἴδητε (Matt 13:14). Aorist subjunctives do not have augments.

The conjunction ὅτι, "that," both here and in the following use, introduces a content clause.

---

[5] But see note 4 above.
[6] Culy, *I, II, III John*, 64.

- γινώσκετε ὅτι καὶ πᾶς ὁ ποιῶν τὴν δικαιοσύνην ἐξ αὐτοῦ γεγέννηται.

The previous use of the verb εἰδῆτε (from οἶδα) instead of γινώσκετε (pres. act. ind. 2nd pl. γινώσκω) is most likely because γινώσκω is never used with the conjunction ἐάν in the NT.

The substantival participle ὁ ποιῶν functions as the subject of the verb γεγέννηται (perf. pass. ind. 3rd sg. γεννάω). Remember that in Greek abstract nouns are usually articular (τὴν δικαιοσύνην).

1 John 3:1

- ἴδετε ποταπὴν ἀγάπην δέδωκεν ἡμῖν ὁ πατὴρ

The verb ἴδετε (aor. act. impv. 2nd pl. βλέπω/ὁράω) is an imperative of command. Baugh notes, "The present imperative (βλέπετε) frequently has a cautionary tone: 'watch out for,' 'keep an eye on' (e.g., Phil 3:2). The sense of this aorist in 1 John 3:1 is more contemplative: 'take a look at . . .' 'consider for a moment. . . .'"[7]

The interrogative pronoun ποταπήν means "how glorious" (BDAG 856) and refers to the quality of God's love for his people.

The verb δέδωκεν (per. act. ind. 3rd sg. δίδωμι) is a consummative perfect, emphasizing the completed past action (see §9.3.2). Thus, "God has lavished his love on those who follow Jesus, love initiated by God the Father in the past and continuing even today."[8]

- ἵνα τέκνα θεοῦ κληθῶμεν, καὶ ἐσμέν.

The conjunction ἵνα introduces a purpose (or, maybe better, a result) statement and triggers the subjunctive mood (κληθῶμεν: aor. pass. subjunc. 1st pl. καλέω; "that [as a result] we might be called children of God"). Note that κληθῶμεν does not have a direct object in the accusative case. Instead, we find the nominative τέκνα. In this construction, τέκνα is similar to a predicate nominative with a copulative verb ("we are children of God" = we are called children of God). Some grammars label τέκνα a nominative of appellation with a verb of calling.

The genitive in the phrase τέκνα θεοῦ is a genitive of relationship: "children *of God*."

---

[7] Baugh, *First John Reader*, 43.
[8] Bateman and Peer, *John's Letters*, 168.

- διὰ τοῦτο ὁ κόσμος οὐ γινώσκει ἡμᾶς ὅτι οὐκ ἔγνω αὐτόν.

The expression διὰ τοῦτο (literally "on account of this") "refers to a reason that supports the proposition it introduces."[9] It can be translated as "for this reason."

Notice that the verbs γινώσκει (pres. act. ind. 3rd sg. γινώσκω) and ἔγνω (aor. act. ind. 3rd sg. γινώσκω) come from the same lexical form. The (second) aorist form is irregular.

1 John 3:2

- Ἀγαπητοί νῦν τέκνα θεοῦ ἐσμεν, καὶ οὔπω ἐφανερώθη τί ἐσόμεθα.

The interrogative pronoun τί is the predicate nominative of the verb ἐσόμεθα (fut. mid. ind. 1st pl. εἰμί).

- οἴδαμεν ὅτι ἐὰν φανερωθῇ, ὅμοιοι αὐτῷ ἐσόμεθα

As is common following a verb of knowledge (e.g., οἴδαμεν: per. act. ind. 1st pl. οἶδα), ὅτι introduces a content clause, "that."

The conjunction ἐάν can introduce a temporal statement (similar to ὅταν) and triggers the subjunctive mood (φανερωθῇ: aor. pass. subjunc. 3rd sg. φανερόω; "*when* he appears").

The personal pronoun αὐτῷ is a dative of reference or respect which limits or qualifies the extent of the verbal action: "we shall be similar [*with respect*] *to him*." After verbs, nouns, or adjectives communicating likeness/similarity, students should expect a dative complement.

- ὅτι ὀψόμεθα αὐτὸν, καθώς ἐστιν.

The conjunction ὅτι here introduces a causal clause, "because."

The verb ὀψόμεθα (fut. mid. ind. 1st pl. ὁράω), like the verb εἰμί (see ἐσόμεθα above), uses a middle form in the future tense. Quite a few Greek verbs follow the middle voice in the future tense. Scholars debate why. Perhaps because the middle voice is preferred for verbs communicating mental conception, it is the mental conceiving of the future (which has not yet happened) that results in this pattern of Greek voice.

---

[9] Culy, *I, II, III John*, 67.

1 John 3:3

- καὶ πᾶς ὁ ἔχων τὴν ἐλπίδα ταύτην ἐπ᾽ αὐτῷ ἁγνίζει ἑαυτόν

  The substantival participle ὁ ἔχων (pres. act. ptc. masc. nom. sg. ἔχω) functions as the subject of the verb ἁγνίζει (pres. act. ind. 3rd sg. ἁγνίζω).

  The prepositional phrase ἐπ᾽ αὐτῷ conveys the basis of the hope: "*upon/in* him."[10] The term ἑαυτόν is a reflexive pronoun.

- καθὼς ἐκεῖνος ἁγνός ἐστιν.

  The conjunction καθὼς expresses a comparison, "just as." The far demonstrative pronoun ἐκεῖνος ("that one" or "he") refers to Jesus (see note at 2:6).

---

[10] See numbered entry "6b" in BDAG for ἐπί, "marker of basis for a state of being, action, or result, on . . . with verbs of believing, hoping trusting."

CHAPTER 7

///////////////

1 JOHN 3:4–10
TENSE AND VERBAL ASPECT

7.1 Vocabulary

ἀνομία, ἡ	lawlessness (15)
ἄρχων, -οντος, ὁ	ruler, authority, judge (37)
διάβολος, ὁ	devil, accuser, slanderous (adj) (37)
πρόβατον, τό	sheep (39)
σπέρμα, -ατος, τό	seed, descendant(s), children (43)
ἐκεῖθεν	from there (37)
καλῶς	well (37)
φανερός, -ά, -όν	manifest, visible, clear (18)
διακονέω	I serve (37)
εὐχαριστέω	I give thanks, am thankful (38)
πειράζω	I tempt, test (38)
ὑποτάσσω	I subject (38)

7.2 Text: 1 John 3:4–10

⁴ Πᾶς ὁ ποιῶν τὴν ἁμαρτίαν καὶ τὴν ἀνομίαν ποιεῖ, καὶ ἡ ἁμαρτία ἐστὶν ἡ ἀνομία.
⁵ καὶ οἴδατε ὅτι ἐκεῖνος ἐφανερώθη, ἵνα τὰς ἁμαρτίας ἄρῃ, καὶ ἁμαρτία ἐν αὐτῷ οὐκ
ἔστιν. ⁶ πᾶς ὁ ἐν αὐτῷ μένων οὐχ ἁμαρτάνει· πᾶς ὁ ἁμαρτάνων οὐχ ἑώρακεν αὐτὸν
οὐδὲ ἔγνωκεν αὐτόν. ⁷ Παιδία, μηδεὶς πλανάτω ὑμᾶς· ὁ ποιῶν τὴν δικαιοσύνην δίκαιός
ἐστιν, καθὼς ἐκεῖνος δίκαιός ἐστιν· ⁸ ὁ ποιῶν τὴν ἁμαρτίαν ἐκ τοῦ διαβόλου ἐστίν, ὅτι
ἀπ᾽ ἀρχῆς ὁ διάβολος ἁμαρτάνει. εἰς τοῦτο ἐφανερώθη ὁ υἱὸς τοῦ θεοῦ, ἵνα λύσῃ τὰ

ἔργα τοῦ διαβόλου. ⁹ Πᾶς ὁ γεγεννημένος ἐκ τοῦ θεοῦ ἁμαρτίαν οὐ ποιεῖ, ὅτι σπέρμα αὐτοῦ ἐν αὐτῷ μένει, καὶ οὐ δύναται ἁμαρτάνειν, ὅτι ἐκ τοῦ θεοῦ γεγέννηται. ¹⁰ ἐν τούτῳ φανερά ἐστιν τὰ τέκνα τοῦ θεοῦ καὶ τὰ τέκνα τοῦ διαβόλου· πᾶς ὁ μὴ ποιῶν δικαιοσύνην οὐκ ἔστιν ἐκ τοῦ θεοῦ, καὶ ὁ μὴ ἀγαπῶν τὸν ἀδελφὸν αὐτοῦ.

7.3 Syntax: Tense and Verbal Aspect

7.3.1 Definitions
Whereas "tense" relates to the *time* of an action (or state), verbal aspect is the *viewpoint* or *perspective* by which an author chooses to portray an action (or state). It is generally recognized that there are three aspects in Koine Greek. An author can portray an action as

1. In process or ongoing (imperfective aspect = present or imperfect tense form)
2. Complete or as a whole (perfective aspect = aorist tense form)
3. A state resulting from a previous action (stative aspect = perfect tense form)

Because *time* is not communicated by the grammatical form of the verb outside of the indicative mood, aspect is primary. That is, since subjunctives and imperatives (as well as participles and infinitives) do not have inherent time, aspect is all that remains to distinguish the tense forms. Thus, regardless of how the action actually happened, the author may choose to portray the action as in progress, as a whole, or as completed with a resulting state.

This basic aspectual distinction, however, does not exist in isolation. There are at least three other factors that influence an author's choice of a particular tense form: (1) lexical factors, (2) grammatical factors, and (3) contextual factors.

7.3.2 Lexical, Grammatical, and Contextual Factors
Lexical Factors. These refer to characteristics restricted to the verb itself that influence the author's choice of one tense form (aspect) over another.[1] This may be in terms of lexical determination or lexical influence. *Lexical determination* is when a verb's usage is limited to certain tense forms. For example, verbs such as εἰμί, κεῖμαι, κάθημαι, and φημί do not occur in the aorist tense form because of their inherent meanings or because of idiomatic influence. Consequently, in some instances, the author's choice of tense form is determined by the verb itself.[2]

Although most verbs are not lexically restricted to only certain tense forms, they typically *prefer* a particular tense form (or forms) over others. *Lexical influence*,

---

[1] In this chapter we often use *tense form* (by which we mean aspect) instead of merely *tense* to reenforce the idea that we are not talking about time.

[2] We are indebted to Baugh for his work in this area; see S. M. Baugh, *Introduction to Greek Tense Form Choice in the Non-Indicative Moods* (PDF edition, 2009). This work can be accessed at dailydoseofgreek.com.

then, refers to the influence of the verbal activity's inherent procedural nature on its usage in the various tense forms. This influence is due to the overlap in function of the verb's aspect and the inherent meaning of the verb.[3] In other words, because the perfective aspect (aorist tense form) is used by the author to portray the action as a whole, it is more natural to use the perfective aspect with verbs whose actions are normally completed in a relatively short period of time. For example, in the NT the imperative of βάλλω occurs fourteen times as an aorist but never as a present. This usage is expected when one considers that the action to "throw" or "put" takes place almost instantaneously. Indeed, it is difficult to conceive of the imperfective aspect being used when there would be virtually no time to portray the action as in progress or incomplete. So, the inherent procedural nature of the activity of "throwing" essentially dictates the tense form choice as aorist (perfective aspect).

Conversely, because the imperfective aspect (present tense form) is used by the author to portray the action as in progress, it is more natural to use the imperfective aspect with verbs whose actions normally are viewed as having no natural endpoint or are stative verbs. For example, in the NT the imperative of γρηγορέω occurs eleven times as a present but only once as an aorist. Again, this usage is expected when one considers that the action of "keeping watch" is not normally completed in a short period of time but is an action that has no natural terminus. Indeed, it is difficult to conceive of the perfective aspect being used when the action is not easily portrayed as a whole.[4]

Most verbs can be categorized into two broad categories: telic or atelic. A telic verb is a verb that has a natural terminus or ending point. These verbs can further be divided into those that convey some perceived duration but express a climax, conclusion, or termination (performance) and those that refer to an action that is done in a moment without taking any perceived or significant time duration (punctual). In contrast, an atelic verb refers to a state (or a condition or relationship) or to an activity that has no natural terminus or no set limit for its completion (i.e., "unbounded").

These distinctions are significant because the lexical or semantic meaning of the verb (i.e., whether it is telic or atelic) limits the choice of the tense form (aspect) used. That is, telic verbs are most semantically compatible with the aorist tense form, whereas atelic verbs are most semantically compatible with the present (or imperfect) tense form. Thus, an author is not simply free to choose the tense form but is often influenced by the verbal activity's inherent procedural nature.

---

[3] The rest of this paragraph and the next are taken from Benjamin L. Merkle, "Verbal Aspect and Imperatives: Ephesians as a Test Case," in *New Testament Philology: Essays in Honor of David Alan Black*, ed. Melton Bennett Winstead (Eugene, OR: Pickwick, 2018), 36–37.

[4] On the other hand, if an ancient Greek speaker commanded someone to "keep watch over this child until the sixth hour," it is likely that the specificity of that command would have been most naturally conceived as a bounded activity, and thus speaker would likely choose an aorist tense form for the imperative of γρηγορέω.

Telic	Performance	Bounded actions with perceived duration	Prefers Aorist
	Punctual	Bounded actions with little perceived duration	
Atelic	Stative	States and relationships	Prefers Present/Imperfect
	Activity	Actions with no inherent termination	

Grammatical Factors. These relate to the particular form (morphemes) of the verb, such as the tense form, voice, and mood. For example, when studying a verb, each mood should be analyzed independently because different factors influence the verb's tense form in the various moods. The tense form of an *indicative* verb is influenced by the time of the action. With the other moods, time is not a factor. With *infinitives*, attention should be given to verb combinations, especially with complementary infinitives. With *subjunctives*, it is important to remember that the aorist tense form outnumbers the present tense form (about a 3:1 ratio). Also, both hortatory subjunctives and prohibitory subjunctives should be analyzed as imperatives (since that is how they function). In addition to mood, other factors, such as the voice of the verb, the nature of the subject or object phrase, the use of various adverbs or prepositional modifiers, and relevant syntactical features, should be considered.

Contextual Factors. Perhaps the most influential contextual factor is the text's *literary genre* since certain literary styles are prone to favor a particular tense forms. For example, when considering imperatives, historical narratives heavily favor the aorist tense form (perfective aspect) whereas epistles favor the present tense form (imperfective aspect). When taking into account all the Epistles and Revelation, the present tense form is used about twice as often as the aorist. Additionally, in prayers where imperatives are used to make requests to God, the aorist is the predominant tense form regardless of the lexical meaning of the verb.[5] A second contextual factor relates to *idiolect*, or a particular author's individual propensity to favor a certain tense form. For example, Paul uses present imperatives about three times more than he uses aorist imperatives. In contrast, 1 Peter contains twenty-five aorist imperatives but only ten present imperatives (a 5:2 ratio).

We can summarize our discussion by noting that a verb's lexical meaning can influence the aspect used because the way an action is *performed* affects the way it can be *portrayed*. Furthermore, both the grammar (especially the mood) and the context (genre and idiolect) also affect the author's aspectual choice.

---

[5] See e.g., Willem Frederik Bakker, *The Greek Imperative: An Investigation into the Aspectual Differences between the Present and Aorist Imperatives in Greek Prayer from Homer up to the Present Day* (Amsterdam: Hakkert, 1966), 12; Fanning, *Verbal Aspect*, 380.

7.3.3 Case Study: 1 John 3:9

In 1 John 3:9, the author writes, "Everyone who has been born of God *does not sin* [ἁμαρτίαν οὐ ποιεῖ], because his seed remains in him; he *is not able to sin* [οὐ δύναται ἁμαρτάνειν], because he has been born of God" (CSB). Does this text mean that true Christians do not sin? This interpretation, however, contradicts both experience and other passages in the Bible such as 1 John 1:8: "If we say, 'We have no sin,' we are deceiving ourselves, and the truth is not in us" (CSB). Additionally, this view is not easily compatible with the repeated injunctions in the epistle to forsake sin and live righteously. Another interpretation states that John is presenting Christians as sinless in view of Christ's atoning work on the cross and is "speaking in terms of a projected eschatological reality."[6] So, even though Christians sin experientially, they do not sin positionally because of Christ's payment for sins on the cross. That is, although we sin, because of Christ's substitutionary atonement, we are viewed as if we have never sinned.

A better interpretation states that John is declaring that true Christians do not continue in sin. First, the idea that John is speaking in light of our eschatological hope does not best fit the context of the letter. In this epistle, John offers a series of three repeated tests that give assurance to true believers and expose false believers. The false believers embrace an ungodly lifestyle, neglect to love others, and consequently continue to live in sin. Thus, John seeks to contrast the lifestyle of the false teachers with those who are genuine Christians.

Second, the present tense is often used with an iterative nuance. In the immediate context, John repeatedly emphasizes the idea of *practicing* sin as a lifestyle:

- πᾶς ὁ ποιῶν τὴν ἁμαρτίαν, "everyone who practices sin" (3:4)
- ὁ ποιῶν τὴν ἁμαρτίαν, "the one who practices sin" (3:8)
- πᾶς ὁ γεγεννημένος ἐκ τοῦ θεοῦ ἁμαρτίαν οὐ ποιεῖ, "everyone who has been born of God does not practice sin" (3:9)

John not only refers to those who sin but specifically to those who practice or *make a practice* of sinning. Thus, John is giving guidelines for knowing who are the true children of God: they are those who are not characterized by habitual disobedience to God.

Finally, and most relevant for our current focus on verbal aspect, this interpretation is confirmed by the use of the infinitive ἁμαρτάνειν in 3:9. John writes that every believer "*is not able to sin* [οὐ δύναται ἁμαρτάνειν], because he has been born of God." The construction δύναμαι + infinitive occurs 174 times in the NT with the infinitive occurring 126 times in the aorist but only forty-eight times in the present. Thus, δύναμαι favors the aorist when in construction with an infinitive.[7]

---

[6] Wallace, *Greek Grammar*, 525.

[7] Cf. μέλλω + infinitive (eighty-four present; seven aorist) and ἄρχομαι + infinitive (eighty-seven present; zero aorist). Statistics are from Baugh, *Greek Tense Form Choice*.

Furthermore, the verb ἁμαρτάνω is a telic verb and so lexically favors the aorist. For example, in the subjunctive mood (which is closest to infinitives among dependent mood verbs), the verb is used six times in the aorist (including twice in 1 John) and never in the present. Based on this data, Baugh comments, "John consciously chose the present infinitive form ἁμαρτάνειν because he wished to convey a special nuance. That nuance is the 'characteristic' nature of the action, a lifestyle of sinning."[8] This interpretation, then, not only fits the historical and literary contexts of 1 John, but there is also grammatical evidence that points in its favor.

7.4 Reading Notes

1 John 3:4

- Πᾶς ὁ ποιῶν τὴν ἁμαρτίαν καὶ τὴν ἀνομίαν ποιεῖ

Throughout the passage, John seems to be emphasizing a continual or habitual type of sinning. He could have written ὁ ἁμαρτάνων "the one who sins," as he does in 3:6. Instead, he uses the verb ποιέω + the noun ἁμαρτία = ὁ ποιῶν τὴν ἁμαρτίαν "the one who practices sin." In addition, the present tense form (imperfective aspect) of the substantival participle lends to the notion of a customary or characteristic action.

John states that the one who practices "sin also practices (ποιεῖ: pres. act. ind. 3rd sg. ποιέω) lawlessness." The context makes it clear that καί here cannot be translated "and" (a coordinating conjunction). Also note that both "sin" and "lawlessness" are abstract nouns but have articles.

- καὶ ἡ ἁμαρτία ἐστὶν ἡ ἀνομία.

Again, καί here is probably not best translated as "and" since the conjunction provides an explanation for what precedes (functioning similar to γάρ). Although some translations leave καί untranslated, the NIV renders it "in fact" and both the KJV and the NLT translate it as "for."

Colwell's Canon is at play here. The predicate nominative (ἡ ἀνομία) retains the article since it follows the verb. The term ἀνομία, "lawlessness," generally means "to behave with complete disregard for the laws and regulations of society" (LN §88.139), though it seems here to have the additional nuance of eschatological hostility toward God (cf. 2 Thess 2:3–7).

---

[8] Baugh, *First John Reader*, 52.

1 John 3:5

- καὶ οἴδατε ὅτι ἐκεῖνος ἐφανερώθη

  The conjunction ὅτι, "that," typically introduces a content clause following a verb of knowledge (i.e., οἴδατε: per. act. ind. 2nd pl. οἶδα).

  This is the third use of the far demonstrative pronoun ἐκεῖνος (masc. nom. sg.). Each time that it occurs in this form in the epistle, the referent is Jesus Christ. The "far" demonstrative pronoun is used when the antecedent is literarily far (i.e., not mentioned in the immediate context). The most immediate reference is πᾶς ὁ ποιῶν τὴν ἁμαρτίαν, "everyone who practices sin," and John obviously is not referring to such a person. Thus, the near demonstrative pronoun οὗτος cannot be used here.

  Every occurrence of the verb ἐφανερώθη (aor. pass. ind. 3rd sg. φανερόω) in 1 John except one (3:2) refers to the first coming of Jesus (see also 1:2 [twice]; 3:8; 4:9).

- ἵνα τὰς ἁμαρτίας ἄρῃ

  The conjunction ἵνα introduces a purpose clause and triggers the subjunctive mood. The verb ἄρῃ (aor. act. subjunc. 3rd sg. αἴρω) is a liquid verb (i.e., a verb whose stem ends in λ, μ, ν, or ρ) and therefore the *sigma* (σ) is rejected, causing the *iota* (ι) to drop.

  The article in τὰς ἁμαρτίας could be functioning as a possessive pronoun, "our sins."

- καὶ ἁμαρτία ἐν αὐτῷ οὐκ ἔστιν.

  John clarifies that Jesus takes away sin but that he is himself still free from sin. Earlier, he emphatically declared that "there is no darkness in him [God] at all" (σκοτία ἐν αὐτῷ οὐκ ἔστιν οὐδεμία, 1:5).

1 John 3:6

- πᾶς ὁ ἐν αὐτῷ μένων οὐχ ἁμαρτάνει·

  The prepositional phrase ἐν αὐτῷ is sandwiched in between a substantival participle (ὁ . . . μένων: pres. act. ptc. masc. nom. sg. μένω).

  The verb ἁμαρτάνει is best understood as an iterative present, communicating an action that is performed repeatedly, regularly, or customarily (see §8.3.1). Some have attempted to interpret the present tense as a gnomic present. In this view, John is speaking in terms of "a projected eschato-logical reality" and therefore presents "in an absolute manner truths that are not yet true, because he is speaking within the context of eschatologi-cal hope (2:28–3:3) and eschatological judgment (2:18–19)."[9] Yet, see the case study above for why the iterative view is best (§7.3.3). In adopting an iterative interpretation, however, we are not denying the paraenetic func-tion of the statement.

- πᾶς ὁ ἁμαρτάνων οὐχ ἑώρακεν αὐτὸν οὐδὲ ἔγνωκεν αὐτόν.

The substantival participle ὁ ἁμαρτάνων functions as the subject of the verb ἑώρακεν (per. act. ind. 3rd sg. ὁράω) and ἔγνωκεν (per. act. ind. 3rd sg. γινώσκω). With both of these perfect verbs, the reduplication of the initial consonant is not used because (1) ὁράω begins with a vowel; and (2) the root of γινώσκω is γνο-, and verbs beginning with double consonants often do not reduplicate (i.e., vocalic reduplication).

1 John 3:7

- Παιδία, μηδεὶς πλανάτω ὑμᾶς·

In 2:26, the author explains that one of the reasons he wrote this letter was to protect his readers against those who were trying to deceive them. Here, he uses an imperative (πλανάτω: pres. act. impv. 3rd sg. πλανάω) to issue a warning (i.e., a prohibition): "let no one deceive you," or "make sure no one deceives you." The pronoun μηδείς, which functions as the subject, is used (and not οὐδείς) because the term serves to negate a nonindicative verb (i.e., an imperative).

- ὁ ποιῶν τὴν δικαιοσύνην δίκαιός ἐστιν, καθὼς ἐκεῖνος δίκαιός ἐστιν·

The substantival participle ὁ ποιῶν (indeed, the entire participial phrase ὁ ποιῶν τὴν δικαιοσύνην) functions as the subject of ἐστιν, with δίκαιος serving as the predicate adjective. The far demonstrative pronoun refers to Jesus (which was needed since the nearest antecedent is πᾶς ὁ ἁμαρτάνων in v. 6).

[9] Wallace, *Greek Grammar*, 525. Culy rightfully rejects this view (*I, II, III John*, 73).

1 John 3:8

- ὁ ποιῶν τὴν ἁμαρτίαν ἐκ τοῦ διαβόλου ἐστίν

In contrast to "the one who practices righteousness" (ὁ ποιῶν τὴν δικαιοσύνην, 3:7), John again mentions "the one practicing sin" (ὁ ποιῶν τὴν ἁμαρτίαν; cf. 3:4).

- ὅτι ἀπ᾽ ἀρχῆς ὁ διάβολος ἁμαρτάνει.

The conjunction ὅτι introduces a causal clause. The verb ἁμαρτάνει (pres. act. ind. 3rd sg. ἁμαρτάνω) is best taken as a durative present (see §8.3.1). This interpretation is based not on the tense form of the verb but on the context. John notes that the devil is not only sinning now but that he has been doing so ἀπ᾽ ἀρχῆς, "from the beginning." As such, in this context the present tense verb conveys not only the current time (from the perspective of the author), but it also conveys a time from the beginning (of the devil's rebellion against God).

- εἰς τοῦτο ἐφανερώθη ὁ υἱὸς τοῦ θεοῦ

The phrase εἰς τοῦτο, "for this reason," is used only here in 1 John and is cataphoric (i.e., it points forward). The demonstrative pronoun τοῦτο is neuter because it refers to a clause (and not a specific noun).

- ἵνα λύσῃ τὰ ἔργα τοῦ διαβόλου.

The conjunction ἵνα introduces a purpose clause and triggers the subjunctive mood (λύσῃ: aor. act. subjunct. 3rd sg. λύω). The expression τοῦ διαβόλου is a subjective genitive ("the works of the devil" = the devil's works).

1 John 3:9

- Πᾶς ὁ γεγεννημένος ἐκ τοῦ θεοῦ ἁμαρτίαν οὐ ποιεῖ

The substantival participle ὁ γεγεννημένος (per. pass. ptc. masc. nom. sg. γεννάω) functions as the subject of the verb ποιεῖ. Again, notice that John does not merely say that everyone born of God does not sin (οὐχ ἁμαρτάνει, as he does in 3:6 and 5:18) but that he does not practice sin (ἁμαρτίαν οὐ ποιεῖ). Even though the two constructions in 1 John are virtual synonyms, the use here emphasizes the habitual nature of the sinful behavior under discussion.

The genitive phrase ἐκ τοῦ θεοῦ conveys source, "*from* God."

- ὅτι σπέρμα αὐτοῦ ἐν αὐτῷ μένει

The conjunction ὅτι, "because," here (and in the following use) introduces a causal clause. The personal pronoun αὐτοῦ refers to God (i.e., "God's seed"), and the second personal pronoun αὐτῷ refers to the believer.

- καὶ οὐ δύναται ἁμαρτάνειν, ὅτι ἐκ τοῦ θεοῦ γεγέννηται.

The verb δύναται (pres. mid. ind. 3rd sg. δύναμαι) is complemented by the infinitive ἁμαρτάνειν (pres. act. inf. ἁμαρτάνω, "not able *to sin*"; see §11.3). John's statement that a true believer is "not able to sin" causes us to pause, as we find a superficial reading of this text contrary to personal experience. Because the expected (default) tense form following the verb δύναμαι is an aorist and because ἁμαρτάνω itself favors the aorist as a telic verb, the present tense form is used to signal a nuanced use (see the case study in §7.3.3). That is, John is once again emphasizing the progressive, habitual, repeated nature of the action. He is not merely presenting the action as a whole but is showing us that those who are born of God do not make a practice of unrepentant, habitual sin (contrary to the false teachers who do not practice righteousness).

1 John 3:10

- ἐν τούτῳ φανερά ἐστιν τὰ τέκνα τοῦ θεοῦ καὶ τὰ τέκνα τοῦ διαβόλου·

The phrase ἐν τούτῳ (neut. dat. sg.) is probably cataphoric (pointing forward). The verb ἐστιν (pres. ind. 3rd sg. εἰμί) is singular even though the subjects are plural (τὰ τέκνα τοῦ θεοῦ καὶ τὰ τέκνα τοῦ διαβόλου). In Koine Greek, it is normal for neuter plural nouns (such as τὰ τέκνα) to take singular verbs. This is known as "the animals run" (τὰ ζῷα τρέχει) rule, a moniker which is itself an example of the rule.

- πᾶς ὁ μὴ ποιῶν δικαιοσύνην οὐκ ἔστιν ἐκ τοῦ θεοῦ, καὶ ὁ μὴ ἀγαπῶν τὸν ἀδελφὸν αὐτοῦ.

The particle μή is sandwiched between the article and the substantival participle (ὁ . . . ποιῶν and ὁ . . . ἀγαπῶν).

Although καί may simply be communicating a parallel idea, it is also possible that it functions epexegetically here: "everyone who does not practice righteousness is not from God, *that is*, the one not loving his brother."

///////////////

CHAPTER 8

1 JOHN 3:11–18
PRESENT, IMPERFECT, AND FUTURE INDICATIVES

8.1 Vocabulary

ἀγρός, ὁ	field, country (36)
ἀνθρωποκτόνος, ὁ	murderer (3)
ὀργή, ἡ	anger, wrath, punishment (36)
σπλάγχνον, τό	compassion, heart (11)
χάριν	for the sake of, on account of (9)
ἐπιστρέφω	I turn (around/back), return (36)
θαυμάζω	I marvel, am amazed, wonder (43)
καυχάομαι	I boast, glory (37)
κλείω	I shut, close, lock (16)
μεταβαίνω	I pass on, depart (12)
παραγίνομαι	I come, arrive, appear (37)
σφάζω	I slaughter (10)

8.2 Text: 1 John 3:11–18

¹¹ Ὅτι αὕτη ἐστὶν ἡ ἀγγελία ἣν ἠκούσατε ἀπ᾽ ἀρχῆς, ἵνα ἀγαπῶμεν ἀλλήλους, ¹² οὐ καθὼς Κάϊν ἐκ τοῦ πονηροῦ ἦν καὶ ἔσφαξεν τὸν ἀδελφὸν αὐτοῦ· καὶ χάριν τίνος ἔσφαξεν αὐτόν; ὅτι τὰ ἔργα αὐτοῦ πονηρὰ ἦν, τὰ δὲ τοῦ ἀδελφοῦ αὐτοῦ δίκαια. ¹³ καὶ μὴ θαυμάζετε, ἀδελφοί, εἰ μισεῖ ὑμᾶς ὁ κόσμος. ¹⁴ ἡμεῖς οἴδαμεν ὅτι μεταβεβήκαμεν ἐκ τοῦ θανάτου εἰς τὴν ζωήν, ὅτι ἀγαπῶμεν τοὺς ἀδελφούς· ὁ μὴ ἀγαπῶν μένει ἐν τῷ θανάτῳ. ¹⁵ πᾶς ὁ μισῶν τὸν ἀδελφὸν αὐτοῦ ἀνθρωποκτόνος ἐστίν, καὶ οἴδατε ὅτι

πᾶς ἀνθρωποκτόνος οὐκ ἔχει ζωὴν αἰώνιον ἐν αὐτῷ μένουσαν. ¹⁶ ἐν τούτῳ ἐγνώκαμεν τὴν ἀγάπην, ὅτι ἐκεῖνος ὑπὲρ ἡμῶν τὴν ψυχὴν αὐτοῦ ἔθηκεν· καὶ ἡμεῖς ὀφείλομεν ὑπὲρ τῶν ἀδελφῶν τὰς ψυχὰς θεῖναι. ¹⁷ ὃς δ᾽ ἂν ἔχῃ τὸν βίον τοῦ κόσμου καὶ θεωρῇ τὸν ἀδελφὸν αὐτοῦ χρείαν ἔχοντα καὶ κλείσῃ τὰ σπλάγχνα αὐτοῦ ἀπ᾽ αὐτοῦ, πῶς ἡ ἀγάπη τοῦ θεοῦ μένει ἐν αὐτῷ; ¹⁸ Τεκνία, μὴ ἀγαπῶμεν λόγῳ μηδὲ τῇ γλώσσῃ, ἀλλὰ ἐν ἔργῳ καὶ ἀληθείᾳ.

8.3 Syntax: Present, Imperfect, and Future Indicatives

8.3.1 Present Indicatives

Present indicative forms (which include more than 35 percent of all indicatives) convey both the time of the action (tense) and the author's portrayal of the action (aspect). The time of the action normally refers to the present time (from the perspective of the author). There are, however, contexts where the present indicative conveys an action that is in the past (e.g., the historical or narrative present), the future, or is omnitemporal (e.g., the gnomic present). The aspect of the present tense form is typically characterized as progressive, internal, or incomplete (imperfective). But other influences often affect a specific use of a verb. Below are some of the uses of present indicative verbs—functions that must be determined by a careful consideration of lexical, grammatical, and contextual factors:

- **Progressive.** An action ongoing or in progress.

    ○ ἡ σκοτία **παράγεται** καὶ τὸ φῶς τὸ ἀληθινὸν ἤδη **φαίνει**, "the darkness **is passing away** and the true light **is** already **shining**" (1 John 2:8).

    ○ ὁ δὲ μισῶν τὸν ἀδελφὸν αὐτοῦ ἐν τῇ σκοτίᾳ ἐστὶν καὶ ἐν τῇ σκοτίᾳ **περιπατεῖ** καὶ οὐκ οἶδεν ποῦ **ὑπάγει**, "But the one who hates his brother is in the darkness and in the darkness **he walks** and he does not know where **he is going**" (1 John 2:11).

- **Durative.** An action that began in the past and continues into the present.

    ○ ἀπ᾽ ἀρχῆς ὁ διάβολος **ἁμαρτάνει**, "the devil **has been sinning** from the beginning" (1 John 3:8).

- **Iterative.** An action performed repeatedly, regularly, or customarily.

    ○ πᾶς ὁ ἐν αὐτῷ μένων οὐχ **ἁμαρτάνει**, "everyone remaining in him **does** not **[continue in] sin**" (1 John 3:6).

    ○ Πᾶς ὁ γεγεννημένος ἐκ τοῦ θεοῦ ἁμαρτίαν οὐ **ποιεῖ**, "everyone who has been born of God **does** not **practice** sin" (1 John 3:9).

- **Gnomic.** A statement that is timeless, universal, or generally true.

  ○ ὁ ἀγαπῶν τὸν ἀδελφὸν αὐτοῦ ἐν τῷ φωτὶ **μένει**, "the one who loves his brother **abides** in the light" (1 John 2:10).

  ○ πᾶς ὁ ἀρνούμενος τὸν υἱὸν οὐδὲ τὸν πατέρα **ἔχει**, "everyone who denies the Son neither **has** the Father" (1 John 2:23).

- **Futuristic.** An action that will occur in the future.

  ○ ἠκούσατε ὅτι ἀντίχριστος **ἔρχεται**, καὶ νῦν ἀντίχριστοι πολλοὶ γεγόνασιν, "you have heard that an antichrist **is coming**, and now many antichrist have come" (1 John 2:18).

  ○ καὶ ὃ ἐὰν αἰτῶμεν **λαμβάνομεν** ἀπ' αὐτοῦ, "and whatever we ask, we **will receive** from him" (1 John 3:22).

- **Other Uses** (not found in 1 John).

  ○ **Instantaneous.** An action done immediately, usually by the very fact that it is spoken: Πάτερ, **εὐχαριστῶ** σοι, "Father, **I thank** you" (John 11:41).

  ○ **Historical/Narrative.** A past event that adds vividness or gives literary prominence to some aspect of the story: καὶ **ἔρχεται** πρὸς τοὺς μαθητάς, "and **he came** to the disciples" (Matt 26:40).

8.3.2 Imperfect Indicatives

The imperfect tense form (which includes only about 10.5 percent of all indicatives) carries the same aspectual significance as the present tense form (imperfective aspect). That is, it portrays that action as progressive, internal, or incomplete. Because it does not occur outside of the indicative mood, the time of the imperfect is almost always past time (which is conveyed by the augment). The categories below are essentially the same as those found with the present tense form. This overlap is due to their aspectual similarity. Note as well that the imperfect tense form *in itself* does not *mean* any of the following categories. Rather, an imperfect indicative form can convey the nuances below when the reader is given the appropriate lexical, grammatical, and contextual clues. There are only seven imperfect indicatives in 1 John (1:1, 2; 2:7, 19 [2×]; 3:12 [2×]), and six are the verb εἰμί (2:7 is from ἔχω). None of the following examples are taken from 1 John.

- **Progressive.** A past action that unfolded progressively over time.

  ○ ἐδίδασκεν γὰρ τοὺς μαθητὰς αὐτοῦ, "For **he was teaching** his disciples" (Mark 9:31).

- **Inceptive.** Highlights the beginning of an action or state.

  ○ ἦρεν τὸν κράβαττον αὐτοῦ καὶ **περιεπάτει**, "he took his mat and **began walking**" (John 5:9).

- **Iterative.** A past action that is repeated or customary.

  ○ κατέκλασεν τοὺς ἄρτους καὶ **ἐδίδου** τοῖς μαθηταῖς αὐτοῦ, "He broke the loaves and **kept giving** [them] to his disciples" (Mark 6:41).

- **Tendential.** A past action was begun, attempted, or proposed but not completed.

  ○ ἐδίωκον τὴν ἐκκλησίαν τοῦ θεοῦ καὶ **ἐπόρθουν** αὐτήν, "I was persecuting the church of God and **was trying to destroy** it" (Gal 1:13).

8.3.3 Future Indicatives

The future tense form (which includes about 10.5 percent of all indicatives) denotes an "occurrence *subsequent* to some reference point."[1] That is, the future grammaticalizes the author's expectation regarding a possible event, an event that has not yet occurred, and thus is future from the author's perspective. The future tense form rarely occurs outside the indicative mood (there are only twelve future participles and five future infinitives). There are only eight uses of the future indicative in 1 John (2:24; 3:2 [3×], 19 [2×]; 5:16 [2×]). Below are some of the uses of the future.

- **Predictive.** Predicts a future event.

  ○ ἐὰν ἐν ὑμῖν μείνῃ ὃ ἀπ᾽ ἀρχῆς ἠκούσατε, καὶ ὑμεῖς ἐν τῷ υἱῷ καὶ ἐν τῷ πατρὶ **μενεῖτε**, "if that which you heard from the beginning remains in you, you also **will remain** in the Son and in the Father" (1 John 2:24).
  ○ οἴδαμεν ὅτι ἐὰν φανερωθῇ, ὅμοιοι αὐτῷ **ἐσόμεθα**, "we know that when he appears, **we will be** like him" (1 John 3:2).

- **Imperatival.** Expresses a command.

  ○ Ἐάν τις ἴδῃ τὸν ἀδελφὸν αὐτοῦ ἁμαρτάνοντα ἁμαρτίαν μὴ πρὸς θάνατον, **αἰτήσει** καὶ δώσει αὐτῷ ζωήν, "If anyone sees his brother sinning a sin not to death, **he will ask** and he will give to him life" (1 John 5:16).

---

[1] Fanning, *Verbal Aspect*, 123.

- **Other Uses** (not found in 1 John):

  - **Deliberative.** Asks a real or rhetorical question: Κύριε, πρὸς τίνα ἀπελευσόμεθα, "Lord, to whom **shall we go**?" (John 6:68).
  - **Gnomic.** Conveys a timeless truth: ἕκαστος γὰρ τὸ ἴδιον φορτίον βαστάσει, "For each one **will bear** his own load" (Gal 6:5).

8.4 Reading Notes

1 John 3:11

- Ὅτι αὕτη ἐστὶν ἡ ἀγγελία ἣν ἠκούσατε ἀπ᾽ ἀρχῆς

  The conjunction ὅτι, "because/for," functions as a causal marker. The subject αὕτη is cataphoric (forward pointing), and the predicate nominative ἡ ἀγγελία retains the article since it follows the verb (Colwell's Canon).

  The antecedent to the relative pronoun ἥν (fem. acc. sg.) is ἡ ἀγγελία (fem. nom. sg.), agreeing in gender and number (but not case since it has a different function in its clause).

- ἵνα ἀγαπῶμεν ἀλλήλους

  The conjunction ἵνα introduces a content (and not a purpose) clause (similar to ὅτι; see BDF §394).[2] The content of the clause is that "we should love" (ἀγαπῶμεν: pres. act. subjunc. 1st pl. ἀγαπάω). The term ἀλλήλους "one another," is a reciprocal pronoun.

1 John 3:12

- οὐ καθὼς Κάϊν ἐκ τοῦ πονηροῦ ἦν καὶ ἔσφαξεν τὸν ἀδελφὸν αὐτοῦ

  The phrase οὐ καθώς introduces a negative comparison. The adjective τοῦ πονηροῦ functions substantivally: "the evil one" (i.e., the devil).

  The verb ἔσφαξεν (aor. act. ind. 3rd sg. σφάζω) is found only in this verse (twice) and eight times in Revelation (5:6, 9, 12; 6:4, 9; 13:3, 8; 18:24). It means "to slaughter, either animals or persons; in contexts referring to persons, the implication is of violence and mercilessness" (LN §20.72).

---

[2] See also Wallace, *Greek Grammar*, 475–76.

- καὶ χάριν τίνος ἔσφαξεν αὐτόν;

  The preposition χάριν serves as "a marker of reason, often with the implication of an underlying purpose" (LN §89.29) and takes its object in the
  genitive case (here τίνος). The phrase χάριν τίνος (unique in the NT) means
  "for what reason" or "why" (literally "because of what") and introduces a
  question. Normally, the preposition χάριν is preceded by its object.

- ὅτι τὰ ἔργα αὐτοῦ πονηρὰ ἦν, τὰ δὲ τοῦ ἀδελφοῦ αὐτοῦ δίκαια.

  The conjunction ὅτι, "because," introduces causal clause.

  The verb ἦν (impf. ind. 3rd sg. εἰμί) is singular even though the subject is
  plural (τὰ ἔργα), a common feature of Greek grammar since neuter plural
  subjects characteristically take singular verbs ("the animals run" rule).[3]
  Both πονηρά and δίκαια function as predicate adjectives: "his works were
  evil but the works of his brother were *righteous.*"

  The second use of the article τά could be said to function as a (demonstrative) pronoun: "but *those* of his brother were righteous." Another way to
  look at it is to see an ellipsis of ἔργα so that the article τά stands for τὰ ἔργα
  "the works." Leaving out obvious words is common in Greek, which is
  further demonstrated by the fact that the verb ἦν is also elided: "but those
  [works] of his brother [were] righteous."

1 John 3:13

- καὶ μὴ θαυμάζετε, ἀδελφοί

  The verb θαυμάζετε (pres. act. impv. 2nd pl. θαυμάζω) is negated by μή and
  is therefore a prohibition: "do not be amazed." A present prohibition does
  not necessarily enjoin stoppage of an action that was currently ongoing. It
  is the context, rather than the tense form of the verb, that expresses such
  information. The present tense form is most likely used for two reasons:
  (1) θαυμάζω is an atelic verb and has no natural terminus, and (2) the author
  intends for the readers to continue to not be amazed as a general practice.

  The noun ἀδελφοί is another use of the vocative case.

---

[3] Wallace, *Greek Grammar*, 399–400.

- εἰ μισεῖ ὑμᾶς ὁ κόσμος.

The conjunction εἰ introduces a first class conditional clause (see §13.3.1).

The verb μισεῖ (pres. act. ind. 3rd sg. μισέω) is best categorized as an iterative or customary present. Bateman and Peer add, "It speaks of a pattern of behavior. The world's system is persistent in its opposition to God and his followers. Therefore, followers of Jesus should not be surprised when it hates them as well. Any believer who finds themselves as an object of the world's hate should not be surprised. The wicked have felt this way about the righteous ever since Cain and Abel."[4] A similar statement was made by Jesus in John 15:18: "If the world hates [μισεῖ] you, understand that it hated me before it hated you" (CSB).

1 John 3:14

- ἡμεῖς οἴδαμεν ὅτι μεταβεβήκαμεν ἐκ τοῦ θανάτου εἰς τὴν ζωήν

The personal pronoun ἡμεῖς is emphatic since the person and number information is embedded in the verb οἴδαμεν (per. act. ind. 1st pl. οἶδα). This pronoun highlights the distinctiveness of God's people as separate from the rebellious world, which is under God's wrath.

Not only is the perfect tense form of the verb μεταβεβήκαμεν (per. act. ind. 1st pl. μεταβαίνω) used in John 5:24, but the phrase ἐκ τοῦ θανάτου εἰς τὴν ζωήν is also found in that verse: "Truly I tell you, anyone who hears my word and believes him who sent me has eternal life and will not come under judgment but has passed [μεταβέβηκεν] from death to life [ἐκ τοῦ θανάτου εἰς τὴν ζωήν]" (CSB).

- ὅτι ἀγαπῶμεν τοὺς ἀδελφούς

Whereas the first use of the conjunction ὅτι, "that," in this verse (see above) introduces a content clause, here it introduces a causal clause (i.e., "because"). Also, the verb ἀγαπῶμεν (pres. act. ind. 1st pl. ἀγαπάω) here is indicative, though the same form in 3:11 is subjunctive. The reason for the similarity of forms is due to the verb ἀγαπάω, which is an *alpha*-contract verb. Consequently, when the *alpha* (α) of the stem contracts with the *omicron* (ο) of the ending, the result is an *omega* (ω): ἀγαπα + ομεν → ἀγαπαομεν → ἀγαπῶμεν.

4 Bateman and Peer, *John's Letters*, 198–99.

The phrase τοὺς ἀδελφούς could be rendered "our brothers" since the article can function as a possessive pronoun.

- ὁ μὴ ἀγαπῶν μένει ἐν τῷ θανάτῳ.

The phrase ὁ ἀγαπῶν (pres. act. ptc. masc. nom. sg. ἀγαπάω) is a substantival participle. The verb μένει is a gnomic present that conveys a timeless fact. The one who refuses to love remains in death.

1 John 3:15

- πᾶς ὁ μισῶν τὸν ἀδελφὸν αὐτοῦ ἀνθρωποκτόνος ἐστίν

The substantival participle ὁ μισῶν (pres. act. ptc. masc. nom. pl. μισέω) functions as the subject of the verb ἐστίν. This verb has a gnomic nuance since the statement is universally or generally true.

The term ἀνθρωποκτόνος is only used in the NT in this verse (twice) and in John 8:44 where the devil is said to be a *murderer* from the beginning.

- καὶ οἴδατε ὅτι πᾶς ἀνθρωποκτόνος οὐκ ἔχει ζωὴν αἰώνιον ἐν αὐτῷ μένουσαν.

The verb οἴδατε (per. act. ind. 2nd pl. οἶδα) functions similar to a present tense verb since the focus is solely on the present state with no antecedent action.

The verb ἔχει (pres. act. ind. 3rd sg. ἔχω) is also used with a gnomic nuance. It is always true that murderers do not have eternal life abiding in them. Of course, John is not suggesting that murderers cannot be forgiven and go to heaven (cf. King David, the apostle Paul). Instead, he is clarifying that those who are actively living the life of a murderer do not have eternal life.

The adjective αἰώνιον (fem. acc. sg.) modifies ζωήν (fem. acc. sg.). Because the personal pronoun αὐτῷ refers to the subject of the verb (i.e., ἀνθρωποκτόνος), this pronoun functions in the same way as a reflexive pronoun (ἑαυτῷ, "in himself").

The participle μένουσαν (pres. act. ptc. fem. acc. sg. μένω) functions attributively, modifying ζωήν: "eternal life *which remains* in him."

1 John 3:16

- ἐν τούτῳ ἐγνώκαμεν τὴν ἀγάπην

The phrase ἐν τούτῳ is cataphoric, pointing forward to the next phrase, and conveys the means by which we know love.

The verb ἐγνώκαμεν (per. act. ind. 1st pl. γινώσκω) conveys an experiential type of love in this context. Again, notice that the abstract noun "love" has an article (τὴν ἀγάπην).

- ὅτι ἐκεῖνος ὑπὲρ ἡμῶν τὴν ψυχὴν αὐτοῦ ἔθηκεν·

This is the fifth (of six) occurrences of ἐκεῖνος with Jesus as the antecedent. The preposition ὑπέρ, "on behalf of," conveys the idea of benefaction or substitution (see BDAG 1030). According to Louw and Nida, ὑπέρ functions as "a marker of a participant who is benefited by an event or on whose behalf an event takes place" (LN §90.36).

The verb ἔθηκεν (aor. act. ind. 3rd sg. τίθημι) with the noun ψυχή is an idiomatic expression meaning "to die, with the implication of voluntary or willing action—'to die voluntarily, to die willingly'" (LN §23.113). This verse is reminiscent of John 15:13: "No one has greater love than this: to lay down his life for his friends" (CSB).

- καὶ ἡμεῖς ὀφείλομεν ὑπὲρ τῶν ἀδελφῶν τὰς ψυχὰς θεῖναι.

The personal pronoun ἡμεῖς is emphatic since the person and number information is embedded in the verb ὀφείλομεν (pres. act. ind. 1st pl. ὀφείλω), highlighting our response in light of Christ's sacrifice on our behalf.

In the phrases τῶν ἀδελφῶν and τὰς ψυχάς, the articles function as possessive pronouns ("our brothers" and "our souls/lives"). Or, another way to conceive of these constructions is that Greek frequently implies possessive pronouns, and in such cases the nouns with implied qualifying pronouns are almost always articular.

The verb θεῖναι (aor. act. inf. τίθημι) is a complementary infinitive linked to the verb ὀφείλομεν: "we ought *to lay down*."

1 John 3:17

- ὃς δ' ἂν ἔχῃ τὸν βίον τοῦ κόσμου

The particle ἄν turns the relative pronoun ὅς into an indefinite relative pronoun (see notes at 2:5), triggering a series of three subjunctive mood verbs connected by καί: ἔχῃ (pres. act. subjunc. 3rd sg. ἔχω), θεωρῇ (pres. act. subjunc. 3rd sg. θεωρέω), and κλείσῃ (aor. act. subjunc. 3rd sg. κλείω). The shift from the present tense form (ἔχῃ and θεωρῇ) to the aorist tense form (κλείσῃ) is due to the lexical meaning of the verbs. Whereas ἔχῃ and θεωρῇ are atelic verbs with no natural terminus, the verb κλείσῃ is a telic verb with a bounded action.

The term βίος (also found in 2:16) here refers to "the resources which one has as a means of living" (LN §57.18) or the "resources needed to maintain life" (BDAG 177) and could be translated "possessions."

The genitive in the phrase τὸν βίον τοῦ κόσμου is probably best taken as an attributive genitive: "*worldly* possessions."

- καὶ θεωρῇ τὸν ἀδελφὸν αὐτοῦ χρείαν ἔχοντα

Frequently in Greek, after a verb of perception (e.g., θεωρῇ), the object or person perceived will be further described with an anarthrous participle. That is, the participle will describe what that person or object is doing as they are perceived. Grammars use different labels for this function of the participle—supplementary, predicate, or the complement in an "object-complement" construction. We will follow the terminology of classical grammars in labeling ἔχοντα (pres. act. ptc. masc. acc. sg. ἔχω) as a supplementary participle.[5]

καὶ κλείσῃ τὰ σπλάγχνα αὐτοῦ ἀπ' αὐτοῦ

The term σπλάγχνον refers to "the inward parts of a body" (BDAG 938), and the phrase κλείσῃ τὰ σπλάγχνα αὐτοῦ is an idiom meaning "to refuse to show compassion" (LN §25.55) or to "close one's heart to someone in need" (BDAG 938).

- πῶς ἡ ἀγάπη τοῦ θεοῦ μένει ἐν αὐτῷ;

This is a rhetorical question that "points to the dissonance between claiming to love God and not demonstrating that love in action toward others in

---

[5] The participle could also function as a temporal adverbial participle: "whoever . . . sees his brother *while having* need."

need."[6] Thus, John is not really looking for an answer but is challenging his readers to think about the disconnect between closing one's heart to the needy while claiming to love God.

The genitive construction in the phrase ἡ ἀγάπη τοῦ θεοῦ is an objective genitive: "the love of God" = someone's love for God.

1 John 3:18

- Τεκνία, μὴ ἀγαπῶμεν λόγῳ μηδὲ τῇ γλώσσῃ

Rather than introduce a new section, the vocative τεκνία concludes the previous section.

The verb μὴ ἀγαπῶμεν (pres. act. subjunc. 1st pl. ἀγαπάω) is a hortatory subjunctive: "let us not love" or "we must not love." Although the form of the verb could be indicative (e.g., see 3:14), because it is negated with μή, it must be subjunctive. A hortatory subjunctive exhorts the readers to join the author in particular actions and functions similar to an imperative.

The dative nouns λόγῳ and τῇ γλώσσῃ are both dative of means: "by [means of] action and tongue."

- ἀλλὰ ἐν ἔργῳ καὶ ἀληθείᾳ.

The noun ἔργῳ is a dative of means: "by [means of] deed." The dative noun ἀληθείᾳ seems to express manner. To love "in truth" means to truly love, not to love in a superficial or insincere way.

---

[6] Culy, *I, II, III John*, 89.

///////////////

CHAPTER 9

1 JOHN 3:19–24

AORIST, PERFECT, AND PLUPERFECT INDICATIVES

9.1 Vocabulary

βιβλίον, τό	book, scroll (34)
μάρτυς, ὁ	witness (35)
οὖς, ὠτός, τό	ear, hearing (36)
περιτομή, ἡ	circumcision (36)
προσευχή, ἡ	prayer (36)
ἅπας, -ασα, -αν	all, everybody, everything (34)
ἀρεστός, -ή -όν	pleasing (4)
ὀπίσω	after, behind (35)
ὥσπερ	(just) as, so (36)
βλασφημέω	I blasphemy, defame, slander (34)
καταγινώσκω	I condemn (3)
ὑποστρέφω	I turn back, return (35)

9.2 Text: 1 John 3:19–24

¹⁹ Καὶ ἐν τούτῳ γνωσόμεθα ὅτι ἐκ τῆς ἀληθείας ἐσμέν, καὶ ἔμπροσθεν αὐτοῦ πείσομεν τὴν καρδίαν ἡμῶν, ²⁰ ὅτι ἐὰν καταγινώσκῃ ἡμῶν ἡ καρδία, ὅτι μείζων ἐστὶν ὁ θεὸς τῆς καρδίας ἡμῶν καὶ γινώσκει πάντα. ²¹Ἀγαπητοί, ἐὰν ἡ καρδία [ἡμῶν] μὴ καταγινώσκῃ, παρρησίαν ἔχομεν πρὸς τὸν θεόν ²² καὶ ὃ ἐὰν αἰτῶμεν, λαμβάνομεν ἀπ' αὐτοῦ, ὅτι τὰς ἐντολὰς αὐτοῦ τηροῦμεν καὶ τὰ ἀρεστὰ ἐνώπιον αὐτοῦ ποιοῦμεν. ²³ καὶ αὕτη ἐστὶν ἡ ἐντολὴ αὐτοῦ, ἵνα πιστεύσωμεν τῷ ὀνόματι τοῦ υἱοῦ αὐτοῦ Ἰησοῦ Χριστοῦ καὶ

ἀγαπῶμεν ἀλλήλους, καθὼς ἔδωκεν ἐντολὴν ἡμῖν. ²⁴ καὶ ὁ τηρῶν τὰς ἐντολὰς αὐτοῦ ἐν αὐτῷ μένει καὶ αὐτὸς ἐν αὐτῷ· καὶ ἐν τούτῳ γινώσκομεν ὅτι μένει ἐν ἡμῖν, ἐκ τοῦ πνεύματος οὗ ἡμῖν ἔδωκεν.

9.3 Syntax: Aorist, Perfect, and Pluperfect Indicatives

9.3.1 Aorist Indicatives

The aorist indicative is the most common tense form in the NT (about 38 percent of all indicatives) and is used when the author desires to portray the action in its entirety without reference to its progress or duration (i.e., perfective aspect). The aorist indicative is also the default tense form used in narratives, often carrying the main storyline. In about 85 percent of instances, the time of the action for aorist indicatives is in the past.[1] This is communicated by the addition of the augment at the beginning of the verb. In combination with lexical, grammatical, and contextual factors, the aorist tense form can be used with the following nuances.

- **Constative.** Portrays the action in its entirety without regard to the process or duration.

  ○ οὐκ οἶδεν ποῦ ὑπάγει, ὅτι ἡ σκοτία **ἐτύφλωσεν** τοὺς ὀφθαλμοὺς αὐτοῦ, "he does not know where he is going because the darkness **blinded** his eyes" (1 John 2:11).

  ○ καθὼς **ἠκούσατε** ὅτι ἀντίχριστος ἔρχεται, "just as **you heard** that the Antichrist is coming" (1 John 2:18).

- **Culminative.** Emphasizes the cessation of an action or state.

  ○ ὃ **ἐθεασάμεθα** καὶ αἱ χεῖρες ἡμῶν **ἐψηλάφησαν** περὶ τοῦ λόγου τῆς ζωῆς, "which **we have seen** and our hands **have touched** concerning the word of life" (1 John 1:1).

  ○ οὐ καθὼς Κάϊν ἐκ τοῦ πονηροῦ ἦν καὶ **ἔσφαξεν** τὸν ἀδελφὸν αὐτοῦ, "not as Cain who was from the evil one and **slew** his brother" (1 John 3:12).

- **Epistolary.** Depicts a present action (usually with the verbs γράφω and πέμπω) using the aorist instead of the present.

  ○ οὐκ **ἔγραψα** ὑμῖν ὅτι οὐκ οἴδατε τὴν ἀλήθειαν ἀλλ' ὅτι οἴδατε αὐτὴν καὶ ὅτι πᾶν ψεῦδος ἐκ τῆς ἀληθείας οὐκ ἔστιν, "**I write** to you not because

---

[1] See e.g., Constantine R. Campbell, "Aspect and Tense in New Testament Greek," in *Linguistics and New Testament Greek: Key Issues in the Current Debate*, ed. David Alan Black and Benjamin L. Merkle (Grand Rapids: Baker Academic, 2020), 46–47.

you do not know the truth, but because you know it and because there is no lie from the truth" (1 John 2:21).

○ Ταῦτα ἔγραψα ὑμῖν περὶ τῶν πλανώντων ὑμᾶς, "**I write** these things to you concerning those who are trying to deceive you" (1 John 2:26; see also 2:14; 5:13).

• **Gnomic.** Conveys a universal statement or one that is generally true.

○ ὁ μὴ ἀγαπῶν οὐκ ἔγνω τὸν θεόν, "the one who does not love **does** not **know** God" (1 John 4:8).

• **Inceptive.** Emphasizes the commencement of an action or a state.

○ Τάδε λέγει ὁ πρῶτος καὶ ὁ ἔσχατος, ὃς ἐγένετο νεκρὸς καὶ ἔζησεν," These things says the first and the last, who was dead and **came to life**" (Rev 2:8).

9.3.2 Perfect Indicatives

The perfect tense form (which accounts for only about 10.5 percent of all indicatives) can be described as a completed action that has continuing results. That is, the action itself is no longer being performed (i.e., it is complete), but the consequences of that action still exist in the present (in relation to the time of the author). Thus, γέγραπται does not simply mean "it has been written" (which focuses on the past action) but "it is written" or "it stands written" (which implies that something was written in the past but still has abiding implications for today). The perfect tense form is typically described as having a stative aspect (i.e., a state of being that results from a previous action). Consequently, some have described the perfect as a combination of the aorist (perfective aspect) and the present (imperfective aspect).[2] Sometimes the focus of a perfect is on the completed action (translated with the helping verb "have/has"), whereas other times the focus is on the resulting state (translated as a present tense verb). Some perfect tense verbs are employed because the author is emphasizing *the relevance of the completed action* for his argument or discussion. Also, roughly 10 percent of perfect verbs in the New Testament are indistinguishable from aorists in nuance. Eventually, in the later Koine period, the perfect became interchangeable with the aorist and, because of this unnecessary overlap, the perfect tense eventually disappeared.

• **Consummative.** Emphasizes the completed action that produced the resulting state.

---

[2] See KMP, *Deeper Greek*, 231; Nicholas J. Ellis, "Aspect-Prominence, Morpho-Syntax, and a Cognitive-Linguistic Framework for the Greek Verb," in *The Greek Verb Revisited: A Fresh Approach for Biblical Exegesis*, ed. Steven E. Runge and Christopher J. Fresch (Bellingham, WA: Lexham, 2016), 122–60.

○ νενικήκατε τὸν πονηρόν, "you **have conquered** the evil one" (1 John 2:13).

○ πολλοὶ ψευδοπροφῆται ἐξεληλύθασιν εἰς τὸν κόσμον, "many false prophets **have gone out** into the world" (1 John 4:1).

- **Intensive.** Emphasizes the resulting state brought about by a past action.

   ▪ ἀφέωνται ὑμῖν αἱ ἁμαρτίαι διὰ τὸ ὄνομα αὐτου, "your sins **are forgiven** on account of his name" (1 John 2:12).

   ▪ ἐν τούτῳ τετελείωται ἡ ἀγάπη μεθ᾽ ἡμῶν, "by this love **is perfected** with us" (1 John 4:17).

- **Present State.** Conveys a present meaning with no completed past action (οἶδα is the most common verb used in this category).

   ○ ὁ δὲ μισῶν τὸν ἀδελφὸν αὐτοῦ ἐν τῇ σκοτίᾳ ἐστὶν . . . καὶ οὐκ οἶδεν ποῦ ὑπάγει, "But the one who hates his brother is in darkness . . . and **does** not **know** where he is going" (1 John 2:11).

   ○ οἴδαμεν δὲ ὅτι ὁ υἱὸς τοῦ θεοῦ ἥκει, "and **we know** that the Son of God has come" (1 John 5:20).

- **Gnomic.** Communicates a general or customary truth.

   ○ ὁ ποιῶν τὴν δικαιοσύνην ἐξ αὐτοῦ γεγέννηται, "the one practicing righteousness **has been born** of him" (1 John 2:29).

   ○ θεὸν οὐδεὶς πώποτε τεθέαται, "no one **has** ever **seen** God" (1 John 4:12; see also 2:5).

9.3.3 Pluperfect Indicatives

The pluperfect (only found eighty-six times in the NT; about 0.5 percent of all indicatives) can be described as "a *past* state of affairs constituted by an action still further in the past."[3] That is, when an author describes an event in the past (typically using the aorist), and then wants to mention an event that occurred prior to that event, the pluperfect is often used. For example, Luke narrates that Jesus traveled (διώδευεν, aorist) from town to town preaching the gospel. The author adds that those traveling with Jesus included the twelve disciples and some women, including Mary Magdalene, from whom "had gone out" (ἐξεληλύθει, pluperfect) seven demons (Luke 8:2). To signify that the exorcism had occurred prior to Jesus's travels, the pluperfect is used. Regarding aspect, significance of the pluperfect emphasizes the resulting (past) state of a prior action or event.

---

[3] Zerwick, *Biblical Greek*, 98 (§290).

- **Consummative.** Emphasizes the completion of a past action.

  ○ οἱ μαθηταὶ αὐτοῦ **ἀπεληλύθεισαν** εἰς τὴν πόλιν, "the disciples **had gone** into the town" (John 4:8).

- **Intensive.** Emphasizes the past results brought about by a past action.

  ○ εἰ γὰρ ἐξ ἡμῶν ἦσαν, **μεμενήκεισαν** ἂν μεθ' ἡμῶν, "for if they were of us, **they would have remained** with us" (1 John 2:19).

- **Past State.** Conveys a past state with no antecedent action with certain verbs (especially οἶδα and ἵστημι).

  ○ πάντες οἱ ἄγγελοι **εἱστήκεισαν** κύκλῳ τοῦ θρόνου, "all the angels **stood** around the throne" (Rev 7:11).

9.4 Reading Notes

1 John 3:19

- **Καὶ ἐν τούτῳ γνωσόμεθα ὅτι ἐκ τῆς ἀληθείας ἐσμέν**

  The phrase ἐν τούτῳ "by this," is anaphoric, pointing back to the previous context (i.e., 3:10–18 or only 3:18).

  Notice that the verb γνωσόμεθα (fut. mid. ind. 1st pl. γινώσκω) shifts to the middle form in the future tense (cf. the future of εἰμί → ἐσόμεθα).

- *καὶ ἔμπροσθεν αὐτοῦ πείσομεν τὴν καρδίαν ἡμῶν*

  Although ἔμπροσθεν, "before" or "in front of," occurs only here in 1 John, it is somewhat common in the NT, occurring forty-eight times. It is known as an improper preposition because it began as an adverb and then only later "improperly" began to be used as a preposition. Improper prepositions are never prefixed to a verb. That is, they are not found as prepositional prefixes on compound verbs.

  The direct object of the verb πείσομεν (fut. act. ind. 1st pl. πείθω) is τὴν καρδίαν (notice that it is singular: "our *heart*"). It is a distributive singular, though, so it is rightly rendered in English as a plural: "our hearts." In John's writings, καρδία is always used figuratively, and here it is used as a synecdoche (i.e., a part used to represent the whole). That is, the heart represents a person's inner being, the "seat of physical, spiritual and mental life" (BDAG 508). The phrase πείθω τὴν καρδίαν is an idiom meaning "to exhibit confidence and assurance in a situation which might otherwise cause dismay and fear" (LN §25.166).

1 John 3:20

- ὅτι ἐὰν καταγινώσκῃ ἡμῶν ἡ καρδία

This verse is difficult to translate. The main problem lies with the two consecutive ὅτι clauses. The first ὅτι, "that," cannot introduce a content clause since the verb πείθω already has a complement (i.e., τὴν καρδίαν). But if the first clause is rendered as a causal clause, then the second clause cannot be rendered as such: "*because* whenever our heart condemns us *because* God is greater than our heart." Consequently, many commentators and English Bible versions think the first three letters should be divided into two words (ὅ τι) instead of one word (ὅτι). Remember that the original manuscript was in majuscule script with no spaces between words! (ΕΝΑΡΧΗΗΝΟΛΟΓΟΣ = Ἐν ἀρχῇ ἦν ὁ λόγος, John 1:1). If the text reads ὅ τι (i.e., a neuter relative pronoun followed by an indefinite pronoun), then the second ὅτι could be causal: "whenever [or with respect to whatever] our heart condemns because God is greater than our heart." This approach is adopted by NASB1995, which reads, "in whatever our heart condemns us; for God is greater than our heart." So too the NRSV renders the verse as, "whenever our hearts condemn us; for God is greater than our hearts." Evidence against this interpretation is that no ancient Greek manuscripts that put spaces between words divide the text in this way.

The conjunction ἐάν introduces a third class conditional clause and triggers the subjunctive mood (καταγινώσκῃ: pres. act. subjunc. 3rd sg. καταγινώσκω).

Also, notice the change in word order: from τὴν καρδίαν ἡμῶν (3:19) to ἡμῶν ἡ καρδία (3:20).

- ὅτι μείζων ἐστὶν ὁ θεὸς τῆς καρδίας ἡμῶν καὶ γινώσκει πάντα.

This second ὅτι is best taken as introducing a causal clause (i.e., "because, for"), especially if the first one is not causal.

The phrase τῆς καρδίας is a genitive of comparison (i.e., "*than* our heart"), a common function in connection with the comparative adjective μείζων.

The καί could be epexegetical: "God is greater than our heart, *that is*, he knows all things." Also, the two present indicative verbs (ἐστίν and γινώσκει) are gnomic presents (i.e., God is always greater than our heart and always knows all things).

1 John 3:21

- Ἀγαπητοί, ἐὰν ἡ καρδία [ἡμῶν] μὴ καταγινώσκῃ

  Although this verse begins with a vocative, it does not begin a new section since the topic and much of the vocabulary remains the same.

  The conjunction ἐάν introduces a third class conditional clause and triggers the subjunctive mood (καταγινώσκῃ: pres. act. subjunc. 3rd sg. καταγινώσκω).

  The term ἡμῶν is disputed. Critical editions of the Greek NT put the term in brackets to indicate that there are significant textual variants. It is possible that the word is not original and was added by scribes to conform to the previous verses. On the other hand, enough significant manuscripts include the term, which led the editorial committee to keep the term in the text but enclose the word in brackets to indicate uncertainty. Additionally, some manuscripts include a second ἡμῶν after καταγινώσκῃ that functions as the genitive direct object of that verb: "does not condemn *us*."

- παρρησίαν ἔχομεν πρὸς τὸν θεόν

  The noun παρρησία refers to "a state of boldness and confidence, sometimes implying intimidating circumstances" (LN §25.158). The term occurs four times in 1 John: believers can have confidence at Jesus's return (2:28), in prayer (3:21; 5:14), and in the day of judgment (4:17).

1 John 3:22

- καὶ ὃ ἐὰν αἰτῶμεν, λαμβάνομεν ἀπ' αὐτοῦ

  The relative pronoun ὅ (neut. acc. sg. "what") followed by ἐάν makes the pronoun indefinite ("whatever" and *not* "what if"), which then triggers the subjunctive mood (αἰτῶμεν: pres. act. subjunc. 1st pl. αἰτέω).

  The verb λαμβάνομεν (pres. act. ind. 1st pl. λαμβάνω) is a futuristic present: "and whatever we ask, we *will receive* [in the future] from him."

- ὅτι τὰς ἐντολὰς αὐτοῦ τηροῦμεν

  The conjunction ὅτι, "because," introduces a causal clause.

  The pronoun αὐτοῦ functions as a subjective genitive: "the commands of him" = he commands.

The verb τηροῦμεν (pres. act. ind. 1st pl. τηρέω) is a contract verb. Consequently, the ending shifts from –ομεν to –ουμεν (τηρε + ομεν → τηρεομεν → τηροῦμεν; cf. ποιοῦμεν in the next clause).

- καὶ τὰ ἀρεστὰ ἐνώπιον αὐτοῦ ποιοῦμεν.

The adjective τὰ ἀρεστά is used substantivally: "the *things* pleasing." Ἐνώπιον is an improper preposition followed by a genitive object (αὐτοῦ).

1 John 3:23

- καὶ αὕτη ἐστὶν ἡ ἐντολὴ αὐτοῦ

The subject αὕτη (feminine near demonstrative pronoun) is cataphoric (forward pointing to the ἵνα clause), and the predicate nominative ἡ ἐντολή retains the article since it follows the verb (Colwell's Canon). It should be noted that nouns that are qualified by possessive personal pronouns are almost always articular. Both a possessive pronoun and an article are indications of specificity/definiteness.

- ἵνα πιστεύσωμεν τῷ ὀνόματι τοῦ υἱοῦ αὐτοῦ Ἰησοῦ Χριστοῦ καὶ ἀγαπῶμεν ἀλλήλους

The conjunction ἵνα introduces a content clause and triggers the subjunctive mood (πιστεύσωμεν: aor. act. subjunc. 1st pl. πιστεύω; ἀγαπῶμεν: pres. act. subjunc. 1st pl. ἀγαπάω): "This is his commandment, [*namely*] *that* we believe."

The use of the aorist subjunctive with πιστεύω is a bit unexpected since that verb is an atelic verb that naturally prefers the present tense form (imperfective aspect), especially when it is used in a parallel construction with a present subjunctive (i.e., ἀγαπῶμεν). Baugh suggests that such a use indicates a nuanced meaning. Thus, he maintains that it has "an inceptive (or 'ingressive') force to it, signifying the entrance into the state of belief. The rendering, '*that we might come to believe*' would bring this out."[4]

The noun τῷ ὀνόματι is a dative direct object (complement) with the verb πιστεύω.

John uses a string of genitive forms here: τοῦ υἱοῦ αὐτοῦ Ἰησοῦ Χριστοῦ. The first (τοῦ υἱοῦ) is a possessive genitive: "the *son's* name"; the second

---

[4] Baugh, *First John Reader*, 62.

(αὐτοῦ) is a genitive of relationship: *"his* son"; and the third (Ἰησοῦ Χριστοῦ) is a genitive of apposition: "his son, *that is, Jesus Christ.*"

- καθὼς ἔδωκεν ἐντολὴν ἡμῖν.

  The verb ἔδωκεν (aor. act. ind. 3rd sg. δίδωμι) is a constative aorist.

1 John 3:24

- καὶ ὁ τηρῶν τὰς ἐντολὰς αὐτοῦ ἐν αὐτῷ μένει καὶ αὐτὸς ἐν αὐτῷ·

  The substantival participle ὁ τηρῶν (pres. act. ptc. masc. nom. sg. τηρέω) functions as the subject of the verb μένει.

- καὶ ἐν τούτῳ γινώσκομεν ὅτι μένει ἐν ἡμῖν

  The phrase ἐν τούτῳ is cataphoric, pointing forward to the phrase ἐκ τοῦ πνεύματος οὗ ἡμῖν ἔδωκεν.

- ἐκ τοῦ πνεύματος οὗ ἡμῖν ἔδωκεν.

  The phrase ἐκ τοῦ πνεύματος refers to agency (i.e., *"by* the Spirit") or per-haps to source (i.e., *"from* the Spirit").

  The relative pronoun οὗ is genitive by attraction. That is, it is attracted to the case of its antecedent τοῦ πνεύματος (which is genitive as the object of the preposition ἐκ). Although relative pronouns need to agree with the gender and number of their antecedent, they do not need to agree with its case since the relative pronoun has its own function in its clause. Because the relative pronoun functions as the direct object of the verb ἔδωκεν, "he gave which [= the Spirit] to us," we would expect it to be in the accusative case. The genitive case is the most common case to which relative pro-nouns are attracted.[5]

  Bateman and Peer label ἔδωκεν a culminative (consummative) aorist, not-ing, "The stress is on the cessation of God's giving the Spirit because the act was already presented as having happened in 2:20, 27."[6]

---

[5] See Wallace, *Greek Grammar*, 338–39.
[6] Bateman and Peer, *John's Letters*, 227.

///////////////////

CHAPTER 10

1 JOHN 4:1–6
PARTICIPLES

10.1 Vocabulary

διαθήκη, ἡ	covenant, decree, last will and testament (33)
διακονία, ἡ	service, office, ministry (34)
μέλος, -ους, τό	member, part, limb (34)
οἶνος, ὁ	wine (34)
πλάνη, ἡ	error, deception (10)
ψευδοπροφήτης, ὁ	false prophet (11)
μήτε	and not, nor (34)
πτωχός, -ή, -όν	poor (34)
ἀσθενέω	I am weak, sick, in need (33)
δείκνυμι	I show (33)
δοκιμάζω	I examine, test, prove (22)
μετανοέω	I repent (34)

10.2 Text: 1 John 4:1–6

¹ Ἀγαπητοί, μὴ παντὶ πνεύματι πιστεύετε ἀλλὰ δοκιμάζετε τὰ πνεύματα εἰ ἐκ τοῦ θεοῦ ἐστιν, ὅτι πολλοὶ ψευδοπροφῆται ἐξεληλύθασιν εἰς τὸν κόσμον. ² ἐν τούτῳ γινώσκετε τὸ πνεῦμα τοῦ θεοῦ· πᾶν πνεῦμα ὃ ὁμολογεῖ Ἰησοῦν Χριστὸν ἐν σαρκὶ ἐληλυθότα ἐκ τοῦ θεοῦ ἐστιν, ³ καὶ πᾶν πνεῦμα ὃ μὴ ὁμολογεῖ τὸν Ἰησοῦν ἐκ τοῦ θεοῦ οὐκ ἔστιν· καὶ τοῦτό ἐστιν τὸ τοῦ ἀντιχρίστου, ὃ ἀκηκόατε ὅτι ἔρχεται, καὶ νῦν ἐν τῷ κόσμῳ ἐστὶν ἤδη. ⁴ ὑμεῖς ἐκ τοῦ θεοῦ ἐστε, τεκνία, καὶ νενικήκατε αὐτούς, ὅτι μείζων ἐστὶν ὁ ἐν

ὑμῖν ἢ ὁ ἐν τῷ κόσμῳ. ⁵ αὐτοὶ ἐκ τοῦ κόσμου εἰσίν, διὰ τοῦτο ἐκ τοῦ κόσμου λαλοῦσιν καὶ ὁ κόσμος αὐτῶν ἀκούει. ⁶ ἡμεῖς ἐκ τοῦ θεοῦ ἐσμεν, ὁ γινώσκων τὸν θεὸν ἀκούει ἡμῶν· ὃς οὐκ ἔστιν ἐκ τοῦ θεοῦ οὐκ ἀκούει ἡμῶν. ἐκ τούτου γινώσκομεν τὸ πνεῦμα τῆς ἀληθείας καὶ τὸ πνεῦμα τῆς πλάνης.

10.3 Syntax: Participles

10.3.1 Attributive Participles

Attributive participles modify an expressed noun (or other substantive) and will typically be articular. The participle will agree with the noun that it modifies in gender, case, and number, and it will often be translated with a relative clause. There are only two attributive participles in 1 John.

- καὶ οἴδατε ὅτι πᾶς ἀνθρωποκτόνος οὐκ ἔχει ζωὴν αἰώνιον ἐν αὐτῷ **μένουσαν**, "and you know that no murderer has eternal life **which remains** in him" (1 John 3:15).

- καὶ αὕτη ἐστὶν ἡ νίκη ἡ **νικήσασα** τὸν κόσμον, "and this is the conquering **which conquers** the world" (1 John 5:4).

10.3.2 Substantival Participles

Substantival participles function as nouns and will typically be articular. They can be translated "the one who," "he who," or "that which" plus the meaning of the participle translated as a finite verb (e.g., ὁ λέγων = "the one who says"). There are about fifty substantival participles in 1 John.

- ὁ ἀγαπῶν τὸν ἀδελφὸν αὐτοῦ ἐν τῷ φωτὶ μένει, **"the one who loves** his brother abides in the light" (1 John 2:10).

- Πᾶς ὁ γεγεννημένος ἐκ τοῦ θεοῦ ἁμαρτίαν οὐ ποιεῖ, "Every**one who has been born** of God does not practice sin" (1 John 3:9).

10.3.3 Adverbial Participles

Adverbial participles are grammatically subordinate to a main verb and are always anarthrous. They answer questions such as "when?" "why?" or "how?" The grammatical form itself does not determine the specific usage. Rather, the lexical nature of the verb and the context (along with the tense form) is what determines the particular use of each participle.

- **Temporal.** The present participle portrays an action as ongoing (usually occurring simultaneously with the main verb), and the aorist participle portrays the action wholistically (usually occurring before the action of the main verb).

- ○ Καὶ **παράγων** εἶδεν Λευίν, "And **as he passed by**, he saw Levi" (Mark 2:14).

- ○ καθαρισμὸν τῶν ἁμαρτιῶν **ποιησάμενος** ἐκάθισεν, "**After making** purification for sins, he sat down" (Heb 1:3).

- **Means.** Answers how the main verb is/was accomplished.

  - ○ μαθητεύσατε πάντα τὰ ἔθνη, **βαπτίζοντες** αὐτοὺς . . . **διδάσκοντες** αὐτούς, "make disciples of all the nations, **by baptizing** them . . . [and] **by teaching** them" (Matt 28:19–20).

- **Manner.** Answers how (related to the emotion or attitude) the main verb was performed.

  - ○ Μαρία δὲ εἱστήκει πρὸς τῷ μνημείῳ ἔξω **κλαίουσα**, "Mary stood outside the tomb **weeping**" (John 20:11).

- **Cause.** Answers why the action is accomplished, providing the reason or grounds.

  - ○ **εἰδότες** ὅτι Χριστὸς ἐγερθεὶς ἐκ νεκρῶν οὐκέτι ἀποθνῄσκει, "**because we know** that Christ, being raised from the dead, no longer dies" (Rom 6:9).

- **Purpose.** Indicates the intended goal of the main verb's action.

  - ○ τοῦτο δὲ ἔλεγεν **πειράζων** αὐτόν, "But he was saying this **to test** him" (John 6:6).

- **Result.** Indicates the result (whether intended or not) of the main verb's action.

  - ○ ἵνα τοὺς δύο κτίσῃ ἐν αὐτῷ εἰς ἕνα καινὸν ἄνθρωπον **ποιῶν** εἰρήνην, "that from the two he might create in himself one new man, **so making** peace" (Eph 2:15).

- **Condition.** Presents the condition on which the main verb depends for its accomplishment.

  - ○ **ἔχοντες** δὲ διατροφὰς καὶ σκεπάσματα, τούτοις ἀρκεσθησόμεθα, "but **if we have** food and clothing, we will be content with these" (1 Tim 6:8).

- **Concession.** Conveys the reason an action should not take place, although it does.

  ○ ὅτι σὺ ἄνθρωπος ὢν ποιεῖς σεαυτὸν θεόν, "because you, **although being** man, make yourself to be God" (John 10:33).

10.3.4 Verbal Participles

Verbal participles often function as main verbs or verbs that are coordinate with a main verb. There are only three verbal participles in 1 John (3:17; 4:2; 5:16).

- **Attendant Circumstance.** A participle that is in a parallel construction with the main verb, thus taking on its mood (usually indicative or imperative).

  ○ ἐγερθεὶς παράλαβε τὸ παιδίον καὶ τὴν μητέρα αὐτοῦ, "**rise** and take the child and his mother" (Matt 2:13).

- **Pleonastic.** A redundant expression usually employing ἀποκριθείς or λέγων.

  ○ καὶ ἀποκριθεὶς ὁ Ἰησοῦς εἶπεν αὐτοῖς, "and **answering** Jesus said to them" (Matt 11:4).

- **Genitive Absolute.** A genitive adverbial participle that provides background information. The subject of the participle will also be in the genitive case.

  ○ ταῦτα αὐτοῦ λαλοῦντος πολλοὶ ἐπίστευσαν εἰς αὐτόν, "**As he was saying** these things, many believed in him" (John 8:30).

- **Indirect Discourse.** An anarthrous accusative participle that expresses what someone said.

  ○ πᾶν πνεῦμα ὃ ὁμολογεῖ Ἰησοῦν Χριστὸν ἐν σαρκὶ ἐληλυθότα ἐκ τοῦ θεοῦ ἐστιν, "every spirit that confesses Jesus Christ **has come** in the flesh is from God" (1 John 4:2).

- **Supplementary Participle.** After verbs of perception, an anathrous participle will provide further details about what the person or object observed is doing.

  ○ ὃς δ' ἂν ἔχῃ τὸν βίον τοῦ κόσμου καὶ θεωρῇ τὸν ἀδελφὸν αὐτοῦ χρείαν ἔχοντα, "But whoever has the possessions of the world and sees his brother **having** need" (1 John 3:17).

○ Ἐάν τις ἴδῃ τὸν ἀδελφὸν αὐτοῦ **ἁμαρτάνοντα** ἁμαρτίαν μὴ πρὸς θάνατον, αἰτήσει καὶ δώσει αὐτῷ ζωήν, "If anyone see his brother **sinning** a sin not to death, he will ask and he will give to him life" (1 John 5:16).

10.3.5 Periphrastic Participles

The term *periphrastic* refers to the "roundabout" way of expressing the verbal idea. A periphrastic construction includes the verb εἰμί plus a participle. Instead of using one verb to express the action (ἔλεγεν = "he was speaking"), a verb plus a participle is used (ἦν λέγων = "he was speaking"). Some common characteristics of periphrastic constructions include the following: (1) the finite verb is usually εἰμί, which can occur in the present, imperfect, or future tense forms; (2) the participle can be either present or perfect, will usually occur in the nominative case, and usually follows the indicative verb; and (3) it is often used to highlight verbal aspect (BDF §352).[1] There are only two periphrastic constructions in 1 John.

- **Perfect Periphrastic** (εἰμί [pres.] + per. ptc.): ὁ θεὸς ἐν ἡμῖν μένει καὶ ἡ ἀγάπη αὐτοῦ ἐν ἡμῖν **τετελειωμένη ἐστίν**, "God abides in us and his love **is perfected** in us" (1 John 4:12).

- **Pluperfect Periphrastic** (ἤμην [impf.] + per. ptc.): καὶ ταῦτα γράφομεν ἡμεῖς, ἵνα ἡ χαρὰ ἡμῶν **ᾖ πεπληρωμένη**, "and we write these things, that our joy **might be complete**" (1 John 1:4).

10.4 Reading Notes

1 John 4:1

- Ἀγαπητοί, μὴ παντὶ πνεύματι πιστεύετε

  Although the form of the verb πιστεύετε (pres. act. impv. 2nd pl. πιστεύω) could be indicative, it must be an imperative (prohibition) since it is negated with μή.

  The phrase παντὶ πνεύματι is a dative direct object (complement) of the verb πιστεύω.

- ἀλλὰ δοκιμάζετε τὰ πνεύματα εἰ ἐκ τοῦ θεοῦ ἐστιν

  The verb δοκιμάζετε (pres. act. impv. 2nd pl. δοκιμάζω) contrasts with the previous imperative: "don't believe but test."

---

[1] See also Porter, *Idioms*, 46.

In this context, εἰ can rightly be translated "whether" as a marker of an indirect question (BDAG 278).

The prepositional phrase ἐκ τοῦ θεοῦ conveys source: "whether they are *from God.*"

The singular verb ἐστιν has an implied plural subject: "whether they [the spirits] are from God." Again, this is an example of "the animals run" rule.

- ὅτι πολλοὶ ψευδοπροφῆται ἐξεληλύθασιν εἰς τὸν κόσμον.

The conjunction ὅτι, "because," introduces a causal clause.

The verb ἐξεληλύθασιν (per. act. ind. 3rd pl. ἐξέρχομαι) is a consummative perfect, emphasizing the completed action that produced the resulting state.

1 John 4:2

- ἐν τούτῳ γινώσκετε τὸ πνεῦμα τοῦ θεοῦ·

The phrase ἐν τούτῳ, "by this," is cataphoric, pointing forward to the next phrase.

The noun τοῦ θεοῦ is a genitive of source: "the Spirit *from God.*"

- πᾶν πνεῦμα ὃ ὁμολογεῖ Ἰησοῦν Χριστὸν ἐν σαρκὶ ἐληλυθότα ἐκ τοῦ θεοῦ ἐστιν

The antecedent for the relative pronoun ὃ (neut. nom. sg.) is πᾶν πνεῦμα, which is the subject of the verb ἐστιν: "*every spirit . . . is from God.*"

The verb ἐληλυθότα (per. act. ptc. masc. acc. sg. ἔρχομαι) is a participle of indirect discourse and is in the accusative case along with Ἰησοῦν Χριστόν because the confession functions as the direct object of the verb ὁμολογεῖ (pres. act. ind. 3rd sg. ὁμολογέω). See 2 John 7 for a similar statement.

The prepositional phrase ἐν σαρκί is a dative of manner indicating that Jesus came as a human.

1 John 4:3

- καὶ πᾶν πνεῦμα ὃ μὴ ὁμολογεῖ τὸν Ἰησοῦν ἐκ τοῦ θεοῦ οὐκ ἔστιν·

The conjunction καί marks both continuity of topic and also (in this context) a contrast with the previous statement.

Interestingly, the indicative verb ὁμολογεῖ is negated with μή, which over-whelmingly negates nonindicative verbs. This may indicate "the subjec-tive conviction of the writer that there are no exceptions to the statement he is making."[2] Or, more likely, it may be because Koine Greek is a tad fuzzy around the edges.

The article τόν in the phrase τὸν Ἰησοῦν points to a previous reference of the name (i.e., the anaphoric use of the article or article of previous ref-erence). In other words, by simply stating that whoever does not confess "this Jesus," the author is pointing back to the previous verse where he stated Ἰησοῦν Χριστὸν ἐν σαρκὶ ἐληλυθότα. Thus, we could translate the phrase: "every spirit that does not confess *this Jesus who has come in the flesh* is not from God."

- καὶ τοῦτό ἐστιν τὸ τοῦ ἀντιχρίστου

The antecedent of the near demonstrative pronoun τοῦτό is πᾶν πνεῦμα.

The word πνεῦμα is elided and should be added to the translation of τὸ τοῦ ἀντιχρίστου: "this is the *spirit* of the Antichrist." The neuter singular arti-cle τό matches the gender and number of πνεῦμα. The genitive phrase τοῦ ἀντιχρίστου functions as a genitive of source: "*from* the Antichrist." John is contrasting "the spirit from God" with "the spirit from the Antichrist."

- ὃ ἀκηκόατε ὅτι ἔρχεται, καὶ νῦν ἐν τῷ κόσμῳ ἐστὶν ἤδη.

The antecedent of the neuter relative pronoun ὅ is τὸ τοῦ ἀντιχρίστου, "the [spirit] of the Antichrist," and is best interpreted as an accusative of respect since the direct object of the verb ἀκηκόατε (per. act. ind. 2nd pl. ἀκούω) is the ὅτι clause.

The verb ἔρχεται (pres. mid. ind. 3rd sg. ἔρχομαι) functions as a futuristic present.

1 John 4:4

- ὑμεῖς ἐκ τοῦ θεοῦ ἐστε, τεκνία, καὶ νενικήκατε αὐτούς

Although the inclusion of the personal pronoun with the verb εἰμί does not usually add emphasis, because the pronoun is fronted John seems to be

---

[2] Culy, *I, II, III John*, 102, citing Robert Law, *The Tests of Life: A Study of the First Epistle of St. John*, 3rd ed. (Edinburgh: T&T Clark, 1914), 396.

contrasting his readers and the spirit of the Antichrist (i.e., "*you* are from God"). The addition of the vocative τεκνία confirms this contrast.

The direct object of the verb νενικήκατε (per. act. ind. 2nd pl. νικάω) is αὐτούς, "you have overcome *them.*" This is perhaps a little surprising since John has been referring to "*the spirit* of the Antichrist," and πνεῦμα is a neuter noun. But instead of a neuter singular pronoun (αὐτό, "it"), John uses a masculine plural form (αὐτούς, "them"). The best explanation is that John is referring back to the many false prophets (πολλοὶ ψευδοπροφῆται) mentioned in 4:1 who speak on behalf of the spirit of the Antichrist.

How do we overcome or conquer these false prophets? Culy writes, "'Conquering' the false prophets (ψευδοπροφῆται, 4:1) and the spirits who inspire them (τὰ πνεύματα, 4:1–3) would apparently involve recognizing their origin and choosing to reject them if they do not 'confess (that) Jesus (Christ has come in human form)' (4:2, 3) and are thus not 'from God' (ἐκ τοῦ θεοῦ, 4:1, 3)."[3]

- ὅτι μείζων ἐστὶν ὁ ἐν ὑμῖν ἢ ὁ ἐν τῷ κόσμῳ.

The conjunction ὅτι, "because," introduces a causal clause.

The term ἤ, "than," is often used in connection with the comparative adjective μείζων. Another option, and one we saw in 3:20, is to use a genitive of comparison.

Both uses of the article ὁ function as substantizers, turning the prepositional phrases into virtual nouns (substantives): "the one in you" and "the one in the world."

1 John 4:5

- αὐτοὶ ἐκ τοῦ κόσμου εἰσίν

The fronting of the personal pronoun αὐτοί adds emphasis (contrast) and refers back to αὐτούς ("them," 4:4) which in turn refers back to the many false prophets (πολλοὶ ψευδοπροφῆται, 4:1).

The preposition ἐκ conveys source: "*from* the world."

---

[3] Culy, *I, II, III John*, 104.

- διὰ τοῦτο ἐκ τοῦ κόσμου λαλοῦσιν καὶ ὁ κόσμος αὐτῶν ἀκούει.

  The phrase διὰ τοῦτο is anaphoric, pointing back to the previous statement. Because they are from the world, two results follow.

  The verbs λαλοῦσιν (pres. act. ind. 3rd pl. λαλέω) and ἀκούει (pres. act. ind. 3rd sg. ἀκούω) are iterative or customary presents: *"they regularly speak* from the world," and "the world *regularly listens to* them."

  The pronoun αὐτῶν is a genitive direct object (complement) of the verb ἀκούω.

1 John 4:6

- ἡμεῖς ἐκ τοῦ θεοῦ ἐσμεν

  The fronting of the personal pronoun ἡμεῖς adds emphasis or contrast: "*they* are of the world; *we* are from God."

- ὁ γινώσκων τὸν θεὸν ἀκούει ἡμῶν

  The substantival participle ὁ γινώσκων (pres. act. ptc. masc. nom. sg. γινώσκω) is the subject of the verb ἀκούει.

  The accusative noun τὸν θεόν is the direct object of the participle ὁ γινώσκων. Even though the participle functions as a noun, it still retains a verbal quality and can take a direct object.

  The pronoun ἡμῶν is a genitive direct object (complement) of the verb ἀκούω.

- ὃς οὐκ ἔστιν ἐκ τοῦ θεοῦ οὐκ ἀκούει ἡμῶν.

  The "headless" (i.e., no antecedent) relative pronoun ὅς functions like an indefinite relative pronoun: "whoever."

- ἐκ τούτου γινώσκομεν τὸ πνεῦμα τῆς ἀληθείας καὶ τὸ πνεῦμα τῆς πλάνης.

  The phrase ἐκ τούτου is anaphoric, pointing back to the previous statement. That is, we know the Spirit of truth and the spirit of deception based on the response of affirming or rejecting the apostolic message.

  The genitives τῆς ἀληθείας and τῆς πλάνης are attributive (adjectival) genitives: "the *truthful* Spirit" and "the *deceptive* spirit."

///////////////

CHAPTER 11

1 JOHN 4:7–12
INFINITIVES

11.1 Vocabulary

ἥλιος, ὁ	sun (32)
ὑπομονή, ἡ	endurance, perseverance, patience (32)
ἀκάθαρτος, -ον	unclean, impure (32)
δυνατός, -ή, -όν	powerful, strong, mighty, able (32)
ἐχθρός, -ά, -όν	hostile, hated (32)
μονογενής, -ές	unique, one of a kind (9)
ναί	yes, certainly, indeed (33)
ποῖος, -α, -ον	of what kind? (33)
πώποτε	ever, at any time (6)
ἀναγινώσκω	I read (aloud) (32)
ἐκπορεύομαι	I go out, come out (33)
παραγγέλλω	I command, charge (32)

11.2 Text: 1 John 4:7–12

⁷ Ἀγαπητοί, ἀγαπῶμεν ἀλλήλους, ὅτι ἡ ἀγάπη ἐκ τοῦ θεοῦ ἐστιν, καὶ πᾶς ὁ ἀγαπῶν ἐκ τοῦ θεοῦ γεγέννηται καὶ γινώσκει τὸν θεόν. ⁸ ὁ μὴ ἀγαπῶν οὐκ ἔγνω τὸν θεόν, ὅτι ὁ θεὸς ἀγάπη ἐστίν. ⁹ ἐν τούτῳ ἐφανερώθη ἡ ἀγάπη τοῦ θεοῦ ἐν ἡμῖν, ὅτι τὸν υἱὸν αὐτοῦ τὸν μονογενῆ ἀπέσταλκεν ὁ θεὸς εἰς τὸν κόσμον, ἵνα ζήσωμεν δι᾽ αὐτοῦ. ¹⁰ ἐν τούτῳ ἐστὶν ἡ ἀγάπη, οὐχ ὅτι ἡμεῖς ἠγαπήκαμεν τὸν θεὸν ἀλλ᾽ ὅτι αὐτὸς ἠγάπησεν ἡμᾶς καὶ ἀπέστειλεν τὸν υἱὸν αὐτοῦ ἱλασμὸν περὶ τῶν ἁμαρτιῶν ἡμῶν. ¹¹ Ἀγαπητοί, εἰ οὕτως

ὁ θεὸς ἠγάπησεν ἡμᾶς, καὶ ἡμεῖς ὀφείλομεν ἀλλήλους ἀγαπᾶν. ¹²θεὸν οὐδεὶς πώποτε τεθέαται. ἐὰν ἀγαπῶμεν ἀλλήλους, ὁ θεὸς ἐν ἡμῖν μένει καὶ ἡ ἀγάπη αὐτοῦ ἐν ἡμῖν τετελειωμένη ἐστίν.

11.3 Syntax: Infinitives

An infinitive is a verbal noun. That is, it is a verb that can function as a noun. Consequently, it has qualities that relate to both parts of speech. As a verb, an infinitive has tense (i.e., aspect) and voice, and as a noun, it can be articular (which is always neuter and singular: τό, τοῦ, and τῷ). The subject of the infinitive occurs in the accusative case, and the infinitive is negated by μή (like all nonindicative verbs). Unlike finite verbs, infinitives are indeclinable, not having person and number. When an infinitive occurs after a preposition in the NT, it is always articular, functioning adverbially. Although infinitives are common in the NT (about 2,300 occurrences), there are only seven infinitives in 1 John: five complementary infinitives (2:6; 3:9, 16; 4:11, 20) and two infinitives of indirect discourse (2:6, 9).

11.3.1 Adverbial Infinitives

* **Complementary.** An anarthrous infinitive that completes the idea of another verb (always with δύναμαι or ὀφείλω in 1 John).

  ○ οὐ δύναται **ἁμαρτάνειν**, ὅτι ἐκ τοῦ θεοῦ γεγέννηται, "he is not able **to sin** because he has been born of God" (1 John 3:9).

  ○ καὶ ἡμεῖς ὀφείλομεν ἀλλήλους **ἀγαπᾶν**, "we also ought **to love** one another" (1 John 4:11).

* **Purpose.** Communicates the goal expressed by the main verb. This use can occur as a simple infinitive (i.e., no article or preposition), after the article τοῦ, or after the prepositions εἰς τό or πρὸς τό.

  ○ μὴ νομίσητε ὅτι ἦλθον **καταλῦσαι** τὸν νόμον ἢ τοὺς προφήτας· οὐκ ἦλθον **καταλῦσαι** ἀλλὰ **πληρῶσαι**, "Do not think that I came **to destroy** the law or the prophets; I did not come **to destroy** but **to fulfill**" (Matt 5:17).

* **Result.** Communicates the actual or conceived result expressed by the main verb. This use can occur as a simple infinitive, after the article τοῦ, after the preposition εἰς τό, or after ὥστε.

  ○ Ἰεζάβελ . . . διδάσκει καὶ πλανᾷ τοὺς ἐμοὺς δούλους **πορνεῦσαι** καὶ **φαγεῖν** εἰδωλόθυτα, "Jezebel . . . teaches and deceives my servants **to commit sexual immorality** and **to eat** food offered to idols" (Rev 2:20).

- **Previous Time.** The action of the infinitive occurs before the main verb (μετὰ τό + inf).

  ○ μετὰ δὲ τὸ παραδοθῆναι τὸν Ἰωάννην ἦλθεν ὁ Ἰησοῦς εἰς τὴν Γαλιλαίαν, "**After** John **was arrested**, Jesus went to Galilee" (Mark 1:14).

- **Contemporaneous Time.** The action of the infinitive occurs simultaneously with the main verb (ἐν τῷ + inf.).

  ○ ἐν δὲ τῷ πορεύεσθαι αὐτοὺς αὐτὸς εἰσῆλθεν εἰς κώμην τινά, "**While** they **were traveling**, he entered a certain village" (Luke 10:38).

- **Subsequent Time.** The action of the infinitive occurs after the main verb (πρὸ τοῦ or πρίν [ἤ] + inf.).

  ○ εἴρηκα ὑμῖν πρὶν γενέσθαι, "I have told you **before it happens**" (John 14:29).

- **Cause.** Communicates the reason for the action of the main verb (διὰ τό + inf.).

  ○ αὐτὸς δὲ Ἰησοῦς οὐκ ἐπίστευεν αὐτὸν αὐτοῖς διὰ τὸ αὐτὸν γινώσκειν πάντας, "But Jesus was not entrusting himself to them **because** he **knew** all [people]" (John 2:24).

11.3.2 Substantival Infinitives

Adverbial infinitives are syntactically linked to verbs. Substantival infinitives, however, function as nouns or other substantives.

- **Subject.** Functions as the subject or predicate nominative of a main verb.

  ○ δεῖ τὸν υἱὸν τοῦ ἀνθρώπου πολλὰ παθεῖν, "For the Son of God **to suffer** much is necessary" (Mark 8:31).

- **Direct Object.** Functions as the direct object of a main verb.

  ○ τῷ υἱῷ ἔδωκεν ζωὴν ἔχειν ἐν ἑαυτῷ, "he has given to the Son **to have** life in himself" (John 5:26).

- **Indirect Discourse.** Follows a verb of speaking to communicate indirect speech.

  ○ ὁ λέγων ἐν αὐτῷ μένειν ὀφείλει καθὼς ἐκεῖνος περιεπάτησεν καὶ αὐτὸς [οὕτως] περιπατεῖν, "The one who claims **to remain** in him, just as that one walked, he himself ought to walk in the same way" (1 John 2:6).

○ ὁ λέγων ἐν τῷ φωτὶ **εἶναι** καὶ τὸν ἀδελφὸν αὐτοῦ μισῶν ἐν τῇ σκοτίᾳ ἐστὶν ἕως ἄρτι, "the one who says that **he is** in the light while hating his brother is in darkness until now" (1 John 2:9).

- **Explanatory.** Defines or clarifies a noun or adjective.

  ○ τοῦτο γάρ ἐστιν θέλημα τοῦ θεοῦ, ὁ ἁγιασμὸς ὑμῶν, **ἀπέχεσθαι** ὑμᾶς ἀπὸ τῆς πορνείας, "for this is the will of God, your sanctification, **[that is,] that** you **abstain** from sexual immorality" (1 Thess 4:3).

Though not common, an infinitive can also function as an imperative (e.g., Rom 12:15) or can be grammatically independent (i.e., an infinitive absolute; e.g., see Acts 23:26).

11.4 Reading Notes

1 John 4:7

- Ἀγαπητοί, ἀγαπῶμεν ἀλλήλους

  The vocative ἀγαπητοί occurs here for the fifth time in 1 John and signals a new paragraph (see note at 2:7).

  The verb ἀγαπῶμεν (pres. act. subjunc. 1st pl. ἀγαπάω) is a hortatory subjunctive, which is used when the author includes himself in the exhortation: "let us love." In 4:19, John will state, "we love because he first loved us." But this verse implicitly makes the same point: those who are beloved (by God) should love one another.

  The reciprocal pronoun ἀλλήλους occurs five times in 1 John, always in connection with the verb ἀγαπάω. It is used twice in a content clause with the conjunction ἵνα (3:11, 23, "that we should love another"), once with a complementary infinitive (4:11, "we ought to love one another"), once with the conditional particle ἐάν (4:12, "if we love one another"), and here in 4:7: "let us love one another."

- ὅτι ἡ ἀγάπη ἐκ τοῦ θεοῦ ἐστιν

  The conjunction ὅτι, "because," introduces a causal clause, providing the reason for the previous exhortation.

  Notice that the article is included with an abstract noun (ἡ ἀγάπη).

The prepositional phrase ἐκ τοῦ θεοῦ indicates the source of love: "love is *from God.*"

• καὶ πᾶς ὁ ἀγαπῶν ἐκ τοῦ θεοῦ γεγέννηται καὶ γινώσκει τὸν θεόν.

The substantival participle ὁ ἀγαπῶν (pres. act. ptc. masc. nom. sg. ἀγαπάω, "the one who loves") is the subject of the verbs γεγέννηται (per. pass. ind. 3rd sg. γεννάω) and γινώσκει (pres. act. ind. 3rd sg. γινώσκω).

1 John 4:8

• ὁ μὴ ἀγαπῶν οὐκ ἔγνω τὸν θεόν

The substantival participle ὁ ἀγαπῶν is negated by μή in a "sandwich construction" (the article and the participle are separated with a modifier in between). Such a construction clearly communicates that μή is negating the participle and was common in Koine Greek. This same construction occurs seven times in 1 John (3:10 [2×], 14; 4:8, 20; 5:10, 12).

The verb ἔγνω (aor. act. ind. 3rd sg. γινώσκω) is negated with οὐ because it is an indicative verb whereas ἀγαπῶν is negated with μή since it is a nonindicative verb (i.e., a participle). John is not simply stating that the person who does not love others *does* not know God, but that they *have* never come to know God. That is, the aorist tense form "describes the person who has never experienced the knowledge of God."[1] For verbs that describe a state, the aorist tense sometimes conveys an inceptive sense. If that nuance is intended here, John would be saying that the person who does not love has not come to know God.

• ὅτι ὁ θεὸς ἀγάπη ἐστίν.

The conjunction ὅτι, "because," introduces a causal clause, providing the reason for the previous statement: the one who does not love does not know God, *because* God is love.

The noun ἀγάπη is anarthrous this time (cf. 4:7, 10: ἡ ἀγάπη), probably because John intends a qualitative sense to the noun. God is, as a characteristic quality and in essence, love.

---

[1] Stephen S. Smalley, *1, 2, 3 John*, WBC 51 (Waco, TX: Word, 1984), 239. Akin draws out the implications even further: "The one who does not love is a stranger to God. He never even began to have a relationship with God; that is, there was never a time when this person could have legitimately claimed that he knew God." See Daniel L. Akin, *1, 2, 3 John*, NAC 38 (Nashville: B&H, 2001), 178.

1 John 4:9

- ἐν τούτῳ ἐφανερώθη ἡ ἀγάπη τοῦ θεοῦ ἐν ἡμῖν

The phrase ἐν τούτῳ, "by this," is cataphoric, pointing forward to the following ὅτι clause.

The subject of the passive ἐφανερώθη (aor. pass. ind. 3rd sg. φανερόω) is ἡ ἀγάπη.

The noun τοῦ θεοῦ is a subjective genitive ("the love of God" = God's love for someone, *not* someone's love for God). The other three uses of this phrase are all objective genitives (2:5; 3:17; 5:3). So how can we be confident that John intends for a different meaning in this noun? The answer, of course, is the context. John continues by describing God's love for us in the sending of his only Son into the world.

The prepositional phrase ἐν ἡμῖν communicates location: "among us."

- ὅτι τὸν υἱὸν αὐτοῦ τὸν μονογενῆ ἀπέσταλκεν ὁ θεὸς εἰς τὸν κόσμον

The conjunction ὅτι, "that," introduces a content clause, providing the substance of how God's love is revealed.

The noun τὸν υἱόν (fronted for emphasis) is modified by the adjective τὸν μονογενῆ with the pronoun αὐτοῦ sandwiched in between. This follows a typical article-noun-article-adjective construction. The adjective μονογενής focuses on Jesus's status as it pertains "to what is unique in the sense of being the only one of the same kind or class" (LN §58.52). Recently, scholars have debated if the adjective μονογενής should be translated "unique/one-of-a-kind" (most modern translations) or "only begotten" (KJV). The issue turns on how early church fathers employed the adjective and whether the adjective teaches the doctrine of the eternal generation of the Son.

The form of this perfect verb ἀπέσταλκεν (per. act. ind. 3rd sg. ἀποστέλλω) needs some explanation. First, it is a compound verb, meaning that it has a prepositional prefix (ἀπό + στέλλω). Thus, any reduplication will take place after the preposition. Second, because the root of the verb begins with a double consonant (στέλλω), it does not fully reduplicate (vocalic reduplication), leaving only the addition of the *epsilon* (ε), which replaces the *omicron* (ο). Finally, because this verb is a liquid verb (i.e., a verb who stem ends in λ, μ, ν, or ρ), when the *kappa* (κ) is added, a *lambda* (λ) drops and the vowel is changed from *epsilon* (ε) to an *alpha* (α).

- ἵνα ζήσωμεν δι' αὐτοῦ.

The conjunction ἵνα introduces a purpose clause and triggers the subjunctive mood (ζήσωμεν: aor. act. subjunc. 1st pl. ζάω). Because this verb lexically favors the present tense form, a nuanced meaning may be intended. For example, in nonindicative forms ζάω occurs eighty-two times in the present but only seven times as an aorist. Verbs that describe stative actions sometimes convey an inceptive idea in their aorist forms. Consequently, Baugh suggests a possible inceptive nuance and offers the following translation: "that we may come to live through him."[2]

1 John 4:10

- ἐν τούτῳ ἐστὶν ἡ ἀγάπη, οὐχ ὅτι ἡμεῖς ἠγαπήκαμεν τὸν θεὸν

The phrase ἐν τούτῳ, "by this," is cataphoric, pointing forward to the following two ὅτι (content) clauses.

The personal pronoun ἡμεῖς is emphatic, contrasting our love with God's love.

The verb ἠγαπήκαμεν (per. act. ind. 1st pl. ἀγαπάω) may appear to be an aorist form, but it is a perfect form. Because the verb begins with a vowel, the reduplication of the first letter does not occur, leaving only the *epsilon* (ε), which causes the initial vowel to lengthen (vocalic reduplication). The *kappa* (κ) at the end of the stem confirms that it is a perfect form.

- ἀλλ' ὅτι αὐτὸς ἠγάπησεν ἡμᾶς

The personal pronoun αὐτός is emphatic, contrasting God's love with ours.

Notice that the tense form of the verb shifted from the perfect (ἠγαπήκαμεν) to the aorist form ἠγάπησεν (aor. act. ind. 3rd sg. ἀγαπάω). The aorist focuses on the act of God in the sending of his Son.

- καὶ ἀπέστειλεν τὸν υἱὸν αὐτοῦ ἱλασμὸν περὶ τῶν ἁμαρτιῶν ἡμῶν.

John again shifts from using the perfect ἀπέσταλκεν (4:9) to the aorist form ἀπέστειλεν (aor. act. ind. 3rd sg. ἀποστέλλω). Note that the augment comes after the prepositional prefix and replaces the *omicron* (ο). Because it is a liquid verb, the *sigma* (σ) is rejected, which causes a *lambda* (λ) to drop and compensatory lengthening of the stem vowel (ε → ει) to occur.

---

2 Baugh, *First John Reader*, 67.

The nouns τὸν υἱόν and ἱλασμόν form a double accusative: "he sent his *son as a propitiation.*" Both the noun ἱλασμός and the phrase περὶ τῶν ἁμαρτιῶν ἡμῶν also occur in 2:2 (cf. Rom 3:25; Heb 9:5).

The pronoun ἡμῶν is a subjective genitive ("our sins" = the sins we commit).

1 John 4:11

• Ἀγαπητοί, εἰ οὕτως ὁ θεὸς ἠγάπησεν ἡμᾶς

The vocative ἀγαπητοί occurs here for the sixth and final time in 1 John. Instead of signaling a new paragraph, it signals the close of the previous paragraph (which is held together by the theme of love).[3]

The adverb οὕτως communicates the *manner* or *way* in which God loved us: "in this way" or "as follows" (BDAG 742). This statement is reminiscent of John 3:16: οὕτως γὰρ ἠγάπησεν ὁ θεὸς τὸν κόσμον, "for in this way God loved the world." The term designates the quality (i.e., "in this manner") and not quantity (i.e., "so much") of God's love.

• καὶ ἡμεῖς ὀφείλομεν ἀλλήλους ἀγαπᾶν.

The personal pronoun ἡμεῖς is emphatic, connecting God's love for us and our love for others.

The verb ἀγαπᾶν (pres. act. inf. ἀγαπάω) is a complementary infinitive connected to the verb ὀφείλομεν (pres. act. ind. 1st pl. ὀφείλω).

1 John 4:12

• θεὸν οὐδεὶς πώποτε τεθέαται.

The noun θεόν is fronted for emphasis. In addition, the adverb πώποτε adds emphasis to the statement. Not only has no one seen God, no one has *ever* seen God.

The verb τεθέαται (per. mid. ind. 3rd sg. θεάομαι) occurred as an aorist form in 1:1 (ἐθεασάμεθα). Verbs that begin with an aspirated consonant (such as θ, φ, χ) will reduplicate the non-aspirated form (τ, π, κ): θ → τ, φ → π, χ → κ.

---

[3] Contra Culy, who sees the vocative beginning a new paragraph (*I, II, III John*, 110).

- ἐὰν ἀγαπῶμεν ἀλλήλους

  The conjunction ἐάν introduces a third class conditional statement and triggers the subjunctive mood (ἀγαπῶμεν: pres. act. subjunc. 1st pl. ἀγαπάω).

- ὁ θεὸς ἐν ἡμῖν μένει καὶ ἡ ἀγάπη αὐτοῦ ἐν ἡμῖν τετελειωμένη ἐστίν.

  The personal pronoun αὐτοῦ is probably best classified as a subjective genitive ("his love" = God's love for us).

  The phrase τετελειωμένη ἐστίν is a perfect periphrastic construction that includes the present tense of εἰμί with a perfect participle (τετελειωμένη: per. pass. ptc. fem. nom. sg. τελειόω).

////////////////

CHAPTER 12

1 JOHN 4:13–21
PRONOUNS, PREPOSITIONS, ADVERBS, CONJUNCTIONS, AND PARTICLES

12.1 Vocabulary

ἄνεμος, ὁ	wind (31)
ἱερεύς, -έως, ὁ	priest (31)
κόλασις, ἡ	punishment (2)
πλῆθος, -ους, τό	multitude, large amount, crowd (31)
ποτήριον, τό	cup (31)
σωτήρ, -ῆρος, ὁ	savior, deliverer (24)
φυλή, ἡ	tribe, nation, people (31)
τέλειος, -α, -ον	perfect, complete, mature, adult (19)
ἐγγύς	near, close to (31)
πλήν	yet, however, but (31)
ἐλπίζω	I hope (31)
ἔξεστιν	it is lawful, permitted (31)

12.2 Text: 1 John 4:13–21

¹³ Ἐν τούτῳ γινώσκομεν ὅτι ἐν αὐτῷ μένομεν καὶ αὐτὸς ἐν ἡμῖν, ὅτι ἐκ τοῦ πνεύματος αὐτοῦ δέδωκεν ἡμῖν. ¹⁴ καὶ ἡμεῖς τεθεάμεθα καὶ μαρτυροῦμεν ὅτι ὁ πατὴρ ἀπέσταλκεν τὸν υἱὸν σωτῆρα τοῦ κόσμου. ¹⁵ ὃς ἐὰν ὁμολογήσῃ ὅτι Ἰησοῦς ἐστιν ὁ υἱὸς τοῦ θεοῦ, ὁ θεὸς ἐν αὐτῷ μένει καὶ αὐτὸς ἐν τῷ θεῷ. ¹⁶ καὶ ἡμεῖς ἐγνώκαμεν καὶ πεπιστεύκαμεν

τὴν ἀγάπην ἣν ἔχει ὁ θεὸς ἐν ἡμῖν. Ὁ θεὸς ἀγάπη ἐστίν, καὶ ὁ μένων ἐν τῇ ἀγάπῃ ἐν τῷ θεῷ μένει καὶ ὁ θεὸς ἐν αὐτῷ μένει. ¹⁷ ἐν τούτῳ τετελείωται ἡ ἀγάπη μεθ᾽ ἡμῶν, ἵνα παρρησίαν ἔχωμεν ἐν τῇ ἡμέρᾳ τῆς κρίσεως, ὅτι καθὼς ἐκεῖνός ἐστιν καὶ ἡμεῖς ἐσμεν ἐν τῷ κόσμῳ τούτῳ. ¹⁸ φόβος οὐκ ἔστιν ἐν τῇ ἀγάπῃ, ἀλλ᾽ ἡ τελεία ἀγάπη ἔξω βάλλει τὸν φόβον, ὅτι ὁ φόβος κόλασιν ἔχει, ὁ δὲ φοβούμενος οὐ τετελείωται ἐν τῇ ἀγάπῃ. ¹⁹ ἡμεῖς ἀγαπῶμεν, ὅτι αὐτὸς πρῶτος ἠγάπησεν ἡμᾶς. ²⁰ ἐάν τις εἴπῃ ὅτι ἀγαπῶ τὸν θεὸν καὶ τὸν ἀδελφὸν αὐτοῦ μισῇ, ψεύστης ἐστίν· ὁ γὰρ μὴ ἀγαπῶν τὸν ἀδελφὸν αὐτοῦ ὃν ἑώρακεν, τὸν θεὸν ὃν οὐχ ἑώρακεν οὐ δύναται ἀγαπᾶν. ²¹ καὶ ταύτην τὴν ἐντολὴν ἔχομεν ἀπ᾽ αὐτοῦ, ἵνα ὁ ἀγαπῶν τὸν θεὸν ἀγαπᾷ καὶ τὸν ἀδελφὸν αὐτοῦ.

12.3 Syntax: Pronouns, Prepositions, Adverbs, Conjunctions, and Particles

Because this chapter includes several parts of speech, each one will be covered with only a cursory treatment.

12.3.1 Pronouns

A pronoun takes the place of a noun. The noun that the pronoun replaces is called the antecedent. There are at least eight types of pronouns found in the Greek of the NT.

Personal		ἐγώ, μου, σύ, ὑμῶν, αὐτός	I, my, you, your [pl], he
Demonstrative	Near	οὗτος, οὗτοι	this, these
	Far	ἐκεῖνος, ἐκεῖνοι	that, those
Relative		ὅς(τις), ἧς, ὅ	who, whose, which
Interrogative		τίς, τίνος, τί	who? whose? what/why?
Indefinite		τις, τινες	anyone/someone, certain ones
Reflexive		ἐμαυτόν, ἑαυτούς, ἑαυτοῖς	myself, yourselves, to themselves
Reciprocal		ἀλλήλων	[of] one another
Correlative		ὅσος, οἷος, ὁποῖος	as many as, such as, what sort of

Three uses of the personal pronoun deserve a brief explanation.

- **Emphatic Use.** The presence of the personal pronoun when it is not needed since the person and number is communicated by the verb's ending. For example, John writes, ἡμεῖς τεθεάμεθα, "we have seen," in 4:14. Because τεθεάμεθα by itself communicates "we have seen," the use of the pronoun ἡμεῖς adds emphasis.

- **Intensive Use.** The use of the third-person personal pronoun (αὐτός, αὐτή, αὐτό) that intensifies an explicit substantive (unlike the emphatic use that has no explicit nominal it is intensifying). For example: αὐτὸς ὁ κύριος . . .

καταβήσεται ἀπ᾽ οὐρανοῦ, "the Lord **himself** will descend from heaven" (1 Thess 4:16).

- **Identical Use.** The use of the third-person personal pronoun placed in the attributive position (i.e., an article directly precedes the pronoun). In such cases, the pronoun is translated "same." For example, Paul states, "There are a variety of gifts, but **the same** Spirit" (τὸ δὲ αὐτὸ πνεῦμα; 1 Cor 12:4).

12.3.2 Prepositions

Prepositions were on the increase during the Koine period. That which could be communicated via case endings alone was made more explicit with prepositions. This usage would have been helpful for nonnative speakers.

Essentially, prepositions help nouns (or other substantives) express their relationship with other components of the sentence. The preposition, along with its object, constitute a prepositional phrase. Most prepositional phrases modify verbs (adverbial), but occasionally they modify nouns or other substantives (adjectival). Adverbial prepositional phrases answer questions related to the verbal action such as "when?" "where?" "why?" or "how?" Adjectival prepositional phrases modify an explicit noun (or other substantive) answering questions such as "which?" or "what kind of?" A prepositional phrase can be turned into a virtual noun or adjective (nominalized or substantivized) by placing an article in front of it, causing the phrase to function as a noun. For example, τὰ ἐν τῷ κόσμῳ, "the things in the world" (1 John 2:15).

Proper prepositions are prepositions that can also be prefixed to a verb, forming compound verbs (e.g., περι + πατέω). There are seventeen proper prepositions in the Greek NT. *Improper* prepositions were originally adverbs that later came to be used "improperly" as prepositions. Improper prepositions are *never* prefixed to a verb. There are forty-two improper prepositions in the Greek NT, but most of them occur very rarely.

12.3.3 Adverbs

An adverb generally modifies a verb, describing how an action was accomplished (e.g., "she was writing *feverishly*"). Adverbs are not typically inflected, maintaining fixed forms. The most common adverbial endings are –ως (e.g., οὕτως) and –ον (e.g., μόνον). Adverbs answer questions such as "when" "where?" "in what way?" and "how often/intensely?" Other parts of speech can also function as adverbs.

- **Adverbs of Time:** ἅπαξ, "once"; αὔριον, "tomorrow"; νῦν, "now"; πάλιν, "again"; πάντοτε, "always"; ποτέ, "formerly"; πότε, "when?"; πρωΐ, "early"; σήμερον, "today"; τότε, "then."

- **Adverbs of Place:** ἄνω, "above"; ἄνωθεν, "from above"; ἐκεῖ, "there"; ἐκεῖθεν, "from there"; κάτω, "down"; κύκλῳ, "around"; ποῦ, "where?"; ὧδε, "here."

- **Adverbs of Manner:** ἀκριβῶς, "accurately"; δωρεάν, "freely"; εὐθύς, "immediately"; καλῶς, "well"; ὁμοθυμαδόν, "with one accord"; οὕτως, "thus"; παραχρῆμα, "immediately"; πῶς, "how?"; ταχέως, "quickly"; ταχύς, "quickly."

- **Adverbs of Degree:** λίαν, "very"; μάλιστα, "especially"; μᾶλλον, "more"; σφόδρα, "exceedingly."

12.3.4 Conjunctions and Particles

Conjunctions are words that connect various literary components together (i.e., words, phrases, clauses, discourse units). Robertson writes that conjunctions "have a very good name, since they bind together (*con-jungo*) the various parts of speech not otherwise connected, if they need connection."[1] The key is to determine the function of the conjunction since it signals the relationship between larger units of the discourse. Indeed, most sentences in NT Greek begin with a conjunction (asyndeton is when a sentence has no conjunction). Essentially, a conjunction indicates whether one unit is composed of a parallel assertion (coordinating conjunction) or whether it is dependent (subordinating conjunction). Below are various types of conjunctions:[2]

- **Copulative:** καί, "and" or "also"; δέ, "and"; οὐδέ, "and not"; μηδέ, "and not"; τέ, "and so"; οὔτε, "and not"; μήτε, "and not."

- **Disjunctive:** ἤ, "or"; εἴτε, "if" or "whether."

- **Adversative:** ἀλλά, "but"; δέ, "but"; μέν, "but"; μέντοι, "nevertheless"; πλήν, "but," "except"; εἰ μή, "except"; ὅμως, "yet"; καίτοι, "yet."

- **Inferential:** οὖν, "therefore" or "so"; ἄρα, "then"; διό, "for this reason"; δή, "therefore."

- **Explanatory:** γάρ, "for."

- **Purpose:** ἵνα, "in order that," "so that"; ὅπως, "that."

- **Result:** ὥστε, "so that"; ὅπως, "that."

- **Causal:** ὅτι, "that," "because"; διότι, "because"; ἐπεί, "because" or "since"; ἐπειδή, "because."

- **Comparative:** ὡς, "as" or "like"; ὥσπερ, "just as"; καθώς, "as," "just as"; καθάπερ, "just as."

- **Conditional:** εἰ, "if"; ἐάν, "if"; εἴπερ, "if indeed."

---

[1] Robertson, *Grammar*, 1177.
[2] The categories for coordinating and subordinating conjunctions, as well as the lists of conjunctions under each category, are (with minor changes) from John D. Grassmick, *Principles and Practice of Greek Exegesis: A Classroom Manual* (Dallas: Dallas Theological Seminary, 1976), 86.

- **Concessive:** εἰ καί, "even if"; καὶ εἰ, "even if"; κἄν, "even though"; καίπερ, "although."
- **Declarative:** ὅτι, "that"; ἵνα, "that."
- **Temporal:** ὅτε, "when"; ἕως, "until"; ὅταν, "whenever"; πρίν, "before."
- **Local:** οὖ, "where"; ὅπου, "where"; ὅθεν, "from where" or "whence."

A particle is a catchall for words that do not fit into any other part of speech. They are usually short (sometimes untranslated) words, which could often also be categorized as adverbs, conjunctions, or interjections.

- **Particles of Negation:** indicative mood = οὐ, οὐκ, οὐχ, οὐχί; nonindicative moods = μή, μήποτε, "never."
- **Particles of Connection:** μέν . . . δέ, "on the one hand . . . on the other hand"; τέ, "and."
- **Particles of Intensification:** ἀμήν, "amen"; γέ, "even"; ναί, "yes!"
- **Particles of Interjection:** ἰδού, "look!"; οὐαί, "woe!"; ὦ, "O!"
- **Particles of the Subjunctive Mood:** ἄν and ἐάν.

12.4 Reading Notes

1 John 4:13

- Ἐν τούτῳ γινώσκομεν ὅτι ἐν αὐτῷ μένομεν καὶ αὐτὸς ἐν ἡμῖν

  The phrase ἐν τούτῳ, "by this," is cataphoric, pointing forward to the second ὅτι clause (ἐκ τοῦ πνεύματος αὐτοῦ δέδωκεν ἡμῖν). The first ὅτι clause introduces a content clause, "we know *that*," whereas the second one introduces a causal clause (i.e., "because").

  The preposition ἐν is used three times in this phrase and conveys means or instrument (ἐν τούτῳ, "by means of this") and metaphorical location (ἐν αὐτῷ, "in him"; ἐν ἡμῖν, "in us").

  There are also four pronouns in this phrase and six in the verse: a near demonstrative pronoun (τούτῳ), three third-person personal pronouns (αὐτῷ, αὐτός, αὐτοῦ), and two first-person personal pronouns (ἡμῖν, ἡμῖν).

  The conjunction καί is coordinate with the previous clause. The second clause has an implied verb, μένομεν.

- ὅτι ἐκ τοῦ πνεύματος αὐτοῦ δέδωκεν ἡμῖν.

The prepositional phrase ἐκ τοῦ πνεύματος conveys source (i.e., "*from* his Spirit"), though some have argued it could be a partitive genitive: "a portion of his Spirit."[3]

The verb δέδωκεν (per. act. ind. 3rd sg. δίδωμι) is perfect, though the aorist was used earlier in a similar phrase: ἐκ τοῦ πνεύματος οὗ ἡμῖν ἔδωκεν (3:24).

1 John 4:14

- καὶ ἡμεῖς τεθεάμεθα καὶ μαρτυροῦμεν

The two uses of καί function as coordinate conjunctions.

The first-person personal pronoun ἡμεῖς is emphatic since that information is embedded in the verbs τεθεάμεθα (per. mid. ind. 1st pl. θεάομαι) and μαρτυροῦμεν (pres. act. ind. 1st pl. μαρτυρέω).

- ὅτι ὁ πατὴρ ἀπέσταλκεν τὸν υἱὸν σωτῆρα τοῦ κόσμου.

The conjunction ὅτι, "that," introduces a content clause.

For more information on the verb ἀπέσταλκεν (per. act. ind. 3rd sg. ἀποστέλλω), see the note on 4:9.

The two nouns τὸν υἱόν and σωτῆρα function as double accusatives: "the Father has sent the *Son as Savior.*" Also, note that τὸν υἱόν could be rendered "his Son," with the article functioning as a possessive pronoun.

The noun τοῦ κόσμου is an objective genitive ("Savior of the world" = he saves the world).

1 John 4:15

- ὃς ἐὰν ὁμολογήσῃ ὅτι Ἰησοῦς ἐστιν ὁ υἱὸς τοῦ θεοῦ

The relative pronoun ὅς, "whoever," in combination with the conjunction ἐάν creates an indefinite relative clause and triggers the subjunctive mood (ὁμολογήσῃ: aor. act. subjunc. 3rd sg. ὁμολογέω).

In 1:9, John states, ἐὰν ὁμολογῶμεν τὰς ἁμαρτίας ἡμῶν, "if we confess our sins," using the present subjunctive of ὁμολογέω. In 4:15, however, he

---

[3] See Culy, *I, II, III John*, 112.

uses an aorist subjunctive. Why the change in tense form (aspect)? Baugh suggests that the present form in 1:9 indicates "a reiteration of discrete events" (we repeatedly confess sins that we commit). The aorist form, on the other hand, expresses "the profession as a discrete event or as a simple fact without explication of any reiteration."[4]

The content (ὅτι) of what is confessed is that "Jesus is the Son of God" (see 5:5). The noun τοῦ θεοῦ is a genitive of relationship: "the son *of God*."

- ὁ θεὸς ἐν αὐτῷ μένει καὶ αὐτὸς ἐν τῷ θεῷ.

This phrase is similar to what John wrote earlier in 3:24 (ἐν αὐτῷ μένει καὶ αὐτὸς ἐν αὐτῷ).

1 John 4:16

- καὶ ἡμεῖς ἐγνώκαμεν καὶ πεπιστεύκαμεν τὴν ἀγάπην ἣν ἔχει ὁ θεὸς ἐν ἡμῖν.

The personal pronoun ἡμεῖς is emphatic.

Although the perfect verb ἐγνώκαμεν (per. act. ind. 1st pl. γινώσκω) was found earlier in 1 John (2:3; 3:16), the perfect πεπιστεύκαμεν (per. act. ind. 1st pl. πιστεύω) occurs first here (and later in 5:10: πεπίστευκεν).

The antecedent for the relative pronoun ἥν (fem. acc. sg.) is τὴν ἀγάπην (fem. acc. sg.).

- Ὁ θεὸς ἀγάπη ἐστίν, καὶ ὁ μένων ἐν τῇ ἀγάπῃ ἐν τῷ θεῷ μένει καὶ ὁ θεὸς ἐν αὐτῷ μένει.

The noun ἀγάπη likely is anarthrous to indicate a qualitative sense for the predicate nominative (see 4:8 for further discussion of the same phrase).

The substantival participle ὁ μένων (pres. act. ptc. masc. nom. sg. μένω) is the subject of the verb μένει.

1 John 4:17

- ἐν τούτῳ τετελείωται ἡ ἀγάπη μεθ' ἡμῶν

The phrase ἐν τούτῳ is anaphoric, pointing back to the previous phrase. Thus, the point is "that through God continuing in relationship with the believer, and perhaps through the believer continuing in relationship with

---

[4] Baugh, *First John Reader*, 68.

God and continuing to live a life of love, love has been brought to maturity among the readers."[5]

The verb τετελείωται (per. pass. ind. 3rd sg. τελειόω) has already occurred in 2:5 and will occur again in the next verse.

The preposition μεθ' is an abbreviated and altered form of μετά. Because the following word (ἡμῶν) begins with a vowel, the ending vowel is dropped (μετ'). And because the following vowel begins with a rough breathing mark (ἡ), the *tau* (τ) is aspirated to a *theta* (θ). The preposition conveys *association*: "with us."

- ἵνα παρρησίαν ἔχωμεν ἐν τῇ ἡμέρᾳ τῆς κρίσεως

The conjunction ἵνα introduces a purpose clause and triggers the subjunctive mood (ἔχωμεν: pres. act. subjunc. 1st pl. ἔχω).

The prepositional phrase ἐν τῇ ἡμέρᾳ communicates time: "in/on the day." The noun τῆς κρίσεως is an attributive genitive: "judgment day."

- ὅτι καθὼς ἐκεῖνός ἐστιν καὶ ἡμεῖς ἐσμεν ἐν τῷ κόσμῳ τούτῳ.

The conjunction ὅτι, "because," introduces a causal clause.

This is the sixth and final time that the far demonstrative pronoun ἐκεῖνός is used as a reference to Jesus.

The prepositional phrase ἐν τῷ κόσμῳ τούτῳ communicates location with a near demonstrative: "in this world."

1 John 4:18

- φόβος οὐκ ἔστιν ἐν τῇ ἀγάπῃ

The prepositional phrase ἐν τῇ ἀγάπῃ is a dative of reference or respect: "there is no fear *with respect to love*." This is also the use of the phrase at the end of the verse: "the one who fears has not been perfected *with respect to love*."

- ἀλλ' ἡ τελεία ἀγάπη ἔξω βάλλει τὸν φόβον

The conjunction ἀλλ' (shortened from ἀλλά) expresses a strong contrast.

[5] Culy, *I, II, III John*, 115.

The adjective τελεία modifies ἡ . . . ἀγάπη, "perfect love."

The adverb ἔξω modifies the verb βάλλει, "casts *out.*"

- ὅτι ὁ φόβος κόλασιν ἔχει

  The conjunction ὅτι introduces a causal clause, "because."

  The first occurrence of φόβος does not possess the article, but this occurrence does. Based on context, the second use with the article communicates previous reference: "this fear."

  The phrase ὁ φόβος κόλασιν ἔχει can literally be translated "fear has punishment" and probably means "fears stems from an expectation of judgment."[6]

- ὁ δὲ φοβούμενος οὐ τετελείωται ἐν τῇ ἀγάπη.

  The substantival participle ὁ φοβούμενος (pres. mid. ptc. masc. nom. sg. φοβέω) is the subject of the verb τετελείωται (per. pass. ind. 3rd sg. τελειόω). Verbs of emotion (e.g., φοβέω) are frequently found in the middle voice.

1 John 4:19

- ἡμεῖς ἀγαπῶμεν, ὅτι αὐτὸς πρῶτος ἠγάπησεν ἡμᾶς.

  The personal pronouns ἡμεῖς and αὐτός are emphatic, highlighting the ability of Christians to love because of having experienced God's love first.

  The conjunction ὅτι, "because," introduces a causal clause.

  The adjective πρῶτος is functioning as an adverb: "he *first* loved."

1 John 4:20

- ἐάν τις εἴπη ὅτι ἀγαπῶ τὸν θεὸν

  The conjunction ἐάν introduces a conditional clause and triggers the subjunctive mood (εἴπη: aor. act. subjunc. 3rd sg. λέγω).

  The conjunction, ὅτι, "that," introduces a content clause of direct discourse. Typically, ὅτι introduces indirect discourse, but here (evidenced

---

6 Culy, *I, II, III John*, 117.

by the first-person verb), direct discourse is used (which some modern Greek versions show by using a capital letter to begin the quote: Ἀγαπῶ). In English, we would communicate this use of ὅτι with quotation marks.

- καὶ τὸν ἀδελφὸν αὐτοῦ μισῇ, ψεύστης ἐστίν·

The conjunction καί links this phrase with the previous one, continuing the subjunctive mood (μισῇ: pres. act. subjunc. 3rd sg. μισέω): "if anyone says *and* hates."

- ὁ γὰρ μὴ ἀγαπῶν τὸν ἀδελφὸν αὐτοῦ ὃν ἑώρακεν

The conjunction γάρ conveys cause, providing the reason for the previous statement.

The relative pronoun ὅν (masc. acc. sg.) is the direct object of ἑώρακεν (per. act. ind. 3rd sg. ὁράω).

- τὸν θεὸν ὃν οὐχ ἑώρακεν οὐ δύναται ἀγαπᾶν.

The noun τὸν θεόν is fronted for emphasis.

The verb ἀγαπᾶν is a complementary infinitive with the verb δύναται: "not able *to love.*"

1 John 4:21

- καὶ ταύτην τὴν ἐντολὴν ἔχομεν ἀπ᾽ αὐτοῦ

The near demonstrative pronoun ταύτην modifies τὴν ἐντολήν: "*this* command."

The preposition ἀπ᾽ communicates source: "*from* him."

- ἵνα ὁ ἀγαπῶν τὸν θεὸν ἀγαπᾷ καὶ τὸν ἀδελφὸν αὐτοῦ.

The conjunction ἵνα, "that," introduces a content clause (see also 3:11) and triggers the subjunctive mood (ἀγαπᾷ: pres. act. subjunc. 3rd sg. ἀγαπάω).

The second use of καί does not function as a coordinating conjunction (see the use in 4:20) but as an adverb: "also."

The pronoun αὐτοῦ functions as a genitive of relationship: "*his* brother."

CHAPTER 13

///////////////

1 JOHN 5:1–12
CONDITIONAL SENTENCES, DISCOURSE
ANALYSIS, AND DIAGRAMMING

13.1 Vocabulary

ἀρνίον, τό	lamb, sheep (30)
γνῶσις, -εως, ἡ	knowledge (29)
διδαχή, ἡ	teaching, instruction (30)
μαρτυρία, ἡ	testimony, witness (37)
μισθός, ὁ	pay, wages, reward (29)
νίκη, ἡ	victory (1)
συνείδησις, -εως, ἡ	conscience (30)
βαρύς, -εῖα, -ύ	heavy, burdensome, severe (6)
ὁμοίως	likewise, similarly (30)
ἀγοράζω	I buy, purchase (30)
ἐπικαλέω	I call (upon), name (30)
συνέρχομαι	I come together, go with, have sexual relations (30)

13.2 Text: 1 John 5:1–12

¹ Πᾶς ὁ πιστεύων ὅτι Ἰησοῦς ἐστιν ὁ Χριστὸς ἐκ τοῦ θεοῦ γεγέννηται, καὶ πᾶς ὁ ἀγαπῶν τὸν γεννήσαντα ἀγαπᾷ καὶ τὸν γεγεννημένον ἐξ αὐτοῦ. ² ἐν τούτῳ γινώσκομεν ὅτι ἀγαπῶμεν τὰ τέκνα τοῦ θεοῦ, ὅταν τὸν θεὸν ἀγαπῶμεν καὶ τὰς ἐντολὰς αὐτοῦ

ποιῶμεν. ³ αὕτη γάρ ἐστιν ἡ ἀγάπη τοῦ θεοῦ, ἵνα τὰς ἐντολὰς αὐτοῦ τηρῶμεν, καὶ αἱ ἐντολαὶ αὐτοῦ βαρεῖαι οὐκ εἰσίν. ⁴ ὅτι πᾶν τὸ γεγεννημένον ἐκ τοῦ θεοῦ νικᾷ τὸν κόσμον· καὶ αὕτη ἐστὶν ἡ νίκη ἡ νικήσασα τὸν κόσμον, ἡ πίστις ἡμῶν. ⁵ τίς δέ ἐστιν ὁ νικῶν τὸν κόσμον εἰ μὴ ὁ πιστεύων ὅτι Ἰησοῦς ἐστιν ὁ υἱὸς τοῦ θεοῦ; ⁶ Οὗτός ἐστιν ὁ ἐλθὼν δι' ὕδατος καὶ αἵματος, Ἰησοῦς Χριστός, οὐκ ἐν τῷ ὕδατι μόνον, ἀλλ' ἐν τῷ ὕδατι καὶ ἐν τῷ αἵματι· καὶ τὸ πνεῦμά ἐστιν τὸ μαρτυροῦν, ὅτι τὸ πνεῦμά ἐστιν ἡ ἀλήθεια. ⁷ ὅτι τρεῖς εἰσιν οἱ μαρτυροῦντες, ⁸ τὸ πνεῦμα καὶ τὸ ὕδωρ καὶ τὸ αἷμα, καὶ οἱ τρεῖς εἰς τὸ ἕν εἰσιν. ⁹ εἰ τὴν μαρτυρίαν τῶν ἀνθρώπων λαμβάνομεν, ἡ μαρτυρία τοῦ θεοῦ μείζων ἐστίν· ὅτι αὕτη ἐστὶν ἡ μαρτυρία τοῦ θεοῦ, ὅτι μεμαρτύρηκεν περὶ τοῦ υἱοῦ αὐτοῦ. ¹⁰ ὁ πιστεύων εἰς τὸν υἱὸν τοῦ θεοῦ ἔχει τὴν μαρτυρίαν ἐν αὐτῷ, ὁ μὴ πιστεύων τῷ θεῷ ψεύστην πεποίηκεν αὐτόν, ὅτι οὐ πεπίστευκεν εἰς τὴν μαρτυρίαν ἣν μεμαρτύρηκεν ὁ θεὸς περὶ τοῦ υἱοῦ αὐτοῦ. ¹¹ καὶ αὕτη ἐστὶν ἡ μαρτυρία, ὅτι ζωὴν αἰώνιον ἔδωκεν ἡμῖν ὁ θεός, καὶ αὕτη ἡ ζωὴ ἐν τῷ υἱῷ αὐτοῦ ἐστιν. ¹² ὁ ἔχων τὸν υἱὸν ἔχει τὴν ζωήν· ὁ μὴ ἔχων τὸν υἱὸν τοῦ θεοῦ τὴν ζωὴν οὐκ ἔχει.

13.3 Syntax: Conditional Sentences, Discourse Analysis, and Diagramming

13.3.1 Conditional Sentences

A conditional sentence is typically an if-then statement: *If* you do this, *then* I will give you that. Conditional clauses are a subset of dependent clauses that set up conditions which, if met, have a particular designated result. They are usually introduced with a conditional particle (εἰ or ἐάν) and can be divided into four *classes*. The *protasis* signifies the "if" clause, whereas the *apodosis* signifies the "then" clause.

- **First Class.** εἰ + protasis (any tense + ind. mood) and apodosis (any tense/ mood). The author presents the reality of the premise true for the sake of argument.

    ○ εἰ οὕτως ὁ θεὸς ἠγάπησεν ἡμᾶς, καὶ ἡμεῖς ὀφείλομεν ἀλλήλους ἀγαπᾶν, "If God in this way loves us, [then] we ought also to love one another" (1 John 4:11).

- **Second Class.** εἰ + protasis (impf., aor., plpf. + ind. mood) and apodosis (impf., aor., plpf. + ἄν and ind. mood). The premise is "contrary-to-fact."

    ○ εἰ γὰρ ἐξ ἡμῶν ἦσαν, μεμενήκεισαν ἂν μεθ' ἡμῶν, "For if they were of us, [then] they would have remained with us" (1 John 2:19).

- **Third Class.** ἐάν + protasis (any tense + subjunc. mood) and apodosis (any tense/mood). The premise is presented by the author as tentative or hypothetical.

○ ἐὰν εἴπωμεν ὅτι ἁμαρτίαν οὐκ ἔχομεν, ἑαυτοὺς πλανῶμεν, "If we say that we have no sin, [then] we deceive ourselves" (1 John 1:8).

● **Fourth Class.** εἰ + protasis (any tense + opt. mood) and apodosis (any tense + opt. mood). The premise is depicted as an unlikely possibility.

○ ἀλλ᾽ εἰ καὶ πάσχοιτε διὰ δικαιοσύνην, μακάριοι, "But even if you should suffer on account of righteousness, [then you are] blessed" (1 Pet 3:14).

13.3.2 Discourse Analysis

Discourse analysis involves analyzing a text in order to understand how it relates to its surrounding context for the purpose of elucidating the author's intended message. As Moisés Silva explains, "Discourse analysis seeks to understand the ways in which clauses, sentences, and paragraphs are formally related to one another in order to convey meaning."[1] Some of the main features to examine include discourse boundaries and prominence.[2]

● **Discourse Boundaries.** The objective basis for dividing sections of a discourse.

○ *Uniformity of Content.* (1) grammatical (same person/number, tense, voice), (2) lexical (same or similar words), (3) informational (same participants, concepts, events, setting, etc.), (4) teleological (same purpose or goal).

○ *Initial Markers.* Stylistic features that an author uses to start a new section, such as (1) orienters ("By this we know," 1 John 3:16, 19; 4:13; "I write these things to you," 1 John 1:26; 5:13), (2) vocatives (ἀγαπητοί, ἀδελφοί, παιδία, τεκνία), (3) topic statements ("now concerning," 1 Cor 7:1, 25; 8:1; 12:1; 16:1, 25), (4) conjunctions (οὖν, διό, δέ), and (5) new settings.

○ *Final Markers.* Stylistic feature that an author uses to conclude a section, such as (1) doxologies (Rom 11:33–36), (2) summaries (Heb 11:39–40), (3) tail-head links ("angels" in Heb 1:4–5 or "endure" in Heb 12:2–3).

● **Prominence.** Explicit markers that emphasize main points or certain themes.

---

[1] Moisés Silva, *Explorations in Exegetical Method: Galatians as a Test Case* (Grand Rapids: Baker, 1996), 82.
[2] Most of the following categories and examples come from Young, *Intermediate Greek*, 251–55, 262–64.

○ *Word Order.* When the expected word order is not followed. For example, when the subject or direct object precedes the main verb.

○ *Certain Words.* Such as emphatic particles (οὐχί, "not!"), emphatic pronouns (ἐμοῦ), or superlatives (λίαν, "very"; σφόδρα, "extremely").

○ *Grammatical Features.* Such as finite verbs, passive voice, relative clauses, and historical present tense.

○ *Figures of Speech.* Such as hyperbole: an exaggeration (e.g., "all Jerusalem"); hendiadys: two terms that represent one reality (e.g., "rejoice and be glad" = be very glad); epizeuxis: a crucial word is repeated for emphasis (e.g., "holy, holy, holy" = very holy); litotes: an understatement (e.g., "no insignificant city" = a very important city).

○ *Rhetorical Questions.* "Should we continue in sin in order that grace may multiply?" (Rom 6:1).

○ *Discourse Proportion.* Larger or longer sections are often more prominent.

13.3.3 Diagramming

Although there are several types of diagramming (e.g., line diagramming and arching), the example below could be labeled phrase diagramming (also sometimes called "sentence-flow" or "thought-flow" diagramming). One of the goals in phrase diagramming is to visually represent the syntactical structure of the Greek text. The idea is to break the text down into phrases with the phrases that contain the main proposition(s) to the far left and dependent or subordinate phrases indented further to the right, usually under the word(s) they modify. If a phrase is grammatically parallel to another phrase, it is indented the same distance.

Example from 1 John 2:12–14

12 γράφω ὑμῖν, τεκνία,
        ὅτι ἀφέωνται ὑμῖν αἱ ἁμαρτίαι
            διὰ τὸ ὄνομα αὐτοῦ.
13 γράφω ὑμῖν, πατέρες,
        ὅτι ἐγνώκατε τὸν ἀπ᾽ ἀρχῆς.
    γράφω ὑμῖν, νεανίσκοι,
        ὅτι νενικήκατε τὸν πονηρόν.
14 ἔγραψα ὑμῖν, παιδία,
        ὅτι ἐγνώκατε τὸν πατέρα.
    ἔγραψα ὑμῖν, πατέρες,
        ὅτι ἐγνώκατε τὸν ἀπ᾽ ἀρχῆς.
    ἔγραψα ὑμῖν, νεανίσκοι,
        ὅτι ἰσχυροί ἐστε
        καὶ ὁ λόγος τοῦ θεοῦ
            ἐν ὑμῖν μένει
        καὶ νενικήκατε τὸν πονηρόν.

13.4 Reading Notes

1 John 5:1

• Πᾶς ὁ πιστεύων ὅτι Ἰησοῦς ἐστιν ὁ Χριστὸς ἐκ τοῦ θεοῦ γεγέννηται

The substantival participle ὁ πιστεύων (pres. act. ptc. masc. nom. sg. πιστεύω) is the subject of the verb γεγέννηται (per. pass. ind. 3rd sg. γεννάω).

The conjunction ὅτι, "that," introduces a content clause of what must be believed, namely, that Ἰησοῦς ἐστιν ὁ Χριστός.

The prepositional phrase ἐκ τοῦ θεοῦ is a genitive of source: "*from* God."

• καὶ πᾶς ὁ ἀγαπῶν τὸν γεννήσαντα ἀγαπᾷ καὶ τὸν γεγεννημένον ἐξ αὐτοῦ.

This phrase contains three more substantival participles (four total in this verse): (1) ὁ ἀγαπῶν (pres. act. ptc. masc. nom. sg. ἀγαπάω), (2) τὸν γεννήσαντα (aor. act. ptc. masc. acc. sg. γεννάω), (3) τὸν γεγεννημένον (per. pass. ptc. masc. acc. sg. γεννάω).

Parsing this verse may be easier than translating it. The second participle in this section functions as the direct object of the first participle. John states, "everyone who loves the one who begets, also loves. . . ." But who is the "one who begets" (or "the begetter")? This is a reference to God the Father, who is the Father of all who believe (Rom 4:11). Thus, John is stating that the one who loves the begetter (the Father), also loves "the one who has been begotten" from him. In other words, the one who loves the Father will also love his other children (i.e., other believers).

1 John 5:2

• ἐν τούτῳ γινώσκομεν ὅτι ἀγαπῶμεν τὰ τέκνα τοῦ θεοῦ

The phrase ἐν τούτῳ, "by this," could be cataphoric, pointing forward to the following ὅταν clause. It is also possible to take it as anaphoric, referring back to the broad proverbial principle in 5:1 that is now applied to the spiritual family of God.

- ὅταν τὸν θεὸν ἀγαπῶμεν καὶ τὰς ἐντολὰς αὐτοῦ ποιῶμεν.

  The conjunction ὅταν introduces an indefinite temporal clause and triggers the subjunctive mood (ἀγαπῶμεν: pres. act. subjunc. 1st pl. ἀγαπάω; ποιῶμεν: pres. act. subjunc. 1st pl. ποιέω).

  This phrase contains a textual variant related to the verb ποιῶμεν, as some manuscripts read τηρῶμεν. The reading of ποιῶμεν is preferred for the following reasons: (1) it is the harder reading that explains the other; (2) the verb τηρέω is often used with τὰς ἐντολάς (see 2:3, 4; 3:22, 24; 5:3); (3) the verb τηρέω is used in the following verse. Thus, it appears that scribes unintentionally substituted the expected τηρέω for ποιῶμεν. In the end, there is no detectable difference in meaning.

1 John 5:3

- αὕτη γάρ ἐστιν ἡ ἀγάπη τοῦ θεοῦ

  The near demonstrative pronoun αὕτη (fem. nom. sg.) is cataphoric, pointing forward to the following ἵνα clause. It is feminine because it refers to *the love* (ἡ ἀγάπη) of God, which is a feminine noun. The noun τοῦ θεοῦ is an objective genitive ("love of God" = our love for God).

- ἵνα τὰς ἐντολὰς αὐτοῦ τηρῶμεν

  The conjunction ἵνα, "that," introduces a content clause and triggers the subjunctive mood (τηρῶμεν: pres. act. subjunc. 1st pl. τηρέω).

  The personal pronoun αὐτοῦ is a subjective genitive: "he commands [something]."

- καὶ αἱ ἐντολαὶ αὐτοῦ βαρεῖαι οὐκ εἰσίν.

  The adjective βαρεῖαι (lexical form βαρύς) means "pertaining to that which is difficult in view of its being burdensome" (LN §22.30) or "pertaining to being a source of difficulty or trouble because of demands made" (BDAG 167).

1 John 5:4

- ὅτι πᾶν τὸ γεγεννημένον ἐκ τοῦ θεοῦ νικᾷ τὸν κόσμον·

  The conjunction ὅτι, "because," introduces a causal clause and provides the reason for the previous statement (i.e., ἵνα τὰς ἐντολὰς αὐτοῦ τηρῶμεν).

The substantival participle τὸ γεγεννημένον (per. pass. ptc. neut. nom. sg. γεννάω) is a bit unexpected since we would expect a masculine form (ὁ γεγεννημένος, 3:9; τὸν γεγεννημένον, 5:1) instead of a neuter form (see note at 1:1; also see John 3:6).

Because the verb νικᾷ (pres. act. ind. 3rd sg. νικάω) is a contract verb, the ending does not follow the regular pattern (νικα + ει = νικαει → νικαι → νικᾳ).

- καὶ αὕτη ἐστὶν ἡ νίκη ἡ νικήσασα τὸν κόσμον, ἡ πίστις ἡμῶν.

The participle ἡ νικήσασα (aor. act. ptc. fem. nom. sg. νικάω) is attributive, modifying the noun ἡ νίκη: "the conquering that conquers." The weakness with using the word *victory* in translating ἡ νίκη is that *victory* does not have a corresponding verbal form, whereas *conquer* can be both a noun (conquering, conquest) or a verb (I conquer). Some of the emphasis is lost when the text is translated "the victory that conquers the world." Culy states, "The writer adds extra rhetorical force through the use of a verb that is cognate to the noun it modifies."[3]

The phrase ἡ πίστις ἡμῶν is in apposition to the demonstrative pronoun αὕτη: "this is the conquering that conquers . . . that is, our faith."

The personal pronoun ἡμῶν is a subjective genitive ("our faith" = we believe).

1 John 5:5

- τίς δέ ἐστιν ὁ νικῶν τὸν κόσμον

The interrogative pronoun τίς introduces a (rhetorical) question, which is also evidenced by the question mark at the end of the verse, and functions as the predicate nominative.

The substantival participle ὁ νικῶν (pres. act. ptc. masc. nom. sg. νικάω) functions as the subject.

- εἰ μὴ ὁ πιστεύων ὅτι Ἰησοῦς ἐστιν ὁ υἱὸς τοῦ θεοῦ;

Taken together, the words εἰ μή mean "unless" and set up the answer for the previous question.

---

[3] Culy, *I, II, III John*, 123.

The exact phrase Ἰησοῦς ἐστιν ὁ υἱὸς τοῦ θεοῦ occurred earlier in 4:15. Once again notice that Colwell's Canon is followed. That is, because the definite predicate nominative (ὁ υἱός) follows the verb, the article is included.

1 John 5:6

- Οὗτός ἐστιν ὁ ἐλθὼν δι' ὕδατος καὶ αἵματος, Ἰησοῦς Χριστός

The grammar and syntax are not as difficult as the meaning and theology of this verse—but the grammar and syntax help determine the correct meaning!

The near demonstrative pronoun οὗτος refers to Jesus. It was used (and not ἐκεῖνός) because Jesus was just mentioned at the end of the previous verse.

The substantival participle ὁ ἐλθών (aor. act. ptc. masc. nom. sg. ἔρχομαι) functions as a predicate nominative. Notice that the aorist tense form (perfective aspect) is used. John is not referring to a characteristic action but is portraying a simple, historical event. (We think John is referring to [1] Jesus's baptism and [2] his death/resurrection.)

The meaning of the phrase ὁ ἐλθὼν δι' ὕδατος καὶ αἵματος, "the one who came by water and blood," is the center of much controversy. The prepositional phrase δι' ὕδατος καὶ αἵματος conveys means: "*by means of* water and blood." The change in the pronouns from διά (δι' ὕδατος καὶ αἵματος) to ἐν (ἐν τῷ ὕδατι καὶ ἐν τῷ αἵματι) is probably a stylistic change.

The nominative noun Ἰησοῦς Χριστός is an apposition to οὗτος.

- οὐκ ἐν τῷ ὕδατι μόνον, ἀλλ' ἐν τῷ ὕδατι καὶ ἐν τῷ αἵματι·

John seems to be emphasizing the blood: he did not come by the water only, but by the water *and the blood*.

The prepositional phrases ἐν τῷ ὕδατι and ἐν τῷ αἵματι convey means.

- καὶ τὸ πνεῦμά ἐστιν τὸ μαρτυροῦν, ὅτι τὸ πνεῦμά ἐστιν ἡ ἀλήθεια.

The substantival participle τὸ μαρτυροῦν (pres. act. ptc. neut. nom. sg. μαρτυρέω) functions as the predicate nominative.

The conjunction ὅτι, "because," introduces a causal clause.

Again, note that the predicate nominative ἡ ἀλήθεια retains the article, consistent with Colwell's Canon.

1 John 5:7

- ὅτι τρεῖς εἰσιν οἱ μαρτυροῦντες

  The conjunction ὅτι, "because," introduces a causal clause.

  The substantival participle οἱ μαρτυροῦντες (pres. act. ptc. masc. nom. pl. μαρτυρέω) functions as the subject of the verb εἰσιν.

  This verse is noticeably shorter than most others in 1 John. The reason for this relates to a textual addition (known as the *Comma Johanneum* or "the Johannine Comma") that is found in a few Greek manuscripts and was included in the KJV. The addition reads, ἐν τῷ οὐρανῷ, ὁ πατὴρ ὁ λόγος καὶ τὸ ἅγιον πνεῦμα, καὶ οὗτοι οἱ τρεῖς ἕν εἰσιν. καὶ τρεῖς εἰσιν οἱ μαρτυροῦντες ἐν τῇ γῇ, "in heaven, the Father, the Word, and the Holy Spirit, and these three are one. And there are three who testify on the earth." This reading is only found in eight Greek manuscripts, none dated before 1400. Furthermore, in four of those manuscripts, the addition is found in the margin (and not in the text itself). The earliest textual witnesses to this reading occur in seventh-century Latin manuscripts. Additionally, no early church Father ever quotes this passage in the first four centuries after the NT was complete. This omission is especially revealing in light of the many early church controversies revolving around the Trinity. Finally, the text reads smoother without the addition. Without doubt, the textual addition, while being true, is not authentic.

1 John 5:8

- τὸ πνεῦμα καὶ τὸ ὕδωρ καὶ τὸ αἷμα

  This phrase is in apposition to the predicate adjective τρεῖς. All three of these "witnesses" are neuter, even though the numeral (τρεῖς) and participle (οἱ μαρτυροῦντες) are masculine, "perhaps due to the fact that the three are personified 'witnesses.'"[4]

- καὶ οἱ τρεῖς εἰς τὸ ἕν εἰσιν.

  The phrase εἰς τὸ ἕν (literally "into the one") is an idiom: "these three are in agreement."

---

[4] Culy, *I, II, III John*, 127.

1 John 5:9

- εἰ τὴν μαρτυρίαν τῶν ἀνθρώπων λαμβάνομεν, ἡ μαρτυρία τοῦ θεοῦ μείζων ἐστίν

  The conjunction εἰ introduces a first class conditional clause (considered true for the sake of the argument).

  The nouns τῶν ἀνθρώπων and τοῦ θεοῦ are both subjective genitives ("testimony of men" = men testify; "the testimony of God" = God testifies).

- ὅτι αὕτη ἐστὶν ἡ μαρτυρία τοῦ θεοῦ, ὅτι μεμαρτύρηκεν περὶ τοῦ υἱοῦ αὐτοῦ.

  The conjunction ὅτι is used two different ways in this verse. The first is *causal* (i.e., "because") whereas the second provides the *content* (i.e., "that") of God's testimony.

  The near demonstrative pronoun αὕτη is cataphoric, pointing forward to the following ὅτι clause.

  The verb μεμαρτύρηκεν (per. act. ind. 3rd sg. μαρτυρέω) is a perfect form (stative aspect), indicating that God testified in the past and that his testimony still stands.

1 John 5:10

- ὁ πιστεύων εἰς τὸν υἱὸν τοῦ θεοῦ ἔχει τὴν μαρτυρίαν ἐν αὐτῷ

  The verb πιστεύω (as a substantival participle) is followed by an accusative prepositional phrase (εἰς τὸν υἱὸν τοῦ θεοῦ).

- ὁ μὴ πιστεύων τῷ θεῷ ψεύστην πεποίηκεν αὐτόν

  The noun τῷ θεῷ is a dative direct object (complement) of the verb πιστεύω. Culy notes, "The dative case may have been chosen here rather than εἰς because the author is now talking about believing something that God has said, rather than believing 'in him.'"[5] If such a distinction exists, it is aided by the context.

  The terms ψεύστην and αὐτόν represent a double accusative direct object construction of the verb πεποίηκεν (per. act. ind. 3rd sg. πιστεύω).

---

[5] Culy, 130.

- ὅτι οὐ πεπίστευκεν εἰς τὴν μαρτυρίαν ἣν μεμαρτύρηκεν ὁ θεὸς περὶ τοῦ υἱοῦ αὐτοῦ.

  The conjunction ὅτι, "because," introduces a causal clause.

  The verb πεπίστευκεν (per. act. ind. 3rd sg. πιστεύω) is followed (again) by an accusative prepositional phrase (εἰς τὴν μαρτυρίαν).

  The antecedent to the relative pronoun ἣν (fem. acc. sg.) is τὴν μαρτυρίαν (fem. acc. sg.).

1 John 5:11

- καὶ αὕτη ἐστὶν ἡ μαρτυρία

  The near demonstrative pronoun αὕτη is cataphoric, pointing forward to the following ὅτι clause.

- ὅτι ζωὴν αἰώνιον ἔδωκεν ἡμῖν ὁ θεός.

  The conjunction ὅτι, "that," introduces a content clause.

- καὶ αὕτη ἡ ζωὴ ἐν τῷ υἱῷ αὐτοῦ ἐστιν.

  The demonstrative pronoun αὕτη is modifying ἡ ζωή: "this life."

1 John 5:12

- ὁ ἔχων τὸν υἱὸν ἔχει τὴν ζωήν·

  This verse follows the same basic pattern as 5:10: two identical substantival participles, with the second participle negated with μή.

- ὁ μὴ ἔχων τὸν υἱὸν τοῦ θεοῦ τὴν ζωὴν οὐκ ἔχει.

  Both uses of "life" (τὴν ζωήν) are articular whereas the reference to "eternal life" (ζωὴν αἰώνιον) in 5:11 was not. These later uses indicate a previous reference use of the article: "this life."

CHAPTER 14

/////////////

1 JOHN 5:13–21
WORD STUDIES

14.1 Vocabulary

αἴτημα, τό	request (3)
διάκονος, ὁ	servant, deacon, assistant (29)
διάνοια, ἡ	understanding, mind (12)
εἴδωλον, τό	idol (11)
μάχαιρα, ἡ	sword (29)
ἴδε	see, look, behold (29)
ἅπτω	Active: I light, kindle; Middle: I touch, take hold of (39)
ἐλεέω	I have mercy on (29)
ἐπιτιμάω	I rebuke, reprove, warn (29)
ἥκω	I have come (26)
κεῖμαι	I lie, recline (24)
φυλάσσω	I guard, protect (31)

14.2 Text: 1 John 5:13–21

¹³ Ταῦτα ἔγραψα ὑμῖν, ἵνα εἰδῆτε ὅτι ζωὴν ἔχετε αἰώνιον, τοῖς πιστεύουσιν εἰς τὸ ὄνομα τοῦ υἱοῦ τοῦ θεοῦ. ¹⁴ καὶ αὕτη ἐστὶν ἡ παρρησία ἣν ἔχομεν πρὸς αὐτόν, ὅτι ἐάν τι αἰτώμεθα κατὰ τὸ θέλημα αὐτοῦ ἀκούει ἡμῶν. ¹⁵ καὶ ἐὰν οἴδαμεν ὅτι ἀκούει ἡμῶν ὃ ἐὰν αἰτώμεθα, οἴδαμεν ὅτι ἔχομεν τὰ αἰτήματα ἃ ᾐτήκαμεν ἀπ᾿ αὐτοῦ. ¹⁶ Ἐάν τις ἴδῃ τὸν ἀδελφὸν αὐτοῦ ἁμαρτάνοντα ἁμαρτίαν μὴ πρὸς θάνατον, αἰτήσει καὶ δώσει αὐτῷ ζωήν, τοῖς ἁμαρτάνουσιν μὴ πρὸς θάνατον. ἔστιν ἁμαρτία πρὸς θάνατον· οὐ

143

περὶ ἐκείνης λέγω ἵνα ἐρωτήσῃ. ¹⁷ πᾶσα ἀδικία ἁμαρτία ἐστίν, καὶ ἔστιν ἁμαρτία οὐ πρὸς θάνατον. ¹⁸ Οἴδαμεν ὅτι πᾶς ὁ γεγεννημένος ἐκ τοῦ θεοῦ οὐχ ἁμαρτάνει, ἀλλ᾽ ὁ γεννηθεὶς ἐκ τοῦ θεοῦ τηρεῖ ἑαυτὸν καὶ ὁ πονηρὸς οὐχ ἅπτεται αὐτοῦ. ¹⁹ οἴδαμεν ὅτι ἐκ τοῦ θεοῦ ἐσμεν καὶ ὁ κόσμος ὅλος ἐν τῷ πονηρῷ κεῖται. ²⁰ οἴδαμεν δὲ ὅτι ὁ υἱὸς τοῦ θεοῦ ἥκει καὶ δέδωκεν ἡμῖν διάνοιαν ἵνα γινώσκωμεν τὸν ἀληθινόν, καὶ ἐσμὲν ἐν τῷ ἀληθινῷ, ἐν τῷ υἱῷ αὐτοῦ Ἰησοῦ Χριστῷ. οὗτός ἐστιν ὁ ἀληθινὸς θεὸς καὶ ζωὴ αἰώνιος. ²¹ Τεκνία, φυλάξατε ἑαυτὰ ἀπὸ τῶν εἰδώλων.

14.3 Syntax: Word Studies

Words studies are a helpful way to dig deeper into a text—if they are done correctly! There are pitfalls and fallacies awaiting the unsuspecting, so we would do well to approach word studies with proven principles and practices. We often do word studies when we are confronted with terms or phrases that are not altogether clear to us. It is often beneficial to study a word in more detail, especially when a word is (1) theologically important, (2) repeated, (3) unclear or difficult, (4) or has a figurative meaning.[1]

14.3.1 Principles for Word Studies

Don't Make Any Word Mean More Than the Author Intends. Linguist Martin Joobs summarizes: "The least meaning is the best meaning."[2] That is, although words all carry a variety of potential meanings, the best meaning for any word is the one that least disturbs the broader literary context. Thus, we should avoid the fallacy called "illegitimate totality transfer." This fallacy involves reading all the possible meanings (glosses) of a word into a single occurrence. Words do not mean the totality of what they could mean in any context; each word only means what the author cues his readers to understand in that particular literary setting.

Prioritize Synchrony over Diachrony. Synchrony is comparing uses of a word from roughly the same time period. Diachrony is comparing the uses of a word throughout various time periods. All languages evolve over time, and part of that evolution is the change in meaning of individual words. This means we have to beware of the etymological fallacy. This fallacy is the false claim that knowing the etymology (historical origins) of a word gives us deeper insights into its meaning. But because the meaning of words change over time, we are not really concerned about what a word meant at an earlier period. Rather we want to know what it meant for the time period of the New Testament writers. The etymological meaning of a word is often most beneficial with rare words (as a last resort) and with proper names (since biblical names are often chosen specifically for their etymological significance).

---

[1] The following material is summarized from KMP, *Deeper Greek*, 483–97.

[2] This linguistic principle is also called "the rule of maximal redundancy." Cited in Moisés Silva, *Biblical Words and Their Meaning: An Introduction to Lexical Semantics*, rev. ed. (Grand Rapids: Zondervan, 1994), 153–54.

Do Not Confuse Words and Concepts. Studying words is a great way to understand a concept but it often is not limited to a particular word (or words). Sometimes a concept could be referenced with different words or indirectly (no explicit word use). For example, when studying the verb προσεύχομαι, "I pray," it is also necessary to study noun forms referring to prayer (e.g., δέησις, εὐχή) or examples where none of those words is used but the concept of prayer is discussed.

Do Not View Word-Study Tools as Inerrant. There are a number of excellent Greek word study tools available. These resources, however, are created by fallible human beings who sometimes show their mental frailty or theological biases.

14.3.2 Resources for Word Studies

- Balz, H., and G. Schneider. *Exegetical Dictionary of the New Testament.* 3 vols. Grand Rapids: Eerdmans, 1990–1993.

- Bauer, Walter, Frederick Danker, William F. Arndt, and F. Wilbur Gingrich. *A Greek-English Lexicon of the New Testament and Other Early Christian Literature.* 3rd ed. Chicago: University of Chicago Press, 2000.

- Louw, Johannes P., and Eugene A. Nida. *Greek-English Lexicon of the New Testament Based on Semantic Domains.* 2 vols. New York: United Bible Societies, 1988. This resource is now mainly available in digital format in Bible software programs.

- Silva, Moisés, ed. *New International Dictionary of New Testament Theology and Exegesis.* 5 vols. Grand Rapids: Zondervan, 2014.

14.3.3 Procedure for Word Studies

Below are seven steps for doing a word study. We will provide both a brief explanation of each step and then illustrate that step using the term παρρησία as used in 1 John.

- **Consider the Immediate and Broader Literary Context in Determining the Meaning of a Word.**

  ○ Words derive their specific nuances from the literary context. Based on the context, what is most likely the author's intended meaning?

  ○ The term παρρησία occurs four times in 1 John: twice in reference to having boldness in prayer (3:21; 5:14), and twice in the eschatological context related to having confidence at the second coming (2:28) and on the day of judgment (4:17).

- **Compare English Bible Translations of the Passage in Question.**

  ○ Choose several different English Bible versions to see how each one renders that particular word. In addition to comparing modern English translations, it may be helpful to look at technical commentaries.

ENGLISH VERSION	2:28	3:21	4:17	5:14
CSB	boldness	confidence	confidence	confidence
ESV	confidence	confidence	confidence	confidence
NIV	confident	confidence	confidence	confidence
NRSV	confidence	boldness	boldness	boldness

Consider the Same Biblical Author's Other Uses of the Word.

  ○ It is more significant to compare the use of the word by the same author than it is to compare those of another author.

  ○ Although John uses this word παρρησία nine times in his Gospel (7:4, 13, 26; 10:24; 11:14, 54; 16:25, 29; 18:20), all these occurrences have a different meaning than in 1 John. That is, each use is found in the dative case (sometimes with the preposition ἐν), functioning as an adverb and meaning "in public," "openly," or "plainly."

- **List the Possible Definitions of the Word According to Standard Lexicons and Word Study Tools.**

  ○ What do BDAG, *NIDNTTE, EDNT,* and LN say about that word?

  ○ BDAG: meaning: "a state of boldness and confidence"; glosses: "courage, confidence, boldness, fearlessness" (781).

  ○ *NIDNTTE*: the term can convey "trust in God, certainty in salvation, the conquest of the consciousness of sin, sanction and power to pray, and expectation of the future" (quoting O. Michel); glosses: "confidence, boldness" (657–60).

  ○ *EDNT*: "The eschatological certainty of deliverance and of having one's prayers heard is grounded in the loving concern of God toward believers, concern experienced as the gift of the Spirit"; glosses: "confidence, forthrightness" (3:45, 47).

  ○ LN: meaning: "a state of boldness and confidence, sometimes implying intimidating circumstances"; glosses: "boldness, courage" (§25.158).

- **Identify Other Words in the Same Semantic Domain.**

  ○ Use LN to help with this as they list words that occur in the same semantic field.

  ○ Semantic Field: Courage, Boldness

    ■ θαρρέω: "to be courageous, to have courage, to be bold" (§25.156).

    ■ λαμβάνω θάρσος: "to take courage" (§25.157).

    ■ παρρησιάζομαι: "to be bold, to have courage" (§25.159).

    ■ ἐπαίρω τὴν κεφαλήν: "to have courage, to lift the head" (§25.160).

    ■ τολμάω: "to dare" (§25.161).

    ■ τολμηρότερον: "boldly" (§25.162).

    ■ ἀποτολμάω: "to be very bold, to be very daring" (§25.163).

    ■ τολμητής: "daring person" (§25.164).

    ■ ἀνδρίζομαι: "to be brave, to be courageous" (§25.165).

    ■ πείθω τὴν καρδίαν: "to be confident, to be assured" (§25.166).

- **Consider Uses of the Word throughout the NT and LXX.**

  ○ This can be done quickly using a Bible program, though a print concordance can be used for this search as well.

  ○ The term παρρησία occurs thirty-one times in the NT: Mark (8:32), John (9×), Acts (5×: 2:29; 4:13, 29, 31; 28:31), Paul (8×: 2 Cor 3:12; 7:4; Eph 3:12; 6:19; Phil 1:20; Col 2:15; 1 Tim 3:13; Phlm 8), Hebrews (4×: 3:6; 4:16; 10:19, 35). The focus of Acts is the open proclamation and testimony of the apostles, a work produced by the Spirit in response to prayer. Paul uses the term to refer to his confidence or boldness in preaching the gospel and fulfilling his ministry or the confidence that all believers have with God. This latter use is characteristic of Hebrews and 1 John.

  ○ The term παρρησία occurs six times in the LXX: Lev 26:13; Esth 8:12; Prov 1:20; 10:10; 13:5; Job 27:10. The use in the LXX ranges from "openly" to "boldly" or "confidence."

- **State Clearly and Succinctly What You Have Discovered about the Word in Question.**

  ○ Give thought to practical exhortation that conveys what you have learned. Also consider other biblical words, concepts, and passages that touch on the topic you are considering.

○ In 1 John, παρρησία is always used to convey a confidence or boldness that believers have before God, especially in relation to prayer and at the final judgment. They can have confidence before God and can receive whatever is asked (3:21–22). They can have confidence that whatever is asked according to God's will, he hears his people (5:14). They can have confidence and not be ashamed in God's presence at the coming of his Son (2:28). And they can have confidence at the day of judgment (4:17). This confidence in prayer is not only rooted in God's love but is also reflected in the life of believers. Their confidence in prayer is rooted in their ongoing filial relationship with God through Christ, as evidenced by their keeping God's commands, doing what is pleasing in his sight (3:22), and asking according to God's will (5:14). Their confidence in the final judgment is because they abide in God (2:28) and because their love is being perfected as they remain in God, enabling them to face the day of judgment without fear (4:17).

14.4 Reading Notes

1 John 5:13

- Ταῦτα ἔγραψα ὑμῖν, ἵνα εἰδῆτε ὅτι ζωὴν ἔχετε αἰώνιον

Because most Greek sentences begin with a conjunction, it is noticeable when there is none (called asyndeton).

The near demonstrative pronoun ταῦτα is anaphoric, pointing back to the entire letter.

The verb ἔγραψα (aor. act. ind. 1st sg. γράφω) is an epistolary aorist, referring not to a previous letter but to the letter of 1 John (cf. John 20:31).

The conjunction ἵνα introduces a purpose clause and triggers the subjunctive mood (εἰδῆτε: per. act. ind. 2nd pl. οἶδα).

- τοῖς πιστεύουσιν εἰς τὸ ὄνομα τοῦ υἱοῦ τοῦ θεοῦ.

The substantival participle τοῖς πιστεύουσιν (pres. act. ptc. masc. dat. pl. πιστεύω) is in apposition to the dative personal pronoun ὑμῖν: "I write these things to you, that is, to those who believe."

1 John 5:14

- καὶ αὕτη ἐστὶν ἡ παρρησία ἣν ἔχομεν πρὸς αὐτόν,

  The near demonstrative pronoun αὕτη is cataphoric, pointing forward to the following ὅτι clause.

  The antecedent of the relative pronoun ἥν (fem. acc. sg.) is ἡ παρρησία (fem. nom. sg.).

  The prepositional phrase πρὸς αὐτόν indicates location: "toward him."

- ὅτι ἐάν τι αἰτώμεθα κατὰ τὸ θέλημα αὐτοῦ ἀκούει ἡμῶν.

  The conjunction ἐάν introduces a third class conditional clause and triggers the subjunctive mood (αἰτώμεθα: pres. mid. subjunc. 1st pl. αἰτέω). Verbs of asking in Greek often occur in the middle voice.

  The personal pronoun αὐτοῦ is a subjective genitive ("his will" = he wills something).

  The first person pronoun ἡμῶν is a genitive of direct object (complement) of the verb ἀκούω (see also 5:15).

1 John 5:15

- καὶ ἐὰν οἴδαμεν ὅτι ἀκούει ἡμῶν ὃ ἐὰν αἰτώμεθα

  The conjunction ἐάν introduces a third class conditional clause, and we would normally expect a subjunctive verb to follow, but instead find an indicative (οἴδαμεν). Various attempts to explain the nuance of this indicative form following ἐάν seem less likely than a general fuzziness around the edges of Greek grammatical patterns. The indefinite relative ὃ ἐάν triggers the subjunctive mood (αἰτώμεθα: pres. mid. subjunc. 1st pl. αἰτέω).

  Ὃ ἐάν is an accusative of reference or respect: "we know that he hears us *with respect to whatever* we ask."

- οἴδαμεν ὅτι ἔχομεν τὰ αἰτήματα ἃ ᾐτήκαμεν ἀπ' αὐτοῦ.

  Once again, whether for rhetorical effect or emphasis, John uses cognate forms. The noun τὰ αἰτήματα, "the requests," and the verb ᾐτήκαμεν (per. act. ind. 1st pl. αἰτέω, "I request") are derived from the same root word. The antecedent of the relative pronoun ἃ (neut. acc. pl.) is τὰ αἰτήματα (neut. acc. pl.).

1 John 5:16

- Ἐάν τις ἴδῃ τὸν ἀδελφὸν αὐτοῦ ἁμαρτάνοντα ἁμαρτίαν μὴ πρὸς θάνατον

The conjunction ἐάν introduces a third class conditional clause and triggers the subjunctive mood (ἴδῃ: aor. act. subjunc. 3rd sg. βλέπω/ὁράω).

The verb ἁμαρτάνοντα (pres. act. ptc. masc. nom. sg. ἁμαρτάνω) functions as a supplementary participle following a verb of perception. The participle gives further information about the observed person. Someone does not just see a person; he sees a person committing a sin.[3]

The noun ἁμαρτίαν is a cognate accusative (with ἁμαρτάνοντα).

The preposition πρός can function as "a marker of result, with focus upon the end point" (LN §89.44). So, here πρὸς θάνατον refers to that which leads (or does not lead) to death.

- αἰτήσει καὶ δώσει αὐτῷ ζωήν, τοῖς ἁμαρτάνουσιν μὴ πρὸς θάνατον.

The subjects of the verbs αἰτήσει (fut. act. ind. 3rd sg. αἰτέω) and δώσει (fut. act. ind. 3rd sg. δίδωμι) are different. The subject of the first verb is *the believer* who asks, and second is *God* who gives. The future αἰτήσει could be classified as imperatival: "he should ask."

The substantival participle τοῖς ἁμαρτάνουσιν (pres. act. ptc. masc. dat. pl. ἁμαρτάνω) is a dative in apposition to αὐτῷ. Although both are in the dative case, αὐτῷ is singular whereas τοῖς ἁμαρτάνουσιν is plural (grammatical discord).

- ἔστιν ἁμαρτία πρὸς θάνατον· οὐ περὶ ἐκείνης λέγω ἵνα ἐρωτήσῃ.

John clarifies that there are two types of sin. Some sin leads to death (which in this context is not physical death but eternal separation from God), and some sin does not. Although it is debated as to the precise nature of the sin that leads to death, it is best to take it as what the false teachers embody. That is, they have rejected the apostolic teaching about Jesus (denying that he has come in the flesh) and therefore are guilty of apostasy (i.e., a sin that leads to eternal death).

The far demonstrative pronoun ἐκείνης is anaphoric, referring back to the sin that leads to death.

---

[3] The participle could also function as a temporal adverbial participle: "If anyone sees his brother *while sinning* a sin that does not lead to death."

The conjunction ἵνα introduces a purpose clause and triggers the subjunctive mood (ἐρωτήσῃ: aor. act. subjunc. 3rd sg. ἐρωτάω). John is not saying that believers should not pray for those who have committed a sin that leads to death (i.e., apostasy). He is simply clarifying that he is not now referring to praying for such a person—not that believers cannot or should not pray for them. In this context, John is giving an example of a confident prayer that believers can offer—that is, a prayer that they know is in accord with God's will. Praying for another genuine believer who has strayed into sin is an example of such a confident prayer.

1 John 5:17

• πᾶσα ἀδικία ἁμαρτία ἐστίν, καὶ ἔστιν ἁμαρτία οὐ πρὸς θάνατον.

The noun πᾶσα ἀδικία functions as the subject and ἁμαρτία as the predicate nominative: "all unrighteousness is sin."

Whereas the prepositional phrase μή πρὸς θάνατον in 5:16 was adverbial (modifying the participle, evidenced by the use of μή and not οὐ), here the phrase is adjectival modifying the noun ἁμαρτία, "a sin that does not lead to death" (evidenced by the change to οὐ).

1 John 5:18

• Οἴδαμεν ὅτι πᾶς ὁ γεγεννημένος ἐκ τοῦ θεοῦ οὐχ ἁμαρτάνει

The substantival participle ὁ γεγεννημένος (per. pass. ptc. masc. nom. sg. γεννάω) is the subject of the verb ἁμαρτάνει (pres. act. ind. 3rd sg. ἁμαρτάνω). This use of the present tense is iterative (or customary) and signifies a repeated or characteristic type of sin: "everyone born of God does not continue in sin" (see note at 3:9).

• ἀλλ' ὁ γεννηθεὶς ἐκ τοῦ θεοῦ τηρεῖ ἑαυτὸν

The substantival participle ὁ γεννηθεὶς (aor. pass. ptc. masc. nom. sg. γεννάω) is the subject of the verb τηρεῖ (pres. act. ind. 3rd sg. τηρέω). There is some debate as to whether the referent of the participle is Jesus or whether it refers to the believer. This ambiguity has caused textual variants (some manuscripts have the personal pronoun αὐτόν instead of ἑαυτόν). If the reading of the text above is correct, then ὁ γεννηθεὶς is a reference to the believer who guards himself (ultimately, guarding himself by the power of God).

- καὶ ὁ πονηρὸς οὐχ ἅπτεται αὐτοῦ.

The adjective ὁ πονηρός is used substantivally: "the evil *one*" (see also 5:19).

The personal pronoun αὐτοῦ is a genitive direct object (complement) of the verb ἅπτεται (pres. mid. ind. 3rd sg. ἅπτω).

1 John 5:19

- οἴδαμεν ὅτι ἐκ τοῦ θεοῦ ἐσμεν καὶ ὁ κόσμος ὅλος ἐν τῷ πονηρῷ κεῖται.

The adjective ὅλος modifies ὁ κόσμος, which is the subject of the verb κεῖται (pres. mid. ind. 3rd sg. κεῖμαι). ὅλος occurs in the predicate position with the noun it is modifying.

1 John 5:20

- οἴδαμεν δὲ ὅτι ὁ υἱὸς τοῦ θεοῦ ἥκει

The verb ἥκει (pres. act. ind. 3rd sg. ἥκω) is often designated as a perfective present since it is a present that is translated as a perfect.[4]

- καὶ δέδωκεν ἡμῖν διάνοιαν ἵνα γινώσκωμεν τὸν ἀληθινόν

The Son of God is the subject of the verb δέδωκεν (per. act. ind. 3rd sg. δίδωμι).

The conjunction ἵνα introduces a purpose (or result) clause and triggers the subjunctive mood (γινώσκωμεν: pres. act. subjunc. 1st pl. γινώσκω).

The adjective τὸν ἀληθινόν is used substantivally ("that one who is true" = God the Father).

- καὶ ἐσμὲν ἐν τῷ ἀληθινῷ, ἐν τῷ υἱῷ αὐτοῦ Ἰησοῦ Χριστῷ.

The prepositional phrase ἐν τῷ υἱῷ is in apposition to the previous phrase ἐν τῷ ἀληθινῷ and Ἰησοῦ Χριστῷ is a dative in apposition to τῷ υἱῷ.

---

[4] Wallace, *Greek Grammar*, 532–33.

- οὗτός ἐστιν ὁ ἀληθινὸς θεὸς καὶ ζωὴ αἰώνιος.

There is debate as to whether John's use of the near demonstrative pronoun (οὗτος) here is a reference to Christ or a reference to God. Because the nearest antecedent is Ἰησοῦ Χριστῷ, the prima facie evidence points in that direction. Additionally, John has been very intentional in his use of demonstrative pronouns. We have seen six times where he uses the far demonstrative pronoun (ἐκεῖνος) to refer to Jesus, but only when Jesus was not in the near context. So for John to use οὗτος here indicates that the referent is literarily close. If John had wanted to refer to God (the Father), he would likely have used ἐκεῖνος to bypass Jesus, the closer referent.

If the referent of οὗτος is in fact Jesus, then he is called ὁ ἀληθινὸς θεός, "the true God," a clear reference to his deity.

1 John 5:21

- Τεκνία, φυλάξατε ἑαυτὰ ἀπὸ τῶν εἰδώλων.

First John ends differently than any other NT letter. There are a number of reasons why John's last verse is somewhat unexpected: (1) there is no connecting conjunction (asyndeton); (2) there is a shift from the indicative mood to the imperative (φυλάξατε: aor. act. impv. 2nd pl. φυλάσσω);[5] (3) the terms φυλάσσω and εἴδωλον are not used elsewhere in 1 John; and (4) there is no formal doxology or concluding farewell.

Why does John warn his audience to keep themselves from idols? Were his readers prone to idolatry? If this issue is so important, why does he wait until the end to mention it? Perhaps John's ending does not introduce a new thought but emphasizes the main point of his letter. That is, John is stating that those who fail the three tests mentioned throughout the letter (the tests of belief, righteousness, and love) are, in essence, guilty of idolatry. In other words, to embrace a form of Christianity that allows one to deny the truth about Jesus, not live a godly life, or not love others is to create an idol—and that is something all Christians must constantly guard themselves against.[6]

---

[5] The aorist imperative may be considered somewhat unexpected since φυλάσσω is best understood as an atelic action. Thus, John may intend an inceptive nuance: "Set your guard out against idols" (see Baugh, *First John Reader*, 81).

[6] For a full defense of this thesis, see Benjamin L. Merkle, "What Is the Meaning of 'Idols' in 1 John 5:21," *Bibliotheca Sacra* 169 (2012): 328–40.

SYNTAX SUMMARY

/////////////

1.3 Koine Greek and Textual Criticism

1.3.1 Koine Greek (300 BC to AD 330)
Changes from Classical to Koine Greek

1. The fading out of the optative mood (used only sixty-eight times in the NT).
2. The increased use of prepositions (instead of merely case endings) to communicate syntactical relationships more explicitly.
3. The disappearance of the letters *digamma* (ϝ) and *koppa* (ϙ), except in numbers and inscriptions.
4. The increased use of the paratactic (coordinate) style over the hypotactic (subordinate) style of writing.
5. The increased use of comparative adjectives to express superlative meanings and superlative forms to express elative meanings.

1.3.2 Textual Criticism
External evidence relates to the age, location, and quantity of the manuscripts that support a particular variant.

1. Favor the older manuscripts.
2. Favor the reading supported by the majority of (significant) manuscripts.
3. Favor the reading best attested across various families of manuscripts.

Internal evidence relates to the context of where the disputed variants are found.

1. Favor the reading that best explains the origin of the other variants.
2. Favor the reading that best fits the literary context.
3. Favor the reading that best corresponds with writings by the same NT author.
4. Favor the more difficult reading.
5. Favor the shorter reading.

2.3 Nominative, Vocative, and Accusative Cases

2.3.1 Nominative Case

- **Subject.** The subject of the finite verb.
- **Predicate Nominative.** Expresses a characteristic or state of the subject with a copulative verb.
- **Apposition.** Additional noun in the nominative with the same referent.
- **Absolute.** Grammatically independent and often used in greetings.
- **Address.** A nominative used in the place of a vocative.

2.3.2 Vocative Case

- **Direct Address.** A person (or a group) is directly addressed (often at the beginning of a paragraph).

2.3.3 Accusative Case

- **Direct Object.** Indicates the recipient/object of the verbal action.
- **Double Accusative.** Sometimes a verb has more than one accusative object to complete the thought. The words *to be* or *as* are often added to the translation.
- **Apposition.** Additional noun in the accusative with the same referent.
- **Respect.** Limits or qualifies the extent of the verbal action.
- **Other Categories** (not found in 1 John):
  - **Measure.** Indicates the extent (time or space) of a verbal action.
  - **Manner.** Specifies the way in which a verbal action is performed.
  - **Subject of Infinitive.** Functions as the subject of an infinitive, indicating the agent performing the action conveyed by the infinitive.

3.3 Genitive Case

- **Possession.** Identifies ownership of the head noun.
- **Relationship.** Signifies a family relationship (e.g., a parent, spouse, or sibling).
- **Attributive.** Conveys an attribute or quality of the head noun.
- **Source.** Designates the origin or source of the head noun.

- **Partitive.** Denotes the whole of which the head noun is a part.
- **Subjective.** Functions as the subject of the verbal idea implied in the head noun.
- **Objective.** Functions as the direct object of the verbal idea implied in the head noun.
- **Separation.** Indicates movement away from, whether literally or figuratively.
- **Comparison.** Denotes comparison with a comparative adjective (e.g., μείζων).
- **Apposition.** Additional noun in the genitive with the same referent.
- **Direct Object.** Verbs of sensation, emotion or volition, sharing, ruling, or separation can take their direct object in the genitive case.
- **Other Categories** (not found in 1 John):

  ○ **Material.** Indicates the material of which an object is made.

  ○ **Content.** Indicates the content of an object.

4.3 Dative Case

- **Indirect Object.** Indicates the one to or for whom an act is performed.
- **Advantage or Disadvantage.** Denotes the person to whose benefit (advantage) or detriment (disadvantage) a verbal action occurs.
- **Reference (Respect).** Limits or qualifies the extent of the verbal action.
- **Sphere (or place).** Identifies the literal or figurative (metaphorical) location.
- **Time.** Indicates the time when the action of a verb is accomplished.
- **Means.** Denotes the impersonal means by which the action of a given verb is accomplished.
- **Manner.** Signifies the way (manner) in which the action of a given verb is accomplished.
- **Apposition.** An additional noun in the dative with the same referent.
- **Direct Object.** Verbs of trusting (e.g., πιστεύω), obeying, serving, worshiping, thanksgiving, or following can take their direct object in the dative case.
- **Other Categories** (not found in 1 John):

  ○ **Possession.** The dative possesses the subject of an equative verb (εἰμί or γίνομαι).

- ○ **Agency.** Indicates the personal agency by which the action of a given verb is accomplished.
- ○ **Association.** Denotes the person or thing with whom (or which) someone is associated.

5.3 Articles and Adjectives

5.3.1 The Article

- **Identification.** The article identifies a particular individual, group, or object from another (or others).

- **Par Excellence.** The article identifies someone who is in a class by himself (or herself). Although there are others in this category, the one referenced is recognizably distinct.

- **Monadic.** The article identifies someone (or something) as unique or one of a kind.

- **With Abstract Nouns.** The article is often used with abstract nouns. When translating such nouns into English, it is appropriate to drop the article (since English does not typically use an article with abstract nouns).

- **Previous Reference (Anaphoric).** The article points back to a substantive that was previously mentioned. It is often appropriate to add "this" or "that" to translation.

- **Generic.** The article identifies one group or a class from another (e.g., "the man on the street").

- **Substantizer.** The article is able to transform various parts of speech into a substantive (noun).

- **As a Pronoun.** The article can function similar to (1) personal, (2) possessive, (3) demonstrative, and (4) alternate pronouns.

- **Granville Sharp Rule.** This rule states that when a single article governs two nouns (substantives) of the same case that are connected by καί, they refer to the same person. This rule only applies to nouns that are (1) singular, (2) personal, and (3) non-proper.

- **Colwell's Canon.** This rule states that when a predicate nominative *precedes* the copulative verb (usually εἰμί or γίνομαι), and the predicate nominative is definite (from contextual analysis), about 90 percent of the time, the noun will be anarthrous. But if the definite predicate nominative *follows* the copulative verb, then the article is expected.

5.3.2 Adjectives

- **Uses**

  - **Predicate.** Predicates a quality to the subject. The adjective is used in conjunction with a copulative verb (such as εἰμί or γίνομαι, stated or implied), and the article will never directly precede the adjective. If the adjective is immediately preceded by the article, it cannot be the predicate use.

  - **Attributive.** Ascribes a certain quality to a noun or substantive. The adjective modifies an expressed noun.

  - **Substantival.** Functions as a noun (substantive).

  - **Adverbial.** Modifies a verb rather than a noun (thus functioning like an adverb).

- **Degrees**

  - **Positive.** Describes the properties of a noun in terms of kind rather than degree (e.g., "the strong man").

  - **Comparative.** Compares two persons or objects by specifying which is higher in degree in relation to the other (e.g., "the stronger man"). Two ways of forming a comparative adjective include (1) a third declension ending on a comparative noun (μείζων) or (2) adding -τερος to a positive degree adjective. These adjectives are often followed by a genitive of comparison or the particle ἤ, "than."

  - **Superlative.** Compares three or more entities and indicates which is the highest in degree (e.g., "the strongest man"). Two ways of forming a superlative include (1) adding -ιστος to a positive degree adjective or (2) adding -τατος to a positive degree adjective.

  - **Elative.** Uses a comparative or superlative adjective to intensify the positive notion (e.g., "the very strong man").

6.3 Subjunctives and Imperatives

6.3.1 Subjunctives

- **Purpose or Result** (ἵνα or ὅπως + subjunctive).
- **Conditional** (ἐάν or ἐὰν μή + subjunctive).
- **Indefinite Relative** (ὅσ[τις] ἄν/ἐάν or ὅς [δ'] ἄν + subjunctive).
- **Temporal** (ὅταν [or ἕως, ἄχρι, μέχρι] + subjunctive).

- **Hortatory.** A first-person plural subjunctive functioning as an imperative.
- **Other Uses** (not found in 1 John).

  - **Deliberative.** Asks a real or rhetorical question.
  - **Emphatic Negation.** Consists of a double negative (οὐ μή).
  - **Prohibitory.** A negated aorist subjunctive that functions as an imperative.

6.3.2 Imperatives

- **Command.** An exhortation or charge.
- **Prohibition.** A negative command (using μή) that forbids an action.
- **Other Uses** (not found in 1 John).

  - **Request.** A plea given to some with a higher social rank.
  - **Permission.** Expresses permission, allowance, or toleration.
  - **Conditional.** Conveys an implied conditional statement.

7.3 Tense and Verbal Aspect

7.3.1 Definitions

- **Verbal Aspect.** The viewpoint or perspective by which an author chooses to portray an action (or state).

  - **Imperfective Aspect.** Presents an action in process or ongoing (present or imperfect tense form).
  - **Perfective Aspect.** Presents the action as complete or as a whole (aorist tense form).
  - **Stative Aspect.** A state resulting from a previous action (perfect tense form).

7.3.2 Lexical, Grammatical, and Contextual Factors

Lexical Factors refer to the verb's semantic meaning that causes it to prefer one tense form (aspect) over another. *Lexical determination* is when a verb's usage is limited to certain tense forms (e.g., εἰμί, κεῖμαι, κάθημαι, and φημί). *Lexical influence* refers to the affect of the verbal activity's inherent procedural nature on the author's choice of tense forms.

Telic	Performance	Bounded actions with perceived duration	Prefers Aorist
	Punctual	Bounded actions with little perceived duration	
Atelic	Stative	States and relationships	Prefers Present/Imperfect
	Activity	Actions with no inherent termination	

Grammatical factors relate to the particular form (morphemes) of the verb—such as the tense form, voice, and mood. **Contextual factors** include the text's *literary genre* since certain literary styles are prone to favor a particular tense form as well as an author's *idiolect* (particular style).

8.3 Present, Imperfect, and Future Indicatives

8.3.1 Present Indicatives

- **Progressive.** An action ongoing or in progress.
- **Durative.** An action that began in the past and continues into the present.
- **Iterative.** An action performed repeatedly, regularly, or customarily.
- **Gnomic.** A statement that is timeless, universal, or generally true.
- **Futuristic.** An action that will occur in the future.
- **Other Uses** (not found in 1 John).
  - ○ **Instantaneous.** An action done immediately, usually by the very fact that it is spoken.
  - ○ **Historical.** A past event that adds vividness or gives literary prominence to some aspect of the story.

8.3.2 Imperfect Indicatives

- **Progressive.** A past action that unfolded progressively over time.
- **Inceptive.** Highlights the beginning of an action or state.
- **Iterative.** A past action that is repeated or customary.
- **Tendential.** A past action was begun, attempted, or proposed, but not completed.

8.3.3 Future Indicatives

- **Predictive.** Predicts a future event.
- **Imperatival.** Expresses a command.

- **Other Uses** (not found in 1 John).

  ○ **Deliberative.** Asks a real or rhetorical question.
  ○ **Gnomic.** Conveys a timeless truth.

9.3 Aorist, Perfect, and Pluperfect Indicatives

9.3.1 Aorist Indicatives

- **Constative.** Portrays the action in its entirety without regard to the process or duration.
- **Culminative.** Emphasizes the cessation of an action or state.
- **Epistolary.** Depicts a present action (usually with the verbs γράφω and πέμπω) using the aorist instead of the present.
- **Gnomic.** Conveys a universal statement or one that is generally true.
- **Inceptive.** Emphasizes the commencement of an action or a state.

9.3.2 Perfect Indicatives

- **Consummative.** Emphasizes the completed action that produced the resulting state.
- **Intensive.** Emphasizes the resulting state brought about by a past action.
- **Present State.** Conveys a present meaning with no completed past action (οἶδα is the most common verb used in this category).
- **Gnomic.** Communicates a general or customary truth.

9.3.3 Pluperfect Indicatives

- **Consummative.** Emphasizes the completion of a past action.
- **Intensive.** Emphasizes the past results brought about by a past action.
- **Past State.** Conveys a past state with no antecedent action with certain verbs (especially οἶδα and ἵστημι).

10.3 Participles

10.3.1 Attributive Participle
An attributive participle modifies an expressed noun (or other substantive) and will typically be articular. The participle will agree with the noun that it modifies in gender, case, and number.

10.3.2 Substantival Participle
A substantival participle functions as a noun and will typically be articular. They can be translated "the one who," "he who," or "that which" plus the meaning of the participle translated as a finite verb (e.g., ὁ λέγων = "the one who says").

10.3.3 Adverbial Participles
Adverbial participles are grammatically subordinate to a main verb and are always anarthrous. They answer questions such as "when?" "why?" or "how?"

- **Temporal.** The present participle portrays an action as ongoing (usually occurring simultaneously as the main verb). The aorist participle portrays the action wholistically (usually occurring before the action of the main verb).

- **Means.** Answers how the main verb is/was accomplished.

- **Manner.** Answers how (related to the emotion or attitude) the main verb was performed.

- **Cause.** Answers why the action is accomplished, providing the reason or grounds.

- **Purpose.** Indicates the intended goal of the main verb's action.

- **Result.** Indicates the result (whether intended or not) of the main's verb action.

- **Condition.** Presents the condition on which the main verb depends for its accomplishment.

- **Concession.** Conveys the reason an action should not take place, although it does.

10.3.4 Verbal Participles

- **Attendant Circumstance.** A participle that is in a parallel construction with the main verb, thus taking on its mood (usually indicative or imperative).

- **Pleonastic.** A redundant expression usually employing ἀποκριθείς or λέγων.
- **Genitive Absolute.** A genitive adverbial participle that provides background information. The subject of the participle will also be in the genitive case.
- **Indirect Discourse.** An anarthrous accusative participle that expresses what someone said.
- **Supplementary.** After verbs of perception, an anarthrous participle will provide further details about what the person or object observed is doing.

10.3.5 Periphrastic Participles

- **Perfect Periphrastic.** (εἰμί [pres.] + per. ptc.).
- **Pluperfect Periphrastic.** (ἤμην [impf.] + per. ptc.).

11.3 Infinitives

11.3.1 Adverbial Infinitives

- **Complementary.** An anarthrous infinitive that completes the idea of another verb (always with δύναμαι and ὀφείλω in 1 John).
- **Purpose.** Communicates the goal expressed by the main verb. This use can occur as a simple infinitive (i.e., no article or preposition), after the article τοῦ, or after the prepositions εἰς τό or πρὸς τό.
- **Result.** Communicates the actual or conceived result expressed by the main verb. This use can occur as a simple infinitive, after the article τοῦ, after the preposition εἰς τό, or after ὥστε.
- **Previous Time.** The action of the infinitive occurs before the main verb (μετὰ τό + inf.).
- **Contemporaneous Time.** The action of the infinitive occurs simultaneously with the main verb (ἐν τῷ + inf.).
- **Subsequent Time.** The action of the infinitive occurs after the main verb (πρὸ τοῦ or πρίν [ἤ] + inf.).
- **Cause.** Communicates the reason for the action of the main verb (διὰ τό + inf.).

11.3.2 Substantival Infinitives

- **Subject.** Functions as the subject or predicate nominative of a main verb.

- **Direct Object.** Functions as the direct object of a main verb.
- **Indirect Discourse.** Follows a verb of speaking to communicate indirect speech.
- **Explanatory.** Defines or clarifies a noun or adjective.

12.3 Pronouns, Prepositions, Adverbs, Conjunctions, and Particles

12.3.1 Pronouns

Personal		ἐγώ, μου, σύ, ὑμῶν, αὐτός	I, my, you, your [pl.], he
Demonstrative	Near	οὗτος, οὗτοι	this, these
	Far	ἐκεῖνος, ἐκεῖνοι	that, those
Relative		ὅς(τις), ἧς, ὅ	who, whose, which
Interrogative		τίς, τίνος, τί	who? whose? what/why?
Indefinite		τις, τινες	anyone/someone, certain ones
Reflexive		ἐμαυτόν, ἑαυτούς, ἑαυτοῖς	myself, yourselves, to themselves
Reciprocal		ἀλλήλων	[of] one another
Correlative		ὅσος, οἷος, ὁποῖος	as many as, such as, what sort of

Three uses of the personal pronoun deserve a brief explanation.

- **Emphatic Use.** The presence of the personal pronoun when it is not needed since the person and number is communicated by the verb's ending.
- **Intensive Use.** The use of the third-person personal pronoun (αὐτός, αὐτή, αὐτό) that intensifies a stated noun.
- **Identical Use.** The use of the third-person personal pronoun in the attributive position (i.e., an article directly precedes the pronoun). The pronoun is translated "same."

12.3.2 Prepositions

- **Adverbial prepositional phrases.** Modify verbs.
- **Adjectival prepositional phrases.** Modify nouns or other substantives.
- **Proper prepositions.** Can also be prefixed to a verb, forming compound verbs.
- **Improper prepositions.** Originally adverbs that now also function as prepositions. They are *never* prefixed to a verb.

12.3.3 Adverbs

- **Adverbs of Time.** ἄπαξ, "once"; αὔριον, "tomorrow"; νῦν, "now"; πάλιν, "again"; πάντοτε, "always"; ποτέ, "formerly"; πότε, "when?"; πρωΐ, "early"; σήμερον, "today"; τότε, "then."

- **Adverbs of Place.** ἄνω, "above"; ἄνωθεν, "from above"; ἐκεῖ, "there"; ἐκεῖθεν, "from there"; κάτω, "down"; κύκλῳ, "around"; ποῦ, "where?"; ὧδε, "here."

- **Adverbs of Manner.** ἀκριβῶς, "accurately"; δωρεάν, "freely"; εὐθύς, "immediately"; καλῶς, "well"; ὁμοθυμαδόν, "with one accord"; οὕτως, "thus"; παραχρῆμα, "immediately"; πῶς, "how?"; ταχέως, "quickly"; ταχύς, "quickly."

- **Adverbs of Degree.** λίαν, "very"; μάλιστα, "especially"; μᾶλλον, "more"; σφόδρα, "exceedingly."

12.3.4 Conjunctions and Particles
Conjunctions

- **Copulative.** καί, "and," "also"; δέ, "and"; οὐδέ, "and not"; μηδέ, "and not"; τέ, "and so"; οὔτε, "and not"; μήτε, "and not."

- **Disjunctive.** ἤ, "or"; εἴτε, "if" or "whether."

- **Adversative.** ἀλλά, "but"; δέ, "but"; μέν, "but"; μέντοι, "nevertheless"; πλήν, "but" or "except"; εἰ μή, "except"; ὅμως, "yet"; καίτοι, "yet."

- **Inferential.** οὖν, "therefore" or "so"; ἄρα, "then"; διό, "for this reason"; δή, "therefore."

- **Explanatory.** γάρ, "for."

- **Purpose.** ἵνα, "in order that" or "so that"; ὅπως, "that."

- **Result.** ὥστε, "so that"; ὅπως, "that."

- **Causal.** ὅτι, "that" or "because"; διότι, "because"; ἐπεί, "because" or "since"; ἐπειδή, "because."

- **Comparative.** ὡς, "as" or "like"; ὥσπερ, "just as"; καθώς, "as" or "just as"; καθάπερ, "just as."

- **Conditional.** εἰ, "if"; ἐάν, "if"; εἴπερ, "if indeed."

- **Concessive.** εἰ καί, "even if"; καὶ εἰ, "even if"; κἄν, "even though"; καίπερ, "although."

- **Declarative.** ὅτι, "that"; ἵνα, "that."

- **Temporal.** ὅτε, "when"; ἕως, "until"; ὅταν, "whenever"; πρίν, "before."

- **Local.** οὗ, "where"; ὅπου, "where"; ὅθεν, "from where" or "whence."

Particles

- **Particles of Negation:** indicative mood = οὐ, οὐκ, οὐχ, οὐχί; nonindicative moods = μή, μήποτε: "never."
- **Particles of Connection:** μέν . . . δέ, "on the one hand . . . on the other hand"; τέ, "and."
- **Particles of Intensification:** ἀμήν, "amen"; γέ, "even"; ναί, "yes!"
- **Particles of Interjection:** ἰδού, "look!"; οὐαί, "woe!"; ὦ, "O!"
- **Particles of the Subjunctive Mood:** ἄν and ἐάν.

13.3 Conditional Sentences, Discourse Analysis, and Diagramming

13.3.1 Conditional Sentences

- **First Class.** εἰ + protasis (any tense + ind. mood) and apodosis (any tense/ mood). The author presents the premise true for the sake of argument.
- **Second Class.** εἰ + protasis (impf., aor., plpr. + ind. mood) and apodosis (impf., aor., plpr. + ἄν and ind. mood). The premise is "contrary-to-fact."
- **Third Class.** ἐάν + protasis (any tense + subjunc. mood) and apodosis (any tense/mood). The premise is presented by the author as tentative or hypothetical.
- **Fourth Class.** εἰ + protasis (any tense + opt. mood) and apodosis (any tense + opt. mood). The premise is depicted as an unlikely possibility.

13.3.2 Discourse Analysis

- **Discourse Boundaries.** The objective basis for dividing sections of a discourse.

  - *Uniformity of Content.* (1) Grammatical (same person/number, tense, voice), (2) lexical (same or similar words), (3) informational (same participants, concepts, events, setting, etc.), (4) teleological (same purpose or goal).

  - *Initial Markers.* Stylistic features that an author uses to start a new section, such as (1) orienters, (2) vocatives (ἀγαπητοί, ἀδελφοί, παιδία, τεκνία), (3) topic statements, (4) conjunctions (οὖν, διό, δέ), and (5) new settings.

  - *Final Markers.* Stylistic feature that an author uses to conclude a section, such as (1) doxologies, (2) summaries, and (3) tail-head links.

- **Prominence.** Explicit markers that emphasize main points or certain themes.

  ○ *Word Order.* When the expected word order is not followed. For example, when the subject or direct object precede the main verb.
  ○ *Certain Words.* Such as emphatic particles (οὐχί, "not!"), emphatic pronouns (ἐμοῦ), or superlatives (λίαν, "very"; σφόδρα, "extremely").
  ○ *Grammatical Features.* Such as finite verbs, passive voice, relative clauses, and historical present tense.
  ○ *Figures of Speech.* Such as hyperbole (e.g., "all Jerusalem"), hendiadys ("rejoice and be glad" = be very glad), epizeuxis ("holy, holy, holy" = very holy), litotes ("no insignificant city" = a very important city).
  ○ *Rhetorical Questions.* "Should we continue in sin in order that grace may multiply?"
  ○ *Discourse Proportion.* Larger or longer sections are often more prominent.

13.3.3 Diagramming
A method that seeks to visually represent the syntactical structure of the Greek text. The idea is to break the text down into phrases with the phrases that contain the main proposition(s) to the far left and dependent or subordinate phrases indented further to the right, usually under the word(s) they modify. If a phrase is grammatically parallel to another phrase, it is indented the same distance.

14.3 Word Studies

14.3.1. Principles for Word Studies

- Don't make any word mean more than the author intends.
- Prioritize synchrony over diachrony.
- Do not confuse words and concepts.
- Do not view word study tools as inerrant.

14.3.2 Resources for Word Studies

- Balz, H., and G. Schneider. *Exegetical Dictionary of the New Testament.* 3 vols. Grand Rapids: Eerdmans, 1990–1993.
- Bauer, Walter, Frederick Danker, William F. Arndt, and F. Wilbur Gingrich. *A Greek-English Lexicon of the New Testament and Other Early Christian Literature.* 3rd ed. Chicago: University of Chicago Press, 2000.

- Louw, Johannes P., and Eugene A. Nida. *Greek-English Lexicon of the New Testament Based on Semantic Domains.* 2 vols. New York: United Bible Societies, 1988.

- Silva, Moisés, ed. *New International Dictionary of New Testament Theology and Exegesis.* 5 vols. Grand Rapids: Zondervan, 2014.

14.3.3 Procedure for Word Studies

- Consider the immediate and broader literary context in determining the meaning of a word.

- Compare English Bible translations of the passage in question.

- Consider the same biblical author's other uses of the word.

- List the possible definitions of the word according to standard lexicons and word study tools.

- Identify other words in the same semantic domain.

- Consider uses of the word throughout the NT and LXX.

- State clearly and succinctly what you have discovered about the word in question.

VOCABULARY

/////////////

The number in brackets [ ] indicates the chapter in which the word is introduced as vocabulary.

ἀγγελία, ἡ	message [2]
ἁγνίζω	I purify, sanctify [6]
ἁγνός, -ή, -όν	pure, holy [6]
ἀγοράζω	I buy, purchase [13]
ἀγρός, ὁ	field, country [8]
ἀδικία, ἡ	unrighteousness, injustice [2]
αἰσχύνω	I am put to shame, disgraced [6]
αἴτημα, τό	request [14]
ἀκάθαρτος, -ον	unclean, impure [11]
ἀλαζονεία, ἡ	arrogance [5]
ἀληθής, -ές	true, honest, genuine [4]
ἀληθινός, -ή, -όν	true, real, genuine [4]
ἀληθῶς	truly, really [3]
ἀναγγέλλω	I report, announce, proclaim [2]
ἀναγινώσκω	I read (aloud) [11]
ἀνάστασις, -εως, ἡ	resurrection [1]
ἄνεμος, ὁ	wind [12]
ἀνθρωποκτόνος, ὁ	murderer [8]
ἀνομία, ἡ	lawlessness [7]
ἀντίχριστος, ὁ	antichrist [5]
ἄξιος, -ία, -ον	worthy, fit, deserving [2]
ἅπας, -ασα, -αν	all, everybody, everything [9]
ἅπτω	Active: I light, kindle; Middle: I touch, take hold of [14]
ἀρεστός, -ή, -όν	pleasing [9]
ἀρνέομαι	I deny, reject [5]
ἀρνίον, τό	lamb, sheep [13]
ἄρτι	now [4]
ἄρχων, -οντος, ὁ	ruler, authority, judge [7]
ἀσθενέω	I am weak, sick, in need [10]
βαρύς, -εῖα, -ύ	heavy, burdensome, severe [13]

βιβλίον, τό	book, scroll [9]
βίος, ὁ	life, means of subsistence [5]
βλασφημέω	I blasphemy, defame, slander [9]
γνῶσις, -εως, ἡ	knowledge [13]
δείκνυμι	I show [10]
διάβολος, ὁ	devil, accuser, slanderous (adj) [7]
διαθήκη, ἡ	covenant, decree, last will and testament [10]
διακονέω	I serve [7]
διακονία, ἡ	service, office, ministry [10]
διάκονος, ὁ	servant, deacon, assistant [14]
διάνοια, ἡ	understanding, mind [14]
διδαχή, ἡ	teaching, instruction [13]
διέρχομαι	I go through, cross over [1]
δοκιμάζω	I examine, test, prove [10]
δυνατός, -ή, -όν	powerful, strong, mighty, able [11]
ἐγγύς	near, close to [12]
εἴδωλον, τό	idol [14]
ἐκεῖθεν	from there [7]
ἐκπορεύομαι	I go out, come out [11]
ἐλεέω	I have mercy on [14]
ἐλπίζω	I hope [12]
ἔξεστιν	it is lawful, permitted [12]
ἐπαγγέλλομαι	I announce, proclaim, promise [5]
ἐπιθυμία, ἡ	lust, craving, desire [5]
ἐπικαλέω	I call (upon), name [13]
ἐπιστρέφω	I turn (around/back), return [8]
ἐπιτίθημι	I lay upon, put upon [6]
ἐπιτιμάω	I rebuke, reprove, warn [14]
ἔρημος, ἡ	desert, wilderness [1]
εὐλογέω	I bless, praise [1]
εὐχαριστέω	I give thanks, am thankful [7]
ἐχθρός, -ά, -όν	hostile, hated [11]
ἥκω	I have come [14]
ἥλιος, ὁ	sun [11]
ἡμέτερος, -α, -ον	our [1]
θαυμάζω	I marvel, am amazed, wonder [8]
θεάομαι	I see, look at, behold [1]
θύρα, ἡ	door, gate, entrance [6]
ἴδε	see, look, behold [14]
ἱερεύς, -έως, ὁ	priest [12]
ἱκανός, -ή, -όν	qualified, able [6]

ἱλασμός, ὁ — propitiation, atoning sacrifice [3]
ἰσχυρός, -ά, -όν — strong, mighty, powerful [4]

καθαρίζω — I cleanse, purify [2]
καινός, -ή, -όν — new, unused [3]
καλῶς — well [7]
καταγινώσκω — I condemn [9]
καυχάομαι — I boast, glory [8]
κεῖμαι — I lie, recline [14]
κλαίω — I weep, cry [3]
κλείω — I shut, close, lock [8]
κοινωνία, ἡ — fellowship, communion [1]
κόλασις, ἡ — punishment [12]

μαρτυρία, ἡ — testimony, witness [13]
μάρτυς, ὁ — witness [9]
μάχαιρα, ἡ — sword [14]
μέλος, -ους, τό — member, part, limb [10]
μέρος, -ους, τό — part, share, district [1]
μεταβαίνω — I pass on, depart [8]
μετανοέω — I repent [10]
μήτε — and not, nor [10]
μισέω — I hate, detest [4]
μισθός, ὁ — pay, wages, reward [13]
μνημεῖον, τό — grave, tomb [5]
μονογενής, -ές — unique, one of a kind [11]

ναί — yes, certainly, indeed [11]
νεανίσκος, ὁ — youth, young man [4]
νικάω — I conquer, overcome [4]
νίκη, ἡ — victory [13]

οἰκοδομέω — I build (up), erect, edify [5]
οἶνος, ὁ — wine [10]
ὀλίγος, -η, -ον — little, few [5]
ὁμοίως — likewise, similarly [13]
ὁμολογέω — I confess, profess [2]
ὀπίσω — after, behind [9]
ὀργή, ἡ — anger, wrath, punishment [8]
οὔπω — not yet [6]
οὖς, ὠτός, τό — ear, hearing [9]
ὀφείλω — I owe, ought [3]

παλαιός, -ά, -όν — old, former [4]
πάντοτε — always [2]
παραγγέλλω — I command, charge [11]
παραγίνομαι — I come, arrive, appear [8]

παράγω	I pass away/by, disappear [4]
παράκλητος, ὁ	advocate, mediator, helper [3]
παραλαμβάνω	I take (to oneself), take with/along [1]
παρίστημι	I place beside, present [3]
παρουσία, ἡ	coming, arrival [6]
παρρησία, ἡ	confidence, boldness [6]
πάσχω	I suffer [1]
πειράζω	I tempt, test [7]
περισσεύω	I exceed, overflow, abound [6]
περιτομή, ἡ	circumcision [9]
πλανάω	I go astray, am misled, wander [2]
πλάνη, ἡ	error, deception [10]
πλῆθος, -ους, τό	multitude, large amount, crowd [12]
πλήν	yet, however, but [12]
πόθεν	from where? [5]
ποῖος, -α, -ον	of what kind? [11]
ποταπός, -ή, -όν	how glorious [6]
ποτήριον, τό	cup [12]
πρόβατον, τό	sheep [7]
προσευχή, ἡ	prayer [9]
πτωχός, -ή, -όν	poor [10]
πώποτε	ever, at any time [11]
σήμερον	today [3]
σκάνδαλον, τό	stumbling block, trap, temptation [4]
σκοτία, ἡ	darkness [2]
σκότος, -ους, τό	darkness [2]
σπέρμα, -ατος, τό	seed, descendants, children [7]
σπλάγχνον, τό	compassion, heart [8]
συνείδησις, -εως, ἡ	conscience [13]
συνέρχομαι	I come together, go with, have sexual relations [13]
σφάζω	I slaughter [8]
σωτήρ, -ῆρος, ὁ	savior, deliverer [12]
τεκνίον, τό	(little) child [3]
τέλειος, -α, -ον	perfect, complete, mature, adult [12]
τελειόω	I complete, make perfect [3]
τέλος, -ους, τό	end, goal [6]
τιμή, ἡ	honor, value, price [3]
τυφλόω	I make blind [4]
ὑπομονή, ἡ	endurance, perseverance, patience [11]
ὑποστρέφω	I turn back, return [9]
ὑποτάσσω	I subject [7]
φαίνω	I shine, appear [4]
φανερός, -ά, -όν	manifest, visible, clear [7]

φυλάσσω — I guard, protect [14]
φυλή, ἡ — tribe, nation, people [12]
φωνέω — I call [1]

χάριν — for the sake of, on account of [8]
χρῖσμα, τό — anointing [5]
χωρίς — without, apart from [3]

ψεύδομαι — I lie [2]
ψευδοπροφήτης, ὁ — false prophet [10]
ψεῦδος, τό — a lie [5]
ψεύστης, ὁ — liar [2]
ψηλαφάω — I touch, handle [1]

ὥσπερ — (just) as, so [9]

AUTHOR INDEX

///////////////

SUBJECT INDEX

///////////////

SCRIPTURE INDEX

/////////////////